Cyber-relationships,
Cracked pots
&
Love

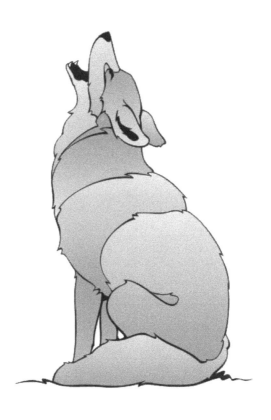

Cyber-relationships, Cracked pots & Love

A transcontinental, cross cultural, virtual, romantic adventure.
A true story.
A happy end.

By
Irene Elizabeth

National Library of Australia Cataloguing-in-Publication data

Elizabeth, Irene, 1959-
Cyber relationships, Cracked pots & Love.
A transcontinental, cross cultural, virtual, romantic adventure.
A true story.
A Happy end

1st ed.
ISBN 9780980431704 (pbk.).

Elizabeth, Irene, 1959- . 2. Online dating.
3. Dating (Social customs) - Computer network resources.
4. Man-woman relationships - Computer network resources.
5. Love - Computer network resources. I. Title.

Dewey Number: 306.70285

US Library of Congress Control Number: 2007906776
ISBN 9781419677243

For Tayna and Raoni

This book would not have been written
without Greg's love and support

Many thanks to Mary Warwick from the
"Tenterfield Writers Ink" for the preliminary editing work

Chapters

Part I

Intro

Someone sent me a joke through an e-mail years ago. It was a drawing of a very ugly, old dog on a computer, talking to a very old, ugly bitch. They were each telling the other how young and beautiful they were. When I received that e-mail, I had been talking to a guy from another country for over three months. I met him on a cyberdating site. We had just started making arrangements for our international meeting.

Some time later, I read an article about cyberdating. It said that people use chat rooms and dating sites to escape from their private and social lives, which, the article assumed, could only be falling apart. These people, the article went on, invested lots of time in conversations with idealized people who may not even exist, instead of using that time to try and fix their real relationships.
It made me think. Does the hat fit and am I wearing it?

This is primarily the account of my transcontinental, cross cultural, virtual, romantic adventure. It had everything to go wrong, but somehow didn't. This is a look back at the whole experience, an attempt to make sense of all that happened and is still happening, a look at what went wrong and what went right.

My need to write this story started as a compulsion, I can't really explain. Maybe because no one wants to listen to what I want to say, or maybe because of all the prejudice around. Maybe writing is just my way of making sense of my own world and myself, but ultimately, I wrote it in the hope that someone may get something positive out of it.
If that happens, even if it is just for one single person, it will have been worth writing it.

Big Decisions

I start this book with a Midnight Oil's song in my head.
They are right. Because we can't know where we are meant to be without knowing where we have been.

The hardest years, the darkest years, the roarin', the fallen years, the wildest, the desperate and divided years. These should not be forgotten years. ("Forgotten years", Blue Sky Mining, 1990)

My cyberdating adventure really starts a lot earlier than the first e-mail I sent to Greg. It began in the mid 80's, when I saw myself trapped in a marriage that didn't feel right, with a diploma I didn't really want to follow, with two beautiful blond angels I didn't know how to handle.
After dragging myself through University in Brazil, in double the normal time, I left for Holland. My younger sister Ursula and one of our best friends, Ilona, had been there for a few years and were apparently, having a great time. I needed to check it out. The boys and their father would come over, as soon as I got organized.

My mother always said I was trying to run away. But for me it wasn't an escape, it was a search. I was not running away from unhappiness, but searching for happiness.
The boys' father used to tell me that I was always running away from responsibility, but it's not fear of responsibility, it's more that I needed to know why and what for I was accepting responsibility.

By mid 1986, I was off to Holland. In the years I spent there, I travelled half the world, completed another University course and got a Master's degree in Nature Conservation. (A Brazilian veterinary degree didn't mean much in Holland). In Amsterdam, I became a singer in a rock band and an acrobat in a circus; I took care of guinea pigs in a hospital for cancer research, cleaned houses of old, grumpy ladies with their heads full of memories of WWII; I baked space cakes for a coffee shop in Amsterdam; I helped break down the Berlin wall and I saw the Joshua Tree in Scotland and many more great concerts. I roamed around in Indonesia's national parks doing research, I learned to speak

English, got divorced from my Brazilian man, fell in love with a Dutch one and then an Australian one and with him I was going to live on a farm in Brazil and off the land.

Back in Brazil, I spent two and a half years, all my money and everything I had on that dream. I bought a few acres of land on the hills of Paraty.
Paraty is a small, picturesque and touristy town, on the border between the states of São Paulo and Rio, where the boys and their father had settled down after our divorce.
I set up a Natural products shop and I married again.
Two years later, I had to go to Holland to sort out some study issues. It was there that I heard that my Australian husband had sold the shop and had run away, back to Australia, without leaving a note, without a trace.
Yes, wild years those were! There were many tough times and many cold days. I laughed a lot and I cried a lot, I did many stupid things and a few wise ones, but happiness I found not.

By May 1995, I was back from Holland, back to ground zero, back in São Paulo, at my parents' home. I was unemployed, the farm lay in tatters and the shop was gone. I was separated from the boys and had no idea whatsoever of what to do with my life. The shards of all my broken dreams and myself scattered all over the place. I had lost everything and I had no real will to live.
All I wanted was some time to get myself together, to redefine views and paths. The same situation I found myself in when I was eighteen. I had just got into Uni. I told my parents then that I needed some time to think, maybe travel a bit. I wasn't ready to take on Uni straight away. But they said no. Almost twenty years later and again, there was no time to stop. The show had to go on and I was telling it to myself this time. Those beautiful boys were growing fast and they needed me.
Somehow, I found the strength and the will to start looking for a job. I soon had to give up hope for a decent job in the Nature Conservation Area. Conservation was not a priority of the Brazilian government at that time and the NGO's were killing for whatever funds they could get.
In no time, I became an English teacher and a translator of Dutch and Portuguese. Long years would drag by, facing uninterested and uninteresting business people in sterile company environments; people I never imagined I could have anything in common with. Yet, a few of them turned out to have

enough in them to earn my respect and tenderness and become very dear to me.

Nonetheless, teaching paid so little that I had to depend on my parents and that hurt.

Dealing with Mum had always been a bumpy task for me all my life and to find myself having the same arguments with her that I used to have twenty years before, seemed all too much. Worse, actually, because unlike twenty years earlier, that time the arguments would always end up with her pointing in the direction of the front door. I could go if I wasn't happy living with her. I didn't have anywhere else to go and she knew it.

Putting up with casual work in Brazil was not easy. I had got used to Holland, where the social security system is one of the best in the world and salaries where good no matter what you did. I missed the respect, the honesty, the libraries and the culture, but I didn't miss the cold, rainy days and the grey skies.

Brazil had its attractions as well: the relaxed, funny people, the sun and the beaches. There were many good moments.

How could I have otherwise, stayed for so long in Brazil?

I watched as the boys grew tall, in a life that looked more like a dream, free like the seagulls in the sky; surfing their youth away along the waves under the Brazilian sun, playing with the turtles in the sea... Precious moments that I will cherish and treasure in my heart forever. There were the big barbecues, now and then, at the oldies farm, where the entire family and many friends would often come together.

Since returning from Holland, I visited the boys in Paraty almost every weekend, but soon, driving the 4-5 hours trip back late at night on a Sunday night, after an exhausting weekend proved to be too risky. I fell asleep behind the wheel twice. So, I started taking the 11:30 p.m. bus, the only night bus available. That meant giving up sleep, because the bus arrived in São Paulo Monday at 6 a.m. My classes started at 7 a.m.

I desperately needed a space to call my own, my own silences and my own noises.

After some time, Tayna came to live with the oldies as well and the need for a space of our own grew exponentially. A space that wouldn't be invaded by little nephews breaking my things, torturing my cat and setting my rubbish bin on fire and not-so-little nieces getting things from my wardrobe without asking.

Family is great when you don't have to deal with them day in, day out. There was friction now and then, I was a lot less able to keep my mouth shut then and I could be poisonous when I wanted to.

Reinforcing weakened ties with long lost, but never forgotten friends from younger times only reminded me more of how far I was from what I wanted to be.

There was no man I could get interested in. There were a few though. Neither stupid nor bad looking, but they were keen to jump in bed with me without even knowing my full name. What I needed was the certainty that they would help me get where I wanted to be and that certainty I never got. I wanted a new life. I wanted to stop doing things I didn't believe in.

Relationships would not be a priority for many years. Twice I had put everything at stake to follow a guy, only to end up losing everything. I got hurt so badly that it took me years to stop feeling sorry for myself. No, I would never follow anyone anymore.

I could have just taken relationships lightly, just have some fun, but somehow, I have never managed to do that. I did try, though. I had my one-night stands, but it was never fun. It's not for me. More than anything else I needed to define my own path and only then would a nice guy be welcome to walk by my side.

After forcing myself to teach for a couple of years that seemed like centuries, I reckoned that the only way I was going to enjoy that, was by doing it my way.

Following stupid school rules that didn't make any sense to me was worse than the teaching and the students themselves.

I thought of an alternative language school.

The oldies' house had several big empty rooms; I could start from there. I would concentrate more on the pedagogical and administrative side of things and less on the teaching. I would make use of literature and cinema, and everything would be based on the Humanistic theory I had just discovered and fallen in love with. A school where the emotional aspect of students had priority over curricular content.

I thought I could, in time, extend that sort of education in the work with street kids.

Starting my own school was the only way I could continue to teach and it was the only way I could see of a meaningful and independent life for me in Brazil. It became my new dream, my new obsession. I worked on it and I made plans for days and months. But, I had forgotten one little detail: my parents. They didn't have any school plans for their house. They had other plans. They had better things to do with their money than help me out again and who could blame them?

How many times did they help me, just to see everything go wrong?

So it was back to square one. I saw no hope for the future.

From then on, I had a constant feeling I was not really living, life was just a struggle.

Then the hot summer of end 1997 arrived. As usual, around Christmas and New Year, Brazil had come to a stop. I was going to spend most of the holiday in Paraty. A friend had invited herself and took her son along, so I had to put up with the arguments between them and her taking over my apartment. The landlord was drunker and more unbearable than usual. I was not enjoying myself.

Then, and I can't remember for what reason, I had another huge argument with the boys' father. Seeing the boys meant seeing him. There was no way around the never-ending arguments, always the humiliating and hurting comments. How can a relationship that was once loving and passionate, deteriorate to such an extent? I didn't understand why we couldn't be friends, like so many couples do after they part.

Going home that afternoon, I sat on the stairs leading to my apartment, prostrated and feeling the weight of the world on my shoulders. Do you know when things are just so overwhelming that you can't even get angry or cry?

I was so sick of that neurotic landlord, the arguing with the ex, the frustrating jobs and the trips up and down the coast. On that moment, I thought to myself, "That's it. This has got to stop! What the hell am I doing with my life? I'm leaving. I will never have a life in this country; surrounded by these people. I have to find a way to leave this country." That argument with the boys' father was going to be the last we would ever have. I was going to leave Brazil, but this time it would be for good. I wanted to start afresh somewhere far away from everything I hated. I worried about the boys too. What would become of them in a small town like Paraty?

I had so many dreams for my life in Brazil when I came back from Holland. I thought I had stayed in Brazil long enough for something, anything, to happen for me, but on that holiday, I lost for good my hope that it ever would.

I was really, really sick of everything. The feeling that I was going nowhere was overwhelming.

To me, Brazil meant a lot of hard and unfulfilling work. It meant being ripped off and not earning enough. I have always believed I'm in life for something bigger. Maybe it's just pretence; conceit, perhaps.

I couldn't see anything changing in Brazil for me. I hated teaching, I always felt uncomfortable in front of a class. I like to learn, not teach and I was doing it for years. There wasn't anyone I would really miss if I left. Come to think about it, I don't think anyone would miss me that much, either. There were only two people in the world I couldn't live without: Tayna and Raoni. Whatever I did, wherever I went they had to be a part of it. I still had so many dreams, so much I wanted to do and be...

I wasn't sure about where to go, though. I thought of Holland of course. I had lived there for almost seven years. It's a good country to live in and I still had friends there, I wouldn't have trouble getting a job, but I would also have to put up with the cold. Those nine months of the year, that used to chill my soul.

I thought of Australia. Until then, Australia was, for me, just a big, sunny island in the Pacific, with kangaroos, Aborigines and beautiful beaches. I started to think of Australia as a possible home. I thought it would have a decent level of social standards without the miserable weather. I thought of the boys, the surf, the beaches and the sun. I thought, "Perfect!" I spent the next two years working on ways to get to Australia and out of Brazil.

I thought of a scholarship for a PhD. Not that I particularly wanted to study again in such a formal way, but a scholarship had helped me before in Holland. It might work again, I thought.

I visited Universities in Brazil and made contacts in Australia, filled out many forms, saw former teachers, put together a research plan and I even managed to get a traineeship at a GIS (Geographic Information Systems) office when it had become evident that I needed to acquire more experience in that area. The thing is, it wasn't that easy to get a government scholarship any more. I wanted to guarantee my first years in Australia through that scholarship but they would only finance the study if there were guarantees that I would get back and use the study in Brazil. Fair enough, but that was not what I was looking for.

I thought about my Australian ex. I hadn't seen him in over three years, but we were still legally married. Just finding him, after several years was a big achievement in itself. Not surprisingly, he was in an even bigger mess than he used to. He could have helped me if he wanted to, he just had to sign some papers, but he didn't. So I tried to get our divorce sorted out, instead.

There was no reason why we should continue to be married.

I made international phone calls, sent letters and telegrams that were never answered. I even sent money so he could send me some papers and forms. He kept the money and I never received any papers.

A scholarship and that ex were the only possibilities I saw of getting to Australia. I spent most of 1998 working obsessively on those projects, sometimes through the night, but it was all in vain. So, I had to give Australia up and turn my thoughts back to Holland.

My plan was to go to Holland, get a job, make some money and get the boys over. The idea was to try and settle in Portugal, where the sun shines more often and the beaches are nicer.

I talked to the boys about it. They got excited with the idea. We kept it secret until I had things better sorted out. I loved those little secret meetings, discussing our plans like a little group of idealists planning a revolution, our own little revolution.

I researched a lot; many more letters came and went to and from Europe. We looked at schools and places to live. Finally, I spoke to their father and after a lot of talking and some arguing, he decided it was probably a good idea and agreed to it, but I should not expect one cent from him for the whole project. It hurt me that the boys took their father's side on this. They too, didn't see there was any need for him to help me.

From then on, I was on a mission. I had to get as much money together as I could. I gave up the flat in Paraty. I began getting as many classes as I could, besides the GIS traineeship. At some stage, I was working for three different schools. The trips down the coast became further between. That meant seeing the boys a lot less and that was hard, but the cause was just.

The GIS Office was fun most of the time; most of the people were really nice. They would often invite me out, although most of them were as young as my sons. When I started there, I was told that there were possibilities for me in the near future but in the almost one year that I stayed there, absolutely nothing happened. There was also something about the manager that didn't click with me, either. One day, he was particularly rude to me, and I decided to quit then and there. I worried about my big mouth; if I stayed there any longer, I would eventually say something I would regret. I did like the boss and I didn't want to hurt the relationship with him, either.

Late one night in February 2000, after I had quit the GIS office and while schools were on holidays, I was bored out of my mind, and started to surf the net. In my head, I had a Brazilian song about being sick of the same damn thing, about wanting to put the apartment on fire and go away... *("Você não entende nada", Caetano e Chico - juntos e ao vivo, 1972).*

A little window popped up on my screen... It landed me on an international dating site. I had never seen or heard about cyberdating before. A thought came to my mind: Imagine if I were to find a guy and end up going to Australia, anyway... Imagine!
I spotted a few guys in Australia and made contact. In this particular site, after you set up your profile, for no cost you could, with one click, send a quick pre-edited e-mail to whomever you chose.

So, on the 16th of February 2000, Greg got an e-mail...

Cyberdating

As I said, it all started as a game, a play, purely out of boredom.

I contacted the guys, either because they looked good or seemed interesting. After a few e-mails, I decided some weren't worth my time and probably some thought the same about me.

One, however, was different. Greg's profile description was sparing, boring in fact. There was no picture and I hadnt'even never heard of the place he lived. Yet, I took a complete gamble on him!

From the first e-mail I received from him, he came over to me as an honest, attentive, intelligent and sincere person. I pictured him as a shy but balanced and thoughtful guy, a bit sensitive, a bit romantic. He was a little bit sad, too. I had a good feeling about him. It didn't take long before the sadness gave place to wit. He didn't seem to be very confident about his looks, so I told him to send me a picture. I must confess I was a bit worried. What if he was really ugly?

It was a very thrilling moment to open that second e-mail and find the face behind the words. I really didn't expect anything astonishing, so I wasn't disappointed to find an average, everyday face. Not handsome, balding and a big nose, but "Nothing to run away from!" I told him. I've never been one to care too much about looks, anyway.

I continued getting e-mails from several other guys and I realized that some of them, including Greg, were serious about a relationship. I couldn't go around playing with people's feelings. I had either to stop that game there and then or get serious as well. If I was to continue talking to Greg, I needed to think about the possibility of a relationship, for he was clear about what he wanted. He was looking for companionship. He was tired of being alone but okay with everything else in his life. So what was I looking for? What did I want?

Relationships weren't at the top of my priority list. Getting my life and the boys sorted out was. The boys had been living with their father since we separated in 1991 and the situation had never been ideal. My vision and hope was that finally, the boys and I would be reunited. My main priority was to help them find their direction in life. Everything else was secondary. From the start, they had always been the major part of my plans.

I also wanted a more fulfilling job and any relationship would have to be placed within this bigger picture.

The way I put it here seems so clear-cut , but it wasn't.

My mind was a constant turmoil of contradictory thoughts and feelings. I had so many dreams, so many things I wanted to do, but I was very confused about how to fit everything into a relationship with Greg. Thoughts raged in excitement when I thought of the possibilities of Australia, but were intertwined with a thousand fears and worries. I knew all the things I wanted to build in Australia would depend on what happened between us and my feelings about him were pretty contradictory.

Some days, I was swept away by dreams of better times, times of happiness and fulfillment.

One late night, alone at the farm, I wrote, "Well, I've made it to my parent's farm. The housekeeper's sleeping already. All I can hear are the crickets outside, a dog barking in the distance... It's so silent and peaceful... There are stars in the sky, Aimee Man is singing softly on the recorder, and I wish you were here... and I think I'm falling in love with you... I will go to bed now and fall asleep while looking at the stars through the window and dreaming of the time we will be looking to the stars together under a different southern sky...

Other days, he came over as this rational, conservative guy and I asked myself how the hell things would ever work between us.

Ursula told me in an e-mail, "You are such a weirdo. How can you fall in love with someone you've never seen?"

Greg too, was a lot more careful about his feelings towards me.

In the three months that we've talked to each other, every time I made a real effort to foresee what my life was going to be in Australia or tried to understand the legal and bureaucratic implications of it all, I would end up writing to Greg that the whole thing was just a stupid dream and that we had better stop talking to each other. Everything looked so overwhelmingly complicated at times.

Not being able to foresee how things were supposed to work for us made my head spin several times. Would I get a job soon enough? Would the boys be able to continue Uni? How was I going to send money to the boys every month and save for their tickets, if I couldn't work? I knew I would be able to sort all this out in Holland, but what about Australia? Greg had never had children, nor had he ever dealt with young people. How was it all supposed to work?

But I did manage to make a few things clear. I did make it clear to him that companionship and sex were not all I was looking for in a relationship. He said that as a man, sex was in his mind more often than he would like. I said I needed room to be myself and to do my things.

What was clear also was that if something were to happen between us, it wasn't going to be based on lies. We would have to really know each other. Honesty had to be complete.

I don't understand how people can pretend they are someone they are not, lying about their looks, age, marital status, financial situation. I think they are screwed up and truly need help; they will surely end up hurting others and themselves. This has never been the case with us.

I had set my mind on Holland when we started to talk, I wanted to get myself sorted out there first and visit him in Australia afterwards, depending on how things went in Holland.

Greg wasn't interested in any of that. He proposed that I came to Australia for a visit. But things weren't that easy for me. As a casual worker, I couldn't just take a holiday from work and then come back. My leaving Brazil, to go to either Holland or Australia would be a definitive thing and I didn't have the money to make both trips. What if I didn't like it? What if it didn't 'click' between us?

"If you decide you don't want to stay, I'll get you to Holland or better still, what if I pay for your ticket from Brazil to Australia? That way you keep your money," Greg suggested. Then, there was the possibility that I wouldn't be able to stay in Australia even if I wanted to. I wouldn't be able to get a work permit for quite a while and I had to consider the boys' expenses in Brazil. Greg said that providing for the boys and me until things got sorted out would not be an issue if I decided to stay.

This was all very disconcerting. I was reluctant. For someone trying to be independent, it just didn't feel right.

For every one of my worries Greg came up with a reasonable solution. He kept giving me the right answers, and I had to give in. It didn't take me long at all to start seeing him as someone I could share a life with and I became more and more excited with the possibility of going to Australia.

But, I still had many things to sort out before I could leave Brazil. Raoni had just started at the Rural University in Rio (the same one that his father and I had attended). For the first time in his life, he was living by himself, having to cook, wash, clean and study. I know him well and I knew how tough it would be for him. I needed to be confident that he was okay in his new life before I could leave. I had also just passed my national translator's exams for Dutch and Portuguese and I had to wait for the certificate (a very complicated and bureaucratic process in Brazil, don't ask me why!) I believed it would be helpful in case I ended up in Holland and I still had all my students and my translation clients. I had an entire life to wrap up.

I penciled down May 2000 as a probable departure date. I needed a time frame to work from and as soon as I did that, life suddenly became a lot busier. I had to make as much money as I could, so I filled all the hours I could at the schools.

Sitting at night in front of the computer to write to Greg became the best thing of the day. The first thing I did when I got home from work was to run to the computer to check my mail. I would even skip dinner. I would spend quite some time inventing new backgrounds, putting bells and whistles on my e-mails.

I always had his picture at hand, so that I could have his face in mind while I wrote. Greg had made my picture his desktop background.

Pictures were very important. Greg was somewhat reluctant to send me pictures of him, but I needed them. This was my way to get used to him. I needed to see him in as many different lights as possible, in his surroundings, at his place, with his family, his dogs. It was funny how in each picture he looked completely different. I didn't know how many Gregs there were, but I needed to make sure I had met as many of them as I could before I got to Australia!

I thought about him more and more. I even began dreaming about him. There were anxious days when computers, servers or providers broke down and e-mails got bounced back, sometimes, for days in a row.

I started to think of opening a restaurant or a café as a job possibility in Australia if nothing else happened. Greg worried about the financial commitment...

We talked about children. Thankfully, Greg didn't want any. We talked about fidelity, aids, pills and vasectomy. We told each other everything about ourselves: past, present, visions for the future, ideas and dreams. We exchanged rants and complaints about almost every issue one can think of.

Lots of questions came and went: "Tell me about a regular day in your life. What time do you usually wake up? What do you have for breakfast, lunch, what time? What do you do in the mornings, afternoons? What time do you go to bed? Do you snore? What's the voltage in Australia, 110 or 220? Are there good programs on TV? How tall are you? How much do you weigh? Do you drive on the wrong side of the road like they do in Britain?" Answers came and went. Jokes and poems came and went. We talked about perfumes and the smells we liked. He ended up buying half a dozen deodorants when I mentioned which one I used. It took me the rest of the year to get through them!

It was embarrassing to explain the mess I was stuck in with my Australian ex.
"...He left before I came back from a long trip to Holland in 1995. I had bought a farm and had started a natural products shop in Paraty. I discovered that he was leaving the country through my father; he didn't find it important to tell me! (I still cannot understand how someone can do something like that!). I've been trying to contact him to sort out the divorce but I never get any answers to my letters. I've talked to a lawyer here and he said that all he has to do is sign a power-of-attorney and everything will be sorted out. The procedure itself should be very simple. I don't know why he doesn't reply. I'm stuck! I don't really know how to sort this out..." Greg tried to contact him but, like me, he didn't succeed.

After Greg and I had been talking for a month or so, I went to the farm with the oldies for the Carnival holidays and told them about the whole cyberdating thing. I'm sure they didn't really understand what it was all about, but they said it sounded good. They hoped I would finally find someone I could really be happy with and so did I.
After that, I felt the need to hear him. I called: engaged...
Then, on a Sunday morning, I was awoken by the phone ringing.
Nobody was home; they had all left for the farm a few days before for yet another long weekend. I had work to do and stayed in São Paulo.
Greg hadn't warned me he was going to call, but I knew it was him. Greg's deep voice had something powerful about it, I liked it.
There we were, two middle-aged people talking to each other like a couple of insecure young teenagers! Pathetic? Maybe, but the truth is that it felt great!

On another long weekend at the farm, late at night, when everyone was asleep and the house was completely silent, I couldn't sleep and lay in bed awake, thinking. That night, the true meaning of "wrap up a life" fell on my head like a bulldozer. The enormity of the step I was about to take had just hit me. My mind started to race. A million things that I needed to sort out crossed my mind. I jumped out of bed and until the early hours, I frantically made plans and lists, putting on paper everything that came to mind. Only after I sent a dozen e-mails, and looked at the finished lists on my bedside table, did I feel relieved enough to get some sleep.

Back home, I stuck the list on the wall of my bedroom where I could see it all the time.

On a Thursday, 23 March, 2000, I made the ticket reservation! Departure from Brazil on the 12th of May and arrival in Australia two days later. Butterflies fluttered in my stomach every time I thought of it. Another huge change in my life! I worried a little bit about not getting my translator certificate in time, but deep inside I didn't really give a damn!

Tracy Chapman was often on my mind in those days.

I had a ticket, I sure, was gonna use it. *("She's got a ticket", Tracy Chapman, 1998)*

I rode on such a high that day that not even the bored and sleepy faces of my students could change my mood. It seemed I had known Greg for a lifetime. It seemed that we had been talking to each other for ages, when in fact it had been only five weeks. The certainty that Greg was the guy for me grew everyday and with every e-mail. I had a feeling it was all meant to be. More and more I dreamt of the beautiful beaches of Australia and Greg at my side.

I thought that if things went wrong between us, the universe would have to have turned upside down and the books that rule nature lost, because there was nothing I wanted more than to be with Greg in Australia.

The boys were both excited and skeptical with the idea. It wouldn't be the first time my plans would end up in nothing.

Another Brazilian song was often on my mind those days: "those who know, set the time, they don't wait for things to happen..." *(Prá Não Dizer Que Não Falei Das Flores, Geraldo Vandré, 1968)*

From the day I made the reservation it was countdown. Things became hectic. I had two months to go through that huge list of things I had made up at the farm. I had to get everything sorted out in the times between classes and translations, in any time that I managed to get free, but every few days I would strike an item off my list.

As it dawned upon the rest of the family that I was serious about going to Australia, I started receiving all the advice I didn't ask for. The boys reckoned it was crazy to go without knowing for sure if I would be able to go to Holland from there. "What if he keeps you as a prisoner? What if he doesn't help you go to Holland?" they knew that for me, going back to Brazil was not an option.

Paulo, my younger brother sent me an e-mail saying I was completely crazy. But, my mind was made and even if things didn't work out the way I hoped, I believed it would have all been worthwhile. I was not going to allow bad thoughts to destroy my hopes of happiness.

Raoni worried about Greg not being able to cope with us. At his young age, he was more aware than I was that we had an issue or two to sort out.

In our talks, Mum told me to try and get it right this time; how I should always wait for the best moment to put things I didn't feel happy about; to think well in advance on how to say things. I wondered why she was telling me that then, because she hadn't said a word when I left the house at eighteen.

But I guess I never gave her the chance. (I showed up pregnant at nineteen, before she could even contemplate the idea of me getting married.) Although she was supportive for a while, criticism from brothers and sisters changed her mind. She avoided the issue "Irene's going to Australia" and every time it came up, her face would turn somber.

For my family, in the long list of weird and stupid things I had done before, this was the maddest. The general idea was that I was being naïve, a sucker, believing in this guy, whoever he may be. I would end up a sex slave in some unknown country. He could only be a sex maniac, quite probably a murderer. One of my friends even went so far as to imagine him getting some bear-suit from the wardrobe and performing some obscene bear act for me! Where on earth do they get all this from? Do they imagine themselves doing these things? Who's the crazy one here?

Nonetheless, the damage was done. I became a bit suspicious. My questions became more direct and I started to demand clear answers. All that nonsense from my family took a lot of the romance away.

I never stopped worrying about the fact that Greg hadn't had any lasting relationships. He blamed it on his shyness, his hearing problems that made him averse to social situations and the isolation of where he lived. I accepted the explanations, but now and then, the thought would creep into my mind: Would there be some other reason for that?

As always, Greg would give me the right answers. If I didn't go to Australia, he would come to Brazil to face the family and put everyone at ease. I told him not to worry about my family. To spend so much money just to convince them was stupid. The decisions were mine - and I didn't need any convincing.

Some say intuition is the ability to hear the voice of wisdom within ourselves. My intuition told me that Greg was all right. I was sure about him from the very first e-mail and my gut feeling has never been wrong – be it good or bad. I get into trouble with people when I don't listen to my intuition. I know many think this is irrational and therefore unreliable, but I think intuition is a gift that most people have lost. I'm not advising anyone to trust solely to this. I'm just saying that I've got a strong intuition, which has never let me down.

I was leaving Brazil without a time to come back. My decision was final and as that decision became more and more a fact and a reality in my mind, I started to look at my family and my life there with different eyes. It dawned upon me that I was leaving my entire life behind, my family, my country and my friends.

I looked at my mother and her eternal worries about not being able to pay all the bills, which she always did anyway, her annoyances with a thousand unavoidable things, her impatience. I can feel an immense tenderness for her at times, but more often I wished I could just run away from her. And non of this has stopped me from having arguments with her. Some say we are too much alike!

My father, so easygoing, so human, so tender sometimes, so down to earth, so hardworking and so happy in his own little world. My brothers and sisters, who have all grown into their different worlds and lives, following their own values and beliefs, so far apart nowadays and yet so close, so different and yet so familiar.

Piveti, our house cleaner for over forty years and her daughters who, some more than others, are also an intrinsic part of the history of this peculiar Dutch-Indonesian-Brazilian family. As I looked at each one of them, my heart filled with an intense tenderness and the thought that I might never see them again crossed my mind many times. I was leaving behind my childhood memories, my cat, all the dreams I once had for Brazil.

That country I love so much, the country I grew up in, the country that's the background of my sweetest memories, the music, the sounds, rhythms, the simple people, the beaches, forests, mountains, the sun, the heat, the mixture of races, the food, tastes and smells, all the things so familiar to my senses. The soccer I used to play almost every day as a kid, houses I lived in with my family and generations and generations of pets, all the friends from happy younger days. Memories of childhood and adolescence that I cherish with so much tenderness. I would miss them all. We never know how much this all means to us, how deep rooted, until we leave it all behind.

Now and then, I would go through my stuff, trying to decide what to pack, what to give away and what to take with me and at times, I felt quite melancholic. My life flicking away in from of my eyes as I turned the pages of my photo albums. Each one of those pictures, a part of my life that I was about to leave behind forever. I was overcome by a feeling of something finishing and I had nothing else to put in its place, just some vague plans for the future. I had a confused and hazy, yet strong feeling that I was about to lose a lot more than just my country and family. At times, it felt as I was about to leave behind a great deal of myself. The tropical autumn in Brazil makes the sky so much bluer; Paraty seemed more beautiful than ever in those last days...

Yet, I knew I had to go. I knew that, as sweet as memories can be, they are only memories, a treasure to keep safely in the heart, memories of the things that made me what I am today, but, we cannot live on memories and dreams; we have to find a destination in life.

There was also the violence, the street kids, the corruption, the madness of the big cities in Brazil that I never managed to handle well. But, most of all was always the restlessness, the dissatisfaction with the life I was leading, very real, always there, screaming, pounding, reminding me with every heart beat, that I had no reason to stay there, that everything I once was, or had, was forever in the past. My heart wasn't beating strongly enough. I still hadn't found what I was looking for...

Days passed and we counted them down, one by one, e-mail by e-mail. I became busier and busier every day, working and sorting out things. My life became incredibly hectic and stressful. In the last month, I was living on the edge most of the time and I tipped over several times. I had some serious arguments with Mum, Tayna and a boss. In the few pauses between, I would become quite melancholic.

By April, we had told everything there was to tell about ourselves, it was becoming harder to find things to talk about, but we had to keep the conversation going. Our e-mails became long conversations about politics, dreams, women's rights, contraception, God and the meaning of life. And it turned out that we did have many differences in some issues and some conversations turned into arguments.

One of these arguments was about maternity leave and the exchanges lasted for several days. Greg thought government money should go to other, more important things, such as alleviation of poverty. I thought that we shouldn't undo women's rights that had been gained at such a cost. He could get really pissed off with mums who got their maternity leave and then didn't come back to work.

"... Honestly, I think you are being hard with those women, because you are too hard to yourself. I think you need to stop worrying about people getting more advantages than they should..."

Then there was something about freedom. I said I needed freedom to do what I wanted. That I didn't want to get into the mutual incrimination many couples fall into when one does not fulfill the other's expectations, where one gets pissed off when the other doesn't want to do the same thing or one does something hating it just to make the other "happy" or to avoid any arguments. That sucks. People should just do what they want to. I was thinking about my parents arguments when my father didn't want to go to mum's choir of elderly women, he would rather play his tennis and mum would get grumpy the whole day. Greg understood I wanted freedom to do things I wouldn't tell him. Things he wouldn't like to know, like seeing other men. We had spoken about faithfulness before and he knew my thoughts about it. I had never believed in an "open" relationship and never would; that's why it really pissed me off and I let him know it.

Immediately after that exchange, coincidentally we both had problems with our e-mail accounts. He sent his reply to an account I had just deleted and I thought he didn't answer me on purpose. I went berserk; I thought the whole thing was over; I even thought of going to Holland again.

A few days later, when we discovered what had happened he wrote, "Yes I do have a damn good idea of what sort of mess your head was in yesterday, as I've been there, even though it may have only been for a few hours... It's not your fault completely either, but trusting me would have saved you a lot of aggravation. I consider it to be a tragic coincidence. I'm sorry for this mistake, forgive me? As soon as I realized what happened I deleted your other names and addresses that had been added automatically by Outlook. I guess it's just bad that you had given me something to think about before this all happened. So, Sweetie, I tell you now, I won't just stop emailing you, okay? And if you do get me pissed off for some reason, I'll send an email to tell you that I'm pissed off, I certainly won't leave you hanging...

There has been a positive out of this negative for me, though and that positive is a confirmation of how you feel about me... When I read the email where you wanted me to define trust, I came within a cat's whisker of ringing you, just to put both of us at ease about it. Maybe I should have, but looking back at it, what has happened has probably ended up doing more good than harm? And no! I can't believe that you would consider going to Holland, without settling with me first!"

A few days later I had to smile to myself, we were already starting to sound like a real couple!

But, in spite of his reassurances, the arguments made me worry a bit. I wouldn't conform to any of his pre-established ideas about women's responsibilities and duties in relationships. I would only live according to what I thought of as correct. These thoughts kept raging in my head for many days. I even dreamt he was a murderer at some stage. In the dream he was telling me he was a murderer as if it was the most normal thing on Earth.

I think the dream had to do with my fear of having to give up on myself, afraid of having to give up my plans, my dreams, afraid of having to walk in his shade.

Ten days before my departure, Greg asked me if I was ready for him. I had no choice but to be honest and make clear again, just what my expectations were in a relationship. I needed my space. I needed to do my own things.

I tried to explain yet again my belief that no one could make another totally happy, that there would always be things that we would have to sort out on our own. I think two together make life a lot easier, but no human being can fill another's heart completely. No matter how long people stay together, they will never stop being two different individuals with different needs. We cannot make someone happy who doesn't do anything to be happy.

I told him I knew exactly what I did and did not want from life. If circumstances were not in my favor, if I couldn't change it I would move on and continue my search for happiness somewhere else.

I wasn't going to Australia to do any stupid jobs. I wasn't going to cross half the world to get into a worse situation than I was in Brazil. For five years, I had done things I didn't believe in and eaten humble pie. I needed to get a decent salary for my work or time to do what I really liked doing. I wanted more time to write, more time to think and read. I wanted to get more involved with social and environmental issues.

I told Greg I truly believed we could be happy together or else I wouldn't be making the huge effort to get to Australia, but I didn't think I would be able to go on if I were to become his sole source of happiness. "I'm not sure if I'm that ready for you and I would really appreciate it if you had a thorough thought on everything I've written here as there's still time for you to change your mind and avoid this lady here because, my dear, I won't take bull... from no one!"

I worried about prejudice in Australia, as well: "the idea of accepting people the way they are even if they don't make any effort to see beyond their limited views scares me to death. As a matter of fact I don't think I can and if I cannot understand someone I'd rather go away."

Finally, the day I got to the end of my list arrived. I had finished all my tasks at the schools and other work commitments, given up my jobs and sorted out a lot of documents and papers. It was time to sort out all my belongings, pack up and put everything away somewhere safe. I wish I had quit my job at least a week earlier so I could have taken care of the packing properly. I will never be able to express how incredibly exhausting that was. I didn't quit work until the day before I left! To have a couple of days to rest before I left would have made a heck of a difference too. In that last week I slept no more than three hours a night, spending many early hours packing and sorting out papers.

I don't think I would have done it without the help of my dear sister Johanna.

The day before I left Brazil, I was packing and racing around in my room, when Dad got in and started to talk. He would come with me if he was thirty years younger. He once dreamt of migrating to Australia. He actually applied for immigration in Holland, as a young man recently married to Mum, but was refused because of his brown Indonesian skin. He said I had screwed up my life so many times, that it was a miracle sent straight from Heaven that I was being given another chance to start anew. He hugged me and said he wished he could always protect us and take care of us, but we had our own lives to live. He told me to be gentle and humble, not to open my big mouth every time I got pissed off. He had tears in his eyes and I told him I wouldn't screw it up this time. His words echoed in my head many times in all these years.

I wasn't certain if it had sunk into Greg what exactly I meant in my last e-mails, but he didn't back off.
Three days later, I was on a plane to Australia.

Big day and first impressions

It was two years later, when I first wrote about the events of that 12th of May of 2000, but the memory was still fresh in my mind. I vividly remembered looking back, while I was going through customs at the International airport in São Paulo: my parents, Tayna, the smile in his face, a vague trace of concern. With my heart pounding strongly, I was a bit sad at leaving them but, at the same time, excited and full of expectations about a new future, sure and confident that I would soon see Tayna again. I remembered the old, shabby airplane, cranky stewards and horrible food; my getting cramped when the front seat went all the way back and I couldn't move mine because it was broken; my impatience waiting for the seat-belt lights to go off, so I could get up and look for another seat. There was chaos at the airport in Buenos Aires as renovations were going on. Our plane to Australia was going to depart in five hours but nobody knew where we were supposed to wait. After a lot of walking, we were placed in a room with a leaking ceiling. I read a book for a while and then I remembered I had promised Greg I would call him during the trip if I got the chance. Personnel at the airport were even crankier than the crew on the flight. Prices in the terminal were sky-high: US$ 5 for a little bottle of water, 20 for a ten minute phone card. By the time I understood how the card worked people started to get up to board the plane.

I could still feel my exhilaration while boarding that huge, brand new and bright Qantas airplane at 1:15 a.m. It felt like another world with smiling faces and decent food. I was quite comfortable; there was an empty seat between a young Brazilian surfer, sitting at the aisle and me, at the window. His mate had problems with his visa and couldn't board; he was supposed to be pretty big too. Then, the sun didn't rise for 24 hours! I first saw daylight again when we got to New Zealand and the plane stopped for two hours. Walking around in the airport in New Zealand, I realized I had lost my wallet. It must have fallen out of my bag when I was trying to get organized to leave the plane. I had all my documents and a lot of money in it. I made my way back into the plane and when I didn't find it, I freaked out. Told my drama to the security guy in the hall and sat down nearby, waiting to see what would eventuate next. He disappeared.

Twenty minutes later, he called me and asked me what I had in it. After I told him, he gave it to me. Man, what a relief!

In Sydney, my young fellow traveler had the opportunity to forgive me for all the times I woke him up to go to the toilet during the flight.

Going through customs was quite intimidating; I had never seen so many dogs sniffing everyone and everything. The officers were quite arrogant. Not really a friendly first impression.

He was getting a bit nervous and looked completely lost. He didn't speak one word of English. I told him to stick to me, not to say a word and pretend we were together. I answered all the questions the officer was asking him and just when the officer was starting to get annoyed and I expected him to ask if he didn't have a tongue I gave him my passport. It was so busy; they couldn't spend that much time with every passenger. When we finally got through, he was very thankful, indeed.

As I walked to the exit door, I noticed I had lost my sunglasses. I looked back and I saw my young fellow passenger, a few meters behind me, pick them up, but a female officer very rudely grabbed them from his hands and gave them to me. She probably thought he was going to keep them and didn't realize we were together. As soon as we got through the exit door, his friends came running to him in excitement and he walked away with them. Continuing on my way I looked back and smiled, I think it was in relief. He was now safe and sound and I didn't need to look after him any more. He waved. I never asked his name.

I had to wait in Sydney for several hours before catching the flight to Brisbane and I had planned to make a boat trip around the harbor. I got rid of my luggage and went to the information desk. As I tried to find my way to the bus stop, my thoughts were interrupted: "Excuse me?" asked a hesitant Brazilian voice behind me. It belonged to a short, simple looking man: "I heard you speaking Portuguese. Could you please help me? I don't speak English..." He went on to explain that he had lost all his luggage and didn't have a clue where to start looking for it. I thought to myself, "Why me?"

I spent over an hour going everywhere with him, searching for his stuff. When I finally managed to put him on his way, I had missed my bus. I could forget the trip around the harbor, so I decided to go to Bondi for a walk, instead.

It was a nice sunny day; there was a gentle, cool breeze.

The ocean was so blue and beautiful; everything looked bright, clean and organized. There was something familiar about it. The feeling was similar to the one I had when I arrived in Amsterdam for the first time: all the colorful and different looking people. In Holland I let myself be dazzled by it all, swallowed by that brand new universe. Not here. This was a different time. The awareness of the obstacles waiting for me was very much with me. Yet, I was happy to be there and I was enjoying myself thoroughly. It surprised me to find several Brazilian soft drinks for sale!

Maybe because it was a Sunday, maybe it's just Bondi, but I didn't find Sydney chaotic and dirty, as one would expect from a big city. In spite of the endless ocean in front of me and the waves hitting the open swimming pool carved in the rocks, it felt a bit like a very big sleepy country town to me.

Is it possible for anyone who grows up in the chaos, noise, pollution and size of São Paulo to be impressed with any other big city in the world?

I sat on the grass like everybody else, enjoying my juice and the view until it was time to go back to the airport and catch my flight.

Back at the Airport, I gave Greg a call.

It's hard to explain what it was like to speak to him. It was comforting to talk to him, to know that in that strange world, there was someone I could count on, someone who was waiting for me and yet, he was also a stranger somehow.

I took all my bags from the lockers and walked a long way through corridors from the international arrivals to the domestic departures. I had to put some stuff from one suitcase into a bag, as it was too heavy for a domestic flight. That was quite a hassle, and it added another bag to my collection of handbags. I think I had five by now, plus two huge suitcases and a guitar.

In the aircraft, I felt confused when I asked the stewardess for one extra sugar for my coffee and she gave me ten bags. I wouldn't have been able to use them all even if the trip had lasted ten instead of an hour and a half. Was she pissed off?

The flight to Brisbane had only a few passengers and by the time I got all my stuff together, everyone was long gone. After 48 hours travelling and no sleep I wasn't in a hurry for anything. I was pretty tired, but still full of excitement. I couldn't even think of sleeping. There was a whole new world to be explored.

When I passed the last bend in the long air bridge into the terminal, I saw Greg at the end of it. I knew it was him from the pictures. Very nonchalant in his shorts from the 70's, cap and thongs. It's very hard to describe what went through my head at that moment. A million things!

There he was, the guy I'd been talking to every single day for the last three months, the guy who knew more of my life than my parents, the guy I knew almost everything about, the guy who had felt so close to me so many times, the guy I came to meet and perhaps start a new life with. My first impulse was to give him a hug, but then somehow, something held me back. I was feeling awkward and that's how my hug must have felt to him.

We spoke about this particular moment over and over. Greg swears to God he gave me a big hug. He remembers my hug as a very cool one. His didn't feel that warm to me either. Still today, I have never managed to recall that moment exactly, no matter how much I tried. Maybe my mind was too wild, maybe the lack of sleep. I was overwhelmed with all the contradictory emotions and thoughts that zipped through my mind.

He was quite shy, smiling all the time, very polite and gentle. The weather was great. There was a cool breeze hanging in the air, that was enough to make my feet and hands go cold (literally), but the sky was blue and the sun bright in the sky. He was surprised with the weather, because it had been overcast for several days before I arrived and I took it as a good omen.

We walked to the car and I paid attention to every little thing: how he opened the door for me, how clean and tidy the car was, his light, graying hair that was once an exuberant auburn mane, the freckled, scorched skin of his arms and hands. He was so different from everyone I knew. I observed him while he drove. He had a stern look on his face; he always looks like that when he drives. I had difficulty understanding him at times and I asked him often if it was a countryside accent or Gregonese.

It was late afternoon; we had to find a place to overnight before dark. We found a motel just outside Brisbane. We did go for a stroll before heading to the motel, but the romantic stroll on the beach I imagined in our e-mails was a stroll on a muddy, mangrove-like beach with rubbish everywhere. There are no beaches in Brisbane!

I remember carrying my huge suitcases up and down the stairs that night and the paper on the lid of the toilet seat that said "cleaned and disinfected", while in fact, there was a big poop floating under it! Very inspiring, very romantic, indeed!

I called home in the evening. The mobile connection was very bad. I called my older brother Ji. The whole family would be there and I hoped I would catch them all, but it was too early for them and he was the only one there. Bummer!

The room had two beds; that made our first night easy. I woke up early the next day, all excited, ready to go to a wildlife park to see koalas, kangaroos, wombats, Tasmanian devils and dingos. It was a really nice day and I bought my Aussie leather hat I dreamt of in Brazil. Much later, when I got to know Greg better, I realized the effort he was making. He's not an early person at all. I used to like having breakfast early and he doesn't eat anything until noon, but then, he was bravely having early breakfasts with me.

Then we headed to the Gold Coast, Surfers Paradise and Kirra. That was more like what I knew of Australia: blue sunny sky, beautiful beaches and crystal clear water. We walked side by side on the edge of the water. I wanted to get my feet wet. It was too cool to swim. I held his hand, but then I felt awkward again and let his hand go. He noticed that. I was still so confused. Who was this guy, really?

We stayed in a high-rise, beachfront hotel. It was very windy, but the view was beautiful, the deep blue ocean extending as far as the eye could see.

We went for a stroll on the beach that evening. There was a University swimming championship going on. We stopped where it was a bit quieter and sat side by side on the sand. I looked at the sky full with stars, there was no moon, the breeze was too cool and I couldn't get comfortable, so we walked back to the hotel. Up in our room, I lit a cigarette and so did Greg. We went to the balcony and he hugged me. The hotel only had double beds available, so we slept in the same bed, but the only things that touched were our toes! Greg says that the thing he will always remember about that night is what I said, just before I turned to my side and fell asleep: "keep your hands to yourself!"

Next, we spent a week in Byron Bay. We stayed in a neat and clean self-contained cabin.

The setting was ideal for us to continue checking each other out. He was so quiet, so humble, a real gentleman. I still couldn't understand everything he said and he had that serious expression that I didn't understand, but I liked him anyway.

His patience certainly didn't go unnoticed. He seemed amused by my always leaving things behind or stuff that kept falling out of the bags all the time; they were always too full or didn't close properly. I had so many bags and I never knew in which one I had put what.

On a phone call from his brother, I heard Greg complain about spending too much money, but he also said that I was lovely. I wondered if he really wanted to be there. When I asked him about it weeks later, he said he didn't expect anything else but to pay for the expenses of that week.

Byron Bay reminded me a lot of Paraty: the alternative scene, beautiful beaches, surfers, greenies, druggies, arts and crafts, musicians, festivals, markets, natural food and people doing tai chi and yoga on the beaches. Yes, it was all too familiar.

There were a few sunny days, which we spent on the beach. The breeze was not too cool. Greg seemed to be cooking under the parasol, his shirt and hat on. I looked at his eyelashes and eyebrows, they were so light, his skin so white. I lay on my towel, sun baking. It amazed him I could just stay in the sun like that. "But, the sun isn't even hot..." I said.

The water was rather cool, but still good for a quick, refreshing dive. Some girls walked around topless and the many pudgy ones kept their clothes on.

We had many strolls on the beach with the pelicans walking by our side. We sat on the lighthouse cliffs, watched the dolphins and turtles playing in the sea below. The ocean had that dark turquoise color I love so much, hard to say if it's blue or green and in the evenings we watched the sunsets. Even though my hands and feet were always cold because of the constant breeze, we both decided that it would be a nice place to start a living.

When the days were overcast, we went to see the surroundings. We visited the Nightcap National Park and passed through Nimbin, a town lost in time, a refuge for all those who lost their way going to or coming back from Woodstock. The colorful buildings, painted with drawings from floor to roof told me that the town moved more on pot than on petrol. Half the shops sold arts and crafts. Greg thought I fitted in pretty well with my army pants and red henna hair, but I told him I'd been there and done that. I was ready for something else.

Nightcap and its waterfalls were gorgeous. It reminded me very much of the tracks we used to follow to the beaches in Paraty, but cooler. There were lots of palm trees and I was surprised to see handrails and walkways if not all the way, at least in those places which were harder to walk. We don't have that in Brazil, even though the bush is thicker and the tracks harder to follow. To venture into the bush in Brazil one needs to be fit!

I also noticed that the sun seems so much brighter here than in other tropical places I've been. It kind of blinds you; I couldn't walk around in the sun without sunglasses. The sun seems to burn more, it feels more scorching on the skin, I wonder if it's because it's so much drier here. In Brazil, I could easily spend all day under a sun of over 40°C, with little protection. I wouldn't think of doing that here! Greg told me that Australia has the highest rate of skin cancer in the world.

I was pleased to find that many of the supermarket items I was used to in Brazil were also available here. In time, I found almost perfect substitutes for everything. Prices of clothing and food were not outrageous, but meat is quite expensive. People in general seemed relaxed and laid-back, everything felt familiar and that was comforting. What was completely new to me was seeing dead kangaroos on the roads, a fair few of them too. In Brazil, we only see dead dogs and cats. It took me some time to get used to the traffic going in the wrong direction and the steering wheel and everything else in the car being on the opposite side. I don't know how many times Greg had to grab me by the arm as I started crossing the road looking the wrong way or had a laugh when I got in the car on the wrong side. Three years later, I was still getting confused at times.

Without those wonderful days, I don't think things between Greg and I would ever have worked. I think it was very important that we were able to forget about everything else, all the usual worries of everyday and spend time getting to know each other, understanding differences, exploring likes and dislikes, going places and talking about worries and fears, in short, plowing the ground for love to grow.

From Byron Bay, we went to Wallangarra. It was a Sunday afternoon. The house and the neighborhood were exactly as in the pictures Greg had sent me. Mumboy received us at the door. There were big hugs and kisses for Greg, for me, a handshake.

Wallangarra is a small town, like so many in Australia. It sits 800 meters high on the Great Dividing Range, with a population of

800 people. A three hours' drive inland from the coast and a four hours drive to the south from Brisbane, on the border between Queensland and New South Wales. A dry and rocky region known as the Granite Belt dotted with wineries and fruit plantations.

Greg lived in the outskirts of town at the edge of the bush, no people around. The intense silence was broken now and then with break time at the primary school nearby and the kookaburras, galahs and lorikeets.

In May temperatures start to drop to near zero in the night, but it's still sunny during the day. The fire was kept burning all day, but doors and windows were also kept open all the time for the dogs and Mumboy. She was always hot and I was always cold! Most of the time I felt out of place, but I loved that silence, the huge backyard and the sunsets over the hills. So many times Greg and I sat on the back door to watch the sunset together, each day a different spectacle. Inside, the house was also exactly as in the pictures I'd seen. No surprises there. Everything would have felt overwhelmingly strange if I hadn't seen those photographs.

Greg's bedroom/office, which I also knew from the pictures, was messy indeed: computers, equipment, wires and boxes everywhere. It had a double bed, where he used to sleep, but Mumboy made us a nice cozy place at the end of the big "L" shaped living room, separated from the rest of the house by a large bookcase and a wardrobe. It gave us a bit of privacy, but we could still hear the TV and what was going on in the rest of the house.

The first time I stepped into the kitchen, I noticed the persimmons in the fruit bowl and I thought of Tayna. He loves them. A few days later, in an e-mail, he asked me if they had them here. I couldn't believe the coincidence! It was not the big red soft one, more common in Brazil, it was a smaller and firmer variety, the kind we call chocolate persimmon in Brazil, so Tayna explained to me.

Our first night in Wallangarra was also our first night together. Greg took the initiative and I let it go. He was very, very tender and sweet. Taking into account the circumstances: two people from opposites sides of the globe, grown up in totally different cultures, with totally different backgrounds, who had seen each other for the first time only ten days before, taking into account Greg's shyness and my worries, it's actually a miracle that things went so well. Nonetheless, it took me some time to feel completely comfortable with him. I still had so many worries: the boys, getting a job, a life, and Greg's true intentions. A bit overwhelmed by all the different things and people I had to get used to. If it were up to me it would have taken a lot more time for something to happen between us. Greg later told me he didn't know where he got the courage from.

After a few days in Wallangarra, the dust started to settle and slowly things got back to normal. Greg had to catch up with his work and I was left to myself for most of the day.
Exactly as Greg had said, the Freshwaters were simple and ordinary people. They were strict about dinnertime. You are supposed to come to table as soon as dinner was called and cleaning-up is supposed to happen immediately after you are finished. At home in Brazil, no one really expected anything of me, so that was a bit of a change.
The relationship between Greg and Mumboy was something completely new to me. I have never seen anything like it. I still don't think I understand it completely.
My relationship with my mother had never been without tension and misunderstanding, as was my relationship with the boys and especially Tayna. Greg and his mother know each other inside out, there's a deep understanding and perfect communication, not a single word spoken to each other is misinterpreted. I find it beautiful, but it was also quite overwhelming at times. She was always there. Greg wasn't the only one I needed to keep happy.

I loved Mumboy's bread making every other day, the wonderful smell of hot bread all over the house. Bread machines were another novelty for me. Like I did so many times before, I had to put up with the laughs when they found out that I used the computer mouse upside down. I don't know why I do that. The manager from the GIS office I worked for thought I was dyslexic, whatever that means. All I know is that I have never had problems learning nor writing. I think I just learned it wrong and the habit became too ingrained to change now. I have tried it several times, but even Greg can't believe how hard it is for me to use it the right way. He even developed software and a little hardware that turned everything upside down, without having to use the mouse upside down, because I did get cramps in my thumb at times, when I used it for too long like that.

Nowadays, there's free software that can make those changes in no time.

I thought of Tayna again when I discovered Vegemite. We used to buy a very similar product in Holland called Marmite, which he loved, but according to Greg, Vegemite is the real thing; it's all vegetarian too, which is a plus. It's a very salty black paste. It makes everything taste great if used in moderation. It is especially tasty on toast but it's one of those things you have to learn to like. Every Aussie grows up with it. It's like the granulated chocolate on bread or the salty licorice from Holland. They, too, can taste strange for those who haven't grown up with them. Interesting how every country's got its own peculiar and unique tastes!

Greg gave me a computer and a scanner and I started to organize the files and pictures I had previously sent to him from Brazil. I discovered the world of digital imagery and I spent many days making letter paper and backgrounds, I scanned and fixed many childhood pictures, some of which were quite damaged. When I sent them to friends and family, it put a smile in the face of some and brought tears to the eyes of others. I could finally give all the original old pictures back to Mum, something she had been asking for and complaining about for ages. I also had hundreds of other pictures I had brought with me. For years, I kept putting them away in a box, hoping to put them into photo books one day. That day had come. I had all the time of the world to sort and organize them. In Byron Bay, I had bought a bagful of postcards to send to friends and family back home but realized that I had forgotten all my addresses. How typical!

I started jogging and I quit smoking, as I had planned. I knew that to quit, all I had to do was to get my blood pumping faster in my veins. I knew that with the influx of oxygen, I wouldn't want to smoke any more. I had to quit coffee and drinks for a while as well. I didn't think I could have those without a cigarette. I can't stand the smoke or the smell of cigarettes ever since. Greg was supposed to have stopped as well, but he never did.

There were days when everything seemed right and familiar, and others when I felt completely out of place. I found it difficult to understand Dadboy and I guess he found it as difficult to understand me; true communication was quite limited, but he was easy-going and happy most of the time. A simple, hardworking man, who reminded me very much of my own father. He would always offer me a drink before dinner.

They were doing their best to be nice to me, to make me feel at ease. Mumboy had been an Avon lady most of her life and she was always spoiling me with creams and other little presents. I appreciated that and in turn, I made an effort to fit in.

All in all my first impressions of Australia, Greg and his family were good. A beautiful country, simple people and life was calm and easy. My dreams weren't shattered. Greg was a sweetie and I had the feeling that I had taken the right step and that I was going to find my destination in Australia.

36 Big Day

Limboland

From the first day I arrived in Wallangarra two things were my main concern: to keep in contact with the boys back in Brazil and to make sense of Greg and me.

The boys seemed to be doing all right. It was easier to talk to Tayna, as he was still with my parents in São Paulo and he had my computer with him. It was so nice exchanging e-mails and ideas with him about everything: the mind and the body, psychotherapy, dreams, films we saw, social issues and so on. But it would be weeks before I heard anything of Raoni and only because he had run out of money. It was hard for him to get to a computer. At Uni, the computer rooms were always jam-packed. At home in Paraty, in the weekends things didn't get much better. Normally the computer is out of order and the telephones often cut out. The house in Paraty was messy and under renovations as usual. Not being able to regularly communicate with him was frustrating and I missed him so much.

Raoni had missed classes and wasn't doing very well at school, but life was fun, anyway. I worried if he had managed to get all his stuff. He had moved into a new house with other students a few days before I left and I didn't have the time to help him move. Shortly after classes started, public servants went on strike in the state and universities stopped soon after. Everything turned into chaos. Nothing was working; restaurant and library were closed, so he went away with friends to the north.

As I settled into the normal routine of the Freshwaters, the afternoons and nights became cooler. The days were so quiet, so sunny. I looked at the endless blue skies in search of clouds, but they wouldn't show up for days on end. I felt so incredibly peaceful in those moments, all the madness of the last previous months in São Paulo, seemed so far away.

Being together felt good and right to Greg and me. A future life together wasn't hard to imagine; we had to begin planning for the future. We had to find out how to formalize our situation in Australia - mine and the boys. So many important decisions had to be made. It soon became clear that I couldn't work without a resident visa and the easiest way to get one was to marry Greg.

That wouldn't happen straight away, so we had several more months to think about it all and to get to know each other better.

We didn't know then, but this was to be the beginning of an unbelievable bureaucratic marathon, which lasted almost a year and spanned three countries. Everything took so long and official information was often contradictory. We never knew if we were doing the best thing.

This made me terribly restless at times. Every day I hoped for a call, a letter, something, anything to make me feel our life was going somewhere. But nothing ever happened; all I could do was wait. Wait for answers from people in Brazil, wait for things to happen here, wait for papers to arrive. Life seemed to be passing me by in slow motion. Like life in Wallangarra, nothing much happened apart from the race in my head. No people in the streets, no people to meet, nothing exciting would ever happen. Meeting Greg's friends didn't help much. I could barely understand them. I wasn't really prepared for the long waiting period that it would take to sort out my situation in Australia. My life had become a deep, thick Limbo. When my mind turned to the future, it all seemed so abstract, so out of reach. Having my own place, having my own life, any life, was just a distant possibility. Days and weeks passed by and it felt like centuries. At times, everything felt surreal. I know of many people that would have gone mad in that situation.

To marry Greg I had to get divorced from my Australian husband and to do that we needed to find him. We searched phone books, called people with the same surname, called people near to where we thought he would be; nothing. He was nowhere to be found and nobody knew of him. So we decided to make the trip to the Sunshine Coast, where he used to live; a five-hour drive north. We found his brother, but he didn't know of him either: "Maybe in Victoria picking fruit". We left messages everywhere we could think of.

The trip in itself was nice. It was a beautiful sunny day and we stopped at the beaches on the way back. It was pitch black when we reached the mountains and saw fire ahead of us. When we got closer, we saw it was a car on fire. Further down the road was the driver. I couldn't believe how calm he was. I suppose he had his insurance well sorted out. We asked if he was all right and needed something. He asked us to call his brother on the mobile when we reached somewhere where we could get a signal and gave us the number. As we drove away, I looked back and saw the car explode just before the whole thing disappeared behind the hill. He had explained to us that it ran on LPG and that the tank was full, he was waiting for it to happen. It was like being in a James Bond movie.

In The Garra (Wallangarra), lots of little annoying problems began to show up in Brazil. I had spent the last months in Brazil running around madly trying to organize everything, trying to finish all my business so that I wouldn't be harassed by it so far away. Nice try! Although I think the most important things were fairly well sorted out, there were a thousand smaller ones: letters would arrive for me that required responses, speeding and parking tickets to pay (I built up quite a collection of them in my last few weeks in Brazil); I had court cases going on, one was a work related issue and the other a car accident; people kept calling about translations; there were tax issues to be sorted out and even results of medical tests that I hadn't had time to pick up.

My bank account in Brazil got into the red at some stage. After many calls to banks and family in Brazil, I came to the conclusion that I had miscalculated the payments of the installments of my plane ticket and they direct debited a last one that I didn't expect. Many more e-mails and phone calls had to come and go before I managed to sort the problem out. Telephone bills skyrocketed. The fax was hot with papers to sign that came and went. Poor Tatol (Tayna) spent a lot of time and effort running around in town to try to sort the mess out.

I had lost control of everything there and I didn't have anything under control over here either. I felt stuck in every possible way and there was nothing I could do.

I filled the long hours and days with a phone call now and then, writing letters to authorities, organizing pictures, playing with digital images, surfing the net, sending e-mails to the boys and friends, receiving error messages, friendship e-mails, jokes, good wishes, wisdom and self-help e-mails, petitions from women in Zimbabwe and Afghanistan to bears in China, virus warnings, pass-on and religious e-mails and all the junk mail you can never be rid of. Much time slipped by fixing computer crashes and virus attacks and watching the National Geographic and Discovery Channels. I spent months, days and hours reading about self-publishing and e-books and dreaming about the future. I helped around in the house here and there and I even helped Mumboy put together a gigantic puzzle, something I hadn't done since childhood. There was the weekly drive to Tenterfield for groceries and an eventual trip to a park nearby.

I started re-reading all the e-mails Greg and I exchanged and a vague idea of using them for a book started to develop in my mind.

One day, to the family's horror, I gave Greg's room a big clean up. Apparently, this hadn't happened in years. I only found out much later, that Greg really doesn't like changing and moving things around. Many more days and hours were spent putting together a 200 page English exercises folder for the boys to do when they got here, progressing from basic to intermediate, but they never ever looked into them. "Too boring" they said.

I missed my pussycat so much. She was a true mongrel one, big and skinny. She had three colors, like only female cats can have. She was a bit messed up as well. She had spent the first two months of her life in hell, in a house full with little children who played, squeezed and threw those little defenseless kittens around as if they were rubber toys. She was so peculiar. She loved to come along when I took the dogs for walks and only drank water straight from the tap, refusing to drink from a bowl. She could also be a little aggressive and wild at times. One of her favorite spots was the top of the big fridge, where she would watch the family eating together at the table below and the old black trunk at the end of the corridor, where Mum kept all the blankets and other winter stuff. She would sit there, waiting for me to pass and then jump on me, sticking her nails through my clothes, to get a ride to the bedroom. She scared the living daylights out of me a few times when I passed there in the dark. I loved to see her playing the piano on Dad's belly before finding the coziest position to lie down. In the morning, she loved jumping on his lap when he was at the table. With her back paws on his lap and the front ones on the edge of the table, she liked to observe very attentively Pa preparing the dogs' breakfast and giving it to them on the floor next to him. She would look at the dogs with an air of superiority as they scoffed down the pieces of bread with spread cheese.
They told me she looked for me like crazy after I left, meowing up and down the corridor. Were they taking good care of her?
It gave me great comfort to hear that she and Dad had become good pals. But alas, it wouldn't be for long. She got very sick and died, less than six months after my departure. I felt I had abandoned her and I felt bad about it.

By the end of June, I was shocked with the temperature dropping to -8 °C while Greg still walked outside barefooted. I always thought Australia was a tropical country!

Even though it's sunny and the sky is blue most of the time, temperatures can drop to −18°C, as we found out in 2002, the chilly winds can pierce through one's soul. It snowed in 1986 and again in 2005.

My money had come to an end and Greg had to start sending money of his own to the boys. I was not happy about it. Sending money over was a big problem too, unless I was prepared to pay A$ 30 to send it over every time. There had to be a cheaper option and I tried different ones, but checks were bounced back, didn't arrive or couldn't be received for one reason or another. It was a nightmare. For every check, half the family in Brazil had to be mobilized; long trips downtown had to be made and fees and other bank costs were subtracted from the amount I sent. It always took so long for them to get the money that often the boys were without a cent. They frequently didn't have money for the bus to school, books or medicines and it upset me very much. At one time, it took about two months before the money could be accessed. The oldies often had to advance it.

With no money in my bank account in Brazil, I decided to close it down and with it my credit card, to avoid any future problems. Such a simple idea, but such a hassle to put in practice. I realized too late that leaving it open would have saved me so much trouble and not having a credit card, would prove to be a bad idea as well.

Hours, days, months passed by in Limboland while the sky was always blue. Nothing seemed to happen in my life, so I lived life through e-mails. With every one that arrived, I could transport myself to somewhere else. I could be in Paraty, watching the boys surf or in their classrooms; I almost heard the laughs when Tayna told me a teacher had asked what his name meant and when he explained, "Planet Venus" another student replied, "That's why he's always spaced out."

I could almost hear the traffic and feel the fog burning my eyes, the sweat and the smells, as Tayna told me how full the buses were to school. I could follow the folks in São Paulo in their trips to the farm and the barbecues or Rubinho (Johanna's hubby) in his new theatre projects.

Raoni's attempts to get himself organized, trying to sort out his bank papers, driver's license and his study tasks exasperated and worried me; his life seemed so chaotic; I wished so much I could help him. He seemed to be a bit lost and overwhelmed in his new life on his own. My eyes filled with tears when I read how hard he found keeping pace with the mad tempo of Uni, how he missed me and life in Paraty and how annoyed he was that it was so difficult to keep in touch. Everything felt unfamiliar and out of place, he said. Paraty didn't feel like home anymore and his father had grown older after their departure, the silence and the emptiness in the house.

I told him his place was here, where I could give him far more support than he was getting over there, but I didn't hear from him for another month and I became more and more convinced that the boys had to come over, the sooner the better.

Then, one night in mid July, we had a phone call from my Australian ex. I explained the whole situation; he understood it and was willing to cooperate. He would be in touch. That was a big relief.

In August I had to leave the country, because my three months' visa was due to expire. The Australian tourist visa is usually for one year, but every three months you have to cross the border. Don't ask me why. We decided to go to Vanuatu, in Melanesia. A decision based upon misguided information, like so many of the information we've got. We had been told that New Zealand, which was cheaper to go to at the time, didn't count as a foreign country. I have since known many tourists cross to New Zealand and back without a problem.

Vanuatu, as a tropical island in the Pacific, has got its attractions. We stayed six days, enjoying incredible crystal clear, blue water and bottomless blue holes amongst the corals surrounding most of the main island. In the main island, there are few sandy beaches.

The hotel had a natural swimming pool with turtles and coral fish; it also had a natural shark aquarium, but service was pretty poor and for the rest I wasn't too impressed.

I got really pissed off with the locals trying to squeeze every cent they could out of us or any other foreigner for that matter.

Everything was absurdly expensive.

Every day of our stay was heavily overcast and we had a lot of rain.

I saw coconut crabs of over one kg and I had to try one at a restaurant in town, only to conclude that the little purple mangrove crabs we have in Brazil taste much better.

I slipped and fell over the corals on the beach, hurting myself pretty badly. But I was lucky, it could have been much worse.

The cameras broke and I lost a whole film of wonderful pictures. Greg and I also had our first argument or something like it, because Greg didn't say a word, but I could see he wasn't happy at all. I wanted to see as much as possible and I was in a hurry to go everywhere. Greg wanted to take it easy, he wasn't feeling well; he's actually, never in a hurry for anything. He had caught a cold in the plane and was feeling miserable most of the time.

I got some satisfaction out of his confusion, when he drove a car we rented. In Vanuatu, they drive on the normal side of the road. He excused himself saying that it would have been easier if the steering wheel was also on the left side.

My feelings towards Greg were still a bit contradictory. I liked being with him very much. He gave me a comfort and peace of mind I had not experienced before in any of my previous relationships. Yet, he was still a bit of a stranger to me. I couldn't figure him out completely. He looked so stern at times. Was he pissed off with something? With me? I can't really explain, but I just knew deep inside that Greg was the guy for me. I think I have always needed someone like him: someone with his feet on the ground and he's always so sweet. I felt so safe with him.

In the plane, in the way back, I watched the sunset in awe. It was breathtaking. We were flying over the clouds and as the sun disappeared through them, it covered them with a million shades of orange. From red and bright orange, the tints around the sun gently faded into a pale shade of yellow the further away from the sun I looked. As I looked up, the yellow reflection of the clouds in the sky slowly mixed in with tones of blue which became deeper and darker the further and higher I looked; all those beautiful tones of blue that no painter will ever be able to reproduce. There was only one star shining bright in the sky: Tayna, the evening star and my mind drifted away back home.

As we approached my new home, Greg started to feel better and I started to feel miserable. I hadn't had a cold that bad in many years.

Back in Brazil, the boys were having so much fun: the money falling into their accounts, a lot of surfing, travelling and partying around with friends.

None of them had ever worked enough to understand what real life in Brazil meant. I'm sure I never got the whole story of what was really going on, but what did get through about their messing around, their mishaps, made them look lost to me and my eyes were often filled with tears. I had the impression they were going nowhere and that couldn't continue. I started to worry so much, time was passing by, and soon they would be too old to be put with me in my immigration application. I couldn't bear the idea of living here separated from them by some stupid country border.

Both were showing reluctance to come. I urged them; I tried to explain that the situation they were living in wouldn't last for ever, that reality would hit one day, and that they would realize that life can't be fun all the time. I tried to explain that life here would be hard in the beginning because of the lack of friends, but that in the long run, they would be better off here. But, I look back at all those e-mails I sent and they seem so chaotic to me today. I think I only confused them and made them even more hesitant about coming, especially Tayna. He was attending Uni; Grandpa was kind enough to lend him the car to go to Paraty on the weekends. He had all he needed and was happy and Raoni wanted to see me more settled, with some sort of life.

I called a few universities to ask about diploma recognition, but when I looked for my folder with all my diplomas and certificates I realized I had left it behind in Brazil. I couldn't believe it. I had that bloody folder on top of everything on my desk. I kept it in sight all the time while I was packing in Brazil, to make sure I wouldn't forget it and yet I did forget it, after all.

The universities would be pleased to help me if I enrolled as an international student in one of their courses, for A\$ 15 to A\$ 30 thousand a year. How kind of them!

It was not until well into 2001 that I found out about NOORS (National Office of Overseas Skills Recognition) and had my Diplomas recognized at no cost. Tell me about learning everything the hard way! Why didn't the universities tell me about it?

I also looked into getting my stuff over. I asked Tayna if he could repack and catalogue everything - about 3 m² of boxes with all sorts of things and then arrange to send it here.

"No way!" I got to hear. I had run away, head over heels. It was my own fault I didn't sort my stuff out, as I should, before I left.

I wondered what I had done wrong to get a reaction like that from my son and Greg thought it unthinkable to give a parent an answer like that. He may be right, but I haven't seen him jumping with joy when requested to do something for his family, either, especially if it's a big job. For me, if it's not given with pleasure, I don't want it. Tayna didn't have to do anything if he didn't want to.

A few e-mails later, Tayna excused himself and said he would do it. As usual, my heart melted, but the whole thing lost its meaning by then. I wouldn't have bothered had I known that six years later I still wouldn't have the money for it or anyone willing to sort things out for me in Brazil.

I also had the brilliant idea of selling the return part of my ticket. I'd seen Ursula and Ilona do it before and I thought I was being clever, but all we got was a big argument with a guy on e-Bay who thought he had got a ticket to Brazil for one dollar, though our advert said to contact seller for details.

For the rest, I couldn't complain really. I was more often happy than not. The family kept trying to please and spoil me. Buster, one of the dogs of the house, became my mate and jogging companion. Actually, I became his possession. Nobody was allowed near me if he was around. I've never seen a dog that looks so much like a cat as he does. If he's not in the mood for you, he'll let you know. I had lost my cat, but I got Buster.

By the end of August, we met my Australian ex at the Family Court in Brisbane. He looked awful: skinny, shabby and smelly. Greg couldn't believe I had married that! I tried to excuse myself by saying that he didn't look that bad then. Anyway, sucker as I am, I just felt so sorry for him. He looked so lost. Will he ever find himself? Does he still smoke so much pot?

After he signed all the papers, we tried to lodge them. They wanted not only the original documents and the translations, but also, with every translation, an affidavit signed by the translator. Out of the more than a dozen papers I gave them, there was one affidavit the translator forgot to sign and because of that, they wouldn't take the application.

We had waited three months for the translations to arrive and two months for an appointment; we had made the four-hour drive to Brisbane to lodge the bloody papers and we had waited half an hour in the queue – and it had all been for nothing. As I tried to convince the clerk to accept the application, pending our sending the last document, I touched her arm. She screamed at me: "keep your hands off me", people waiting in the queues and other clerks behind the counter looked back as if I had grabbed her and was assaulting her or something.

"Holy cow" I thought. That woman was really screwed up, I think. I wanted to scream, but I kept telling myself, that it all must have a reason.

Why do I hate these bureaucratic people so much? What am I supposed to be learning here? Why is this all happening?

Getting that one little paper signed by the original translator was unbelievable. I sent copies of the papers to that government translating mob, TIS (Translating and Interpreting Services). In all public instances, in every piece of paper, form and leaflet from the Government, you'll see that mob's contact address and number in case you need a translation.

I sent them by express post; they didn't receive them. I sent them by fax, same thing, by fax again. When they finally got it, they didn't want to do it. They couldn't understand why I was not satisfied with the translation. According to them, it had been checked and re-checked and was considered to have no problems whatsoever. They couldn't understand what they had to do with an affidavit for the Family Court. I ended up having to pay for an entire new translation that took another few months to be done. The whole thing seems to me even more absurd today than it felt then.

Half way through September, spring arrived. The air filled with a thousand sweet smells from an explosion of flowers, cheerful noises of lorikeets, singing of birds and busy bees.

The Olympics began as well. I had bet with Greg that Brazil would take at least the soccer and the beach volley, but Brazil kept frustrating my hopes and soon my interest was replaced by annoyance due to the overdose of the whole thing on TV.

I moved my desk and stuff from Greg's working room to the living room, where it was much warmer.

I could forget about everything looking at the blue sky through the window, the sun and its blessing rays covering everything with light and warmth and the many colorful lorikeets and galahs looking for insects and seeds in that vast backyard.

Life seemed so peaceful, but in my head, the storms never stopped raging: thunder, lightning and heavy, dark clouds. There were days when I was cranky all day and I couldn't really come up with any decent excuse for it or I would burst into tears for no apparent reason. Now and then, I would go mad with doubts. I had suspicions about Greg's real intentions; I would think he only wanted a woman, any woman, nothing more; all my needs and aspirations didn't matter at all.

Somewhere in October, I had a crisis. I felt increasingly vulnerable, my resistances and defenses started to crumble down. Much about Greg and me was still quite confusing in my mind. One night he was a bit tired, things in bed didn't go very well and Greg fell quickly asleep, afterwards. It was the second time that had happened; we had spoken about it before. Doubt came back to my mind with all its strength. I wanted to run away, but I couldn't. A rage came from I don't know where and took me over.

As I watched him sleep, a thousand thoughts came to my mind: do you give a damn? Should I talk to you? Do I keep all these thoughts to myself? I don't want to hurt you. Am I being an idiot? Is it all going to go wrong again in my life? What do I mean to you? Are we playing hide and seek? I don't know... I know nothing anymore. I don't know if all this is right. Will we ever be able to accept, understand and love each other completely or are we from different worlds? I still feel a stranger amongst you, after all these months. I may be wrong, only confused. I better wait, I better silence.

The turmoil in my head lasted several days until I eventually, burst into tears uncontrollably. Mumboy asked Greg what was going on. I had a hard time explaining my feelings to him; it wasn't easy at all. Greg got really upset that I had let it get that far. He said he felt pushed away and he was sincerely sorry. I never had another crisis like that in regards to us and from then on, I became convinced he truly loved me.

I often thought things would have been a lot easier for me if we had have our own space from the start, but we both knew we couldn't afford it.

Living with the family was so hard at times. I had been living with my own family in Brazil for so long. I had to fit in and make sense not of Greg only, but of an entire family. I longed so much for my own space.

I held my horses, I kept my mouth shut and I kept out of the way so many times. God knows how hard that has been. Those who know me well grew used to my big mouth.

But here, I had to ignore all the little things that annoyed me, comments made, opinions and ideas contrary to mine. How many times, did I get close to freaking out with one thing or another?

Sometimes it would be the smallest of things, little complaints about things I did.

There were days when I felt a complete stranger in a strange house with strange people, in a strange world. Like a wild animal in a cage, wishing I wasn't there. I asked myself so many times what the hell I was doing there and what the hell I was doing with my life. Where was the warmth of Brazil? Where were all my people? The people who accept me for what I am, people who don't look at me amused, as if I am a chimp in the zoo.

One day as they often did, Mumboy watched as I made my sandwich, I asked, "What's so interesting?" She started to cry and ran away and I felt even worse.

Tayna's feelings about coming here went from one pole to the other. One day he seemed sure about wanting to come after finishing Uni and the other he didn't have a clue if what he was doing was what he really wanted. I didn't think he was happy there and he didn't seem too sure where he was heading. I asked my brothers to try to have a talk with him, try to show him that finishing his studies here would be better for him. Meanwhile, my mother became serious about selling the house; she had been talking about it for quite a while and had already spoken to a few real estate agents while I was still there. She was sick of cleaning and taking care of such a big house, she was sick of São Paulo and they wanted to move to the farm.

Today I wonder if selling the house wasn't just her way of coping with the loneliness she felt in the house, but back then, I truly believed she was just waiting for me to leave, so she could get rid of the house. I felt like a stone in her shoe all my life. I didn't want Tayna to feel the same

Where was Tayna going to live if they sold the house? He could live with Johanna, who lived nearby, but she didn't think his father would help her with the extra expenses of having him there. Tayna would have to go to Rio, rent a place. It all sounded so complicated. I began to get anxious.

It took Tayna some time, but when he realized he would eventually have to leave São Paulo before finishing his studies, he got quite upset about it.

Like his brother, he also worried about me not being ready to receive them, but I had it all sorted out in my head. I reckoned the whole immigration and divorce thing would be over by the end of November and that I would be able to start working straight after that. We were informed by an officer from DIAC (Immigration Dept.) that the boys didn't have to be here to lodge their visa applications together with me. That would make it possible for me to work for four months before they arrived. I would be able to save money to rent a house and receive the boys in March. They would then study English in their first year here and work a bit for a while, until they were sure what study they wanted to follow. In time, they would go to Uni. They would be able to study and work part-time to make ends meet. It would be hard for a year or two, but things would eventually, get easier. When our visas were sorted out, they would be able to get some assistance from the government with their studies. They were aware that they would have to help in the household and they were okay with it in theory.

I was thoroughly convinced life for the boys here would be better. I had a vision and hoped that finally, we would be reunited once more, even if it was to be only for a short time, so that I could help them find their direction in life.

I needed so much to see them going in the right direction. Most of all I wanted them to come here to rethink their choices, to find their true calling. I thought an education here would help them a long way, even if they decided to go back to Brazil in a few years. But, they didn't have plans to stay here for long. They just wanted to study some English and check things out and their reluctance killed me.

I didn't want to force them. I wanted them to make the decision by themselves, but as time passed, I worried more and more. Even though they were not sure yet about anything, we had to start to sort out papers, because we didn't have a lot of time.

Another cross-country marathon of papers and translations started and Tayna hated every moment of it. He had to go back and forth to pick up papers and even postpone trips to Paraty. Come to think about it, it's actually a miracle that he did all he did!

After my nightmarish experiences with translations here, I tried to translate papers in Brazil, in the hope it would be faster there. What a mistake!

Then October came to an end, another three months had gone by and I had to cross the border again. Things were taking so long to get sorted out, papers so long to arrive. I didn't have a clue any more when I would ever be able to start looking for work. Time was passing and I was worried I wouldn't be able to receive the boys properly when they arrived. That's when I proposed to Greg for the first time, that I go to Holland for a while, earn some money and then come back, but he found the idea unthinkable. Instead, off I go to Vanuatu again, this time, on my own.

A few minutes into the flight, I saw a cockroach coming out of the upper bag compartment, in front of me. I lost my peace of mind for the rest of the trip. I had to keep an eye on it and know where it was heading. Lucky it was a little one. If it was a bigger one, I would have to call the stewardess.

The trip package included a stay in a bungalow. When I opened the bedroom door, two big geckos, ran from behind it and I almost had a heart attack, as I was still jumpy from the cockroach in the plane. The bath was more like a little swimming pool and the bed was just right for my size, if Greg was there, his feet would be hanging over the edge!

I slept badly. It felt strange being alone again. Greg had been such an overwhelming presence in my life in the last six-seven months.

It was heavily overcast most of the time, but now and then, blue spots appeared in the sky and the sun came through, so I went to the beach anyway. It was completely empty. I had a long walk looking for shells and watching the hermit crabs playing their funny games. I walked in the shallow sea over the corals to get to the edge where the coral reef finishes suddenly, forming a sharp steep cliff down into the sea. It becomes very deep all of a sudden. As I got closer, I imagined the coral reef breaking under my weight and me getting trapped under it, so I backed off.

In the afternoon, back at the bungalow, I saw that one of the shells I caught was still inhabited, so I went back to the beach to take Mr. Hermit Crab back and was surprised by a wonderful sunset.

The night turned into a beautiful tropical starry night. I watched the sky and the big full moon silvering the leaves of the coconut trees, while enjoying a cup of coffee on the verandah.

It was warm, and I could hear the sea nearby. My mind drifted away in memories of younger, worry-free days travelling in the northeast of Brazil; the same stars in the sky but, different coconut trees. I was bitten back to reality by the mozzies, so I went to bed hoping the sky would stay clear. I thought a lot about Greg. I think I could say I loved him by then. My life without him felt strange. I thought of all our plans for the future; all the things we still had to sort out.

My last night was cut short at 4:30 a.m. by the driver of the hotel. He was taking us to the airport to catch the flight back to Australia at 7 a.m.

We flew over the beautiful reefs and islands of New Caledonia. How disappointing it was to see the pictures afterwards. What the lens was able to capture through the cramped, dull window of the plane was but a faint, hazy glimpse of the beauty that I saw.

Back in Australia, customs didn't like my army pants. They went through every bag, every pocket, every single thing I had. My bag of dirty undies and even my sanitary napkins, every nook and cranny in my bags was emptied and turned inside out.

How much money have you got? Where are you going to stay? How long? What's this? What's it for?

When I thought they were finished I was asked to accompany another officer who took me to a room and left me there without saying a word. I waited for about twenty minutes and a woman came and started questioning me. She went through every single piece of paper she could find on me, read them all and asked me to read the ones written in Dutch and Portuguese. Man, she asked so many questions!

I thought it was all normal procedure and didn't think much about it. Calmly, I explained my whole situation with Greg, our plans, the divorce procedure, our marriage plans, even my writing plans. It was only when I looked at the time and realized I had been in there for 1½ hours that I said I wanted to talk to Greg who was waiting outside. He must have been worried by then. She said, "Okay, I will let you land, but ..." she kept talking but I wasn't listening anymore. All I could think was, "what do you mean, let me land? Have I not landed yet?" It was only after Greg explained it to me that I realized what had really gone on.

These people send people back to the country they came from, without letting them leave the airport. Only then, I became angry. Who do they think they are, invading people's privacy like that?

It became clear to me later, that the biggest threat to the nation Australian Customs could think of in a pre 09/11 world was someone ripping off the taxman. Everyone that looks to them like a potential illegal worker is stopped and the major suspects are longhaired students, people with dark skin, Asians and people wearing army pants. Don't they know that the real crooks always dress impeccably?

As soon as I got home, I ran to the computer to check my mail. The first one I got was from Tayna and it was a big one...
"Hi mum. How was Vanuatu?
We've been talking to Dad. You know mum, you are a bit crazy, with your adventures all over the world. You say you like it there, that you'll get a job, but the fact is that you still didn't, how can you be sure you'll get one after we arrive?
That's what you told our father when you went to Holland, but when he got there, you told him to bugger off. You screwed him up; he was down and out with nowhere to go.
You change with the moon, mum, we cannot really trust you. What if you get sick of Greg after a while, or he doesn't want you anymore, what if he doesn't want to put up with all the problems with us, I don't know... Then, you will go somewhere else again. In Holland, that's what happened. You met a guy there, then you dumped my father, then the Dutch guy dumped you. With the Aussie guy, it was exactly the same. You took him home and then wanted to get rid of us. Okay, you were separated then, you fell in love with him. And when we are in love, we only see that person and we don't really want anyone else around. We went to Brazil and then you came because of us. Then you decide to go back to Holland to study again and abandoned the guy. Then he pissed off back to Australia. What I want to say is that you change with the moon and we cannot trust you.
Raoni's not sure at all about going, either. I wanted to wait for him till March, for us to go together but he told me to go first. He didn't give me any of the doc's you asked him.
I haven't got anything to lose, my life sucks, and I'll go against my father's wish.
My father proposed I live in Rio. Not a bad idea. I told him that if I came back and that wouldn't probably be before a year, I would do just that. He will rent an apartment for me. Uni will be free, because the director of the University's a friend of his and he can get me a scholarship.
Now I want to know one thing and that will be the decisive point for me:
If I don't like it there, will I be able to get back to Brazil? If I can't I won't go, but I will work to pay my ticket back if needs be.
The other thing my father said that made us really insecure was

about our situation there. You haven't got your visa yet. How can we stay there, on a tourist visa, for only a year? Why is it only valid for three months? You know Mum; I'm not sure about anything anymore. Especially Raoni, he's so happy here. Studying at Uni, going places, surfing a lot... As I said, I'm going, even if I regret it later, I want to check it out.

My doc's are all sorted out. I went yesterday with Johanna to the Notary and all docs are certified. We also got your papers that you had asked for and everything's going to the translator. This is all costing money, too, you know? Besides the certifications, I also had to pay for parking, petrol and photocopies.

And there's a lot more to come.

Anyway, I think everything's more or less under way. How do you know I tried to call you? I sent you an e-mail but I got an error message back saying that it wasn't delivered. The phone rang once and then it fell. And I didn't get any messages. It's a holyday on Wednesday and I'm going to Paraty.

I found all your diplomas. I'll send you everything together with all the other doc's when they are ready.

My surfboard is so old. Is it worth taking? Can I buy one over there?

Well, I'll have a shower now and get some sleep. I took the night bus from Paraty and I haven't slept last night.

Big Kiss, Tayna."

I was shocked and flabbergasted. I couldn't think of any reasonable word in reply for many days. It felt so unfair. Their father had given them the entire version of our separation and my relationships after that without me being able to say a word. I had never spoken with the boys about any of these things, no one, especially not with their father. It hurt me so much that the boys wouldn't even ask me for my side of the story. I was floored.

I tried to explain myself. I tried to be cool and rational, but all I did was feel upset and not know what to say. I sent a few very confusing e-mails, that didn't really say much but eventually, I managed to express a few coherent thoughts:

"I have never ever sent you away, Tayna. I have never wanted to get rid of you as you said. That never crossed my mind. You didn't like the Aussie guy. You decided to go back to your father in Brazil and I let you go. Maybe I made a mistake then; maybe I shouldn't have let you go. I really didn't know what to do, then.

You know Tol (Tayna), since I let you go to Brazil from Holland, this whole story has always been very sad to me. All those years

in Brazil, all these absurd things your father tells you. Have you ever asked your father why I abandoned him? Do you really believe he's a saint, a poor innocent thing?
I believe God's watching everything and the truth will prevail.
I know my intentions towards you are pure. I always thought of your good. You are my sons, the most precious things to me. The only reason I want you here is because from the depth of my heart I believe you are going to be happier here. This is my only intention.
Have you asked yourself why your father wants you so much to stay in Brazil, finish your Tourism course? Is it really what you want to do? Does he really worry about you or does he want someone to take care of his new resort? The proposition about an apartment in Rio is really strange to me. He didn't want Raoni to go to the south to study Oceanography in a public, unpaid Uni, because he didn't have the money to pay for the rent of an apartment there. Where is he going to get the money for accommodation for you in Rio, which is a lot more expensive than in the south?
You worry about Greg. He has accepted you both, since the first time I spoke about you. I'll never find a better guy for me. You know who is sending you money every month, don't you? I have no intentions of leaving here. I'm forty-one, Tol, one day one gets tired of running around. I want to let my roots grow here, with a great man by my side, in a good country and with my two loves.
Tol, I told you already that if you want to go back to Brazil, we'll find a way. You won't have to work to pay your ticket back. Have you looked for tickets, yet?
I can't say I was happy with your e-mail, with all the bull... your father's telling you. But at least you say you are coming.
Take care
Love you heaps
Irene

C3 CR C3 CR C3

Things between their father and me started to go wrong very early in the marriage. When Raoni was just four months old, he had to go to the Ivory Coast, in Africa for a training course of four months. I would never have thought of anything, I never did before. But my sister in law kept asking me if I trusted him, if I didn't worry he would do something. So, when he came back, I insisted so much, that he ended up telling me that he had gone to a brothel there several times. Many of the women there were under age as they are in so many of these poor countries. He said he was the only married man in his group, as if that justifies anything.

My marriage until then had an aura of sacredness. Tayna and Raoni were the most beautiful babies in the world. He was the first man I had ever have sex with. It had been the first time we'd been apart for such a long time and I really missed him. It had taken me so long to get to that point, to trust him so completely. I was so in love with him then. I had put my entire life into his hands. I had come to believe that our relationship was something really special. But, from one day to another, I felt totally stupid. I had been sending him passionate and beautiful, carefully chosen postcards all those months. I would fill the letters with drawings and kisses, which he would show off to his colleagues. It felt as such a precious love had just been trampled upon, thrown in the rubbish bin, discarded as trash. In his entire account of the events, there wasn't any sign of shame, nor regret, not one tear. A sharp dagger pierced through my heart, it really hurt.

If I had any sense of self then, I would have taken that episode very, very seriously. I would have either left him there and then and the long, dragged-out mess that our relationship has always been could have ended with a lot less pain to everyone involved, because the younger the children are, the less painful the separation of the parents is, or I would have set out the rules of how I expected things to be from then on. But instead, I didn't do anything. I didn't cry. I didn't get angry. There were no arguments. I just pretended the pain I was feeling deep inside wasn't really happening. I just disconnected myself from my feelings and I continued doing that ever since! All I managed to do instead was to ask with a hesitating, rather pathetic voice, "Will I be number one?" He just smiled.

It wasn't clear to me then, but today I can see that my whole paradigm about the meaning of love and any certainties I had about his love for me were seriously shaken. The idea I had of what I meant for him became totally blurred.

I will never be able to separate sex from love. And I cannot understand people who do. Who was I really married to?

How can people do this? Have sex simply out of pure lust; use another body for the simple thrill of it, pleasure without any responsibility, apart from the need to throw a few coins on a table?

A lot of the respect I had for him was destroyed at that moment. I can also see today that my inadequate reaction that day was the green light for him to take me for granted. If I could accept that, what could I possibly not?

It's not that he had changed. He had always been like that, I just didn't see. I didn't want to see, because, at eighteen, I was too desperately in need of a life. I told myself then (like so many young girls do), "he loves me, he'll change and everything will be all right". Marrying him and starting a family was the solution I found, at nineteen, to all my problems.

I never knew if he had other women after that. I never asked anything any more. I couldn't stand to hear the truth. I can see clearly today that the wound never healed. It got infected and over the years, it slowly developed into a gangrenous cancer that killed our marriage in the most painful way possible.

Years passed and, for me, every little mishap, every little misunderstanding reinforced that neither I, nor family life meant much to him. His social life, his friends, his political activities and work came always first. He never changed one broken light bulb in the house, never got up, not even once, when the kids woke up at night. "If men were supposed to take care of children, they would have breasts", he often told me. After we had an argument, he would close our joint bank account without telling me. I found myself a few times, looking stupid in the supermarket with a trolley full with groceries not understanding why the card wouldn't work.

I could fill pages with all the things that proved to me that he didn't really care.

The thought of leaving him crossed my mind a few times, but I was too proud to go back to my parents and I didn't have a clue about what to do with my life on my own with two little children who, after all, loved their father. There was no social security in Brazil. I was trapped.

More and more I saw that marriage getting away from any acceptable idea I had about a life together, about raising children. I felt incredibly lonely, at times. It had never been a partnership. I was to be a passenger, not a co-pilot. I was not expected to ask where we were going; he never asked me where I wanted to go, not even if I was enjoying the ride. In fact, he never really listened when I said anything. On my twenty fifth birthday, I was totally aware of how terribly unhappy I was in that relationship and yet, I didn't know what to do. I had a feeling that I was supposed to be going somewhere, doing something, being someone. But instead, I felt I was going nowhere, I felt insignificant and living a mediocre life. That's why, at twenty-six, as soon as I finished Uni I took off to Holland. There I would prepare things for them to come, everything would change and life would be great!

Yet, in Holland, the awareness that my marriage was a mess only grew. I felt as lost as I ever did. I fell in love with another guy. It was a pretty messy business from beginning to end. I told him the truth about my situation from the start, but he didn't. Only later on I found out he also had a girlfriend. I never enjoyed anything about that affair but, again, I was looking for someone to save me, someone to provide a solution for all my problems, when in fact, he was just another problem. I had to force myself into that affair. If I could have affairs like he did, maybe I would feel as confident as him.

It had never been my intention to take things too far. It had always been my intention to tell him the whole story in due time, but it all went wrong. He got to know about the affair through someone else. He became insecure, angry and emotional. All our life together he had told me that infidelity wasn't a big deal. That one shouldn't have to repress sexual feelings for someone else.

Every time I told him I wouldn't be able to do anything with anybody else, he told me I had a problem and even encouraged me to try it.

And then that! So it is a big deal, after all?! It was all right for him to have sex with other people, but now that the roles were reversed it was all a different story. So he did feel hurt, as I did. He did feel insecure about himself as I did. I begged him for time. I didn't want to break up the family. I told him everything would sort itself out fine; he just needed to back off a little, give me some time, some space.

But he wouldn't. He started pressing me, charging me and his reaction made me lose any respect I still had for him. Without respect, love is not possible. I decided our relationship was over.

Yet it was to the Dutch guy that I said goodbye. I knew that was a dead-end alley, too.

I can still see that grey, misty, cold, winter day in Holland. The line of leafless trees. In the car parked on the side of the highway, I told him what was going on, told him I loved him and said farewell. I hugged him tenderly and got out of the car. I looked back from the other side of the road; he had his hands on the steering wheel and his forehead on his hands. I don't know how long he stayed there before he drove away. My heart felt heavy with sadness and guilt. But I thought of the boys and I hastened my pace out of the piercing cold.

That was the last time I ever saw or heard of him. Wherever he's now, I hope he's all right.

The situation at home became unbearable. It was not a relationship any more; it had become a neurotic entanglement. So in 1987 I decided to separate. We lived apart for a year. Without a doubt, it was the most difficult year of my life, in every possible way and I think it was pretty hard on him as well. He was in a strange country, where he had no one and didn't even speak the language. For a couple of months, he stayed with some Brazilian friends he had made, and then he managed to get a scholarship and started a Masters course in another town. I don't think I would do that to anyone today, but at the time, I felt he was really tormenting me. I was feeling very hurt and he just kept putting more pressure on me.

By the end of that year, he convinced me to give it another try. We got together again. I even gained new hopes. Things were all right for a few months but then the same nightmare began again. In the year we were apart, he had met several women, some from our common circle of friends. They would just continue to call and come to see him as if I wasn't there. He didn't even hide his escapades anymore. I kept finding photos, notes and even condoms. I felt like trash. We didn't talk to each other anymore, we just screamed.

But, it wasn't until September 1991, after several long years hurting each other beyond repair, that he finished his studies and finally agreed that separating would probably be a good thing to do. He left for Brazil and I stayed in Holland to finish my studies.

I really didn't think, then, that the relationship had any chance of salvation. I was convinced nothing would ever change. I was convinced he didn't love me. Staying in that marriage meant having to accept that I wasn't worth anything better. I would rather die.

Too shortly, after he left, three months if I'm not mistaken, I gave a ride to a hitch-hiker in the outskirts of Amsterdam, a young Australian guy. It was winter, it was freezing and he wasn't dressed properly for that weather. He looked like a lost, hungry, frozen dog and like I have always done with lost, stray animals I took him in. After a few days, he asked if he could stay a little longer to try and get some work and I let him. I felt a big tenderness for him; something strongly attracted me to him.

I had never felt that way before and I thought it was special.

Tayna hated him from the start; he and the boys in the same house never worked.

The boys didn't know exactly what had happened between their father and me. They only knew he had left, but that had happened before and he had come back. They didn't know it was permanent this time. I had planned to explain everything to them when I got back to Brazil in a few months time, after I finished my studies. So they were confused with this new guy in the house. Only much later did I realize how deeply this had impacted on them. They had concluded that I didn't want to be their mother any more, that I was only interested in this guy. I never ever dreamt that any such thoughts were going on in their minds. Of course, I was giving this new guy attention, but I didn't stop doing any of the things I have always done for the boys. I couldn't understand it; I thought it was just jealousy. I did nothing to ease their anxieties, fears and confusion. How could I, if that was exactly how I was feeling myself?

As weeks, months passed by, and nothing changed for the better for the boys, Raoni decided to go to his father in Brazil and off he went. Tayna, as usual, was waiting that little bit longer to see if I would understand. But I never did and so he also left, two months after his brother, in tears, not knowing if his father would be waiting for him. As usual, I couldn't reach his father, although I tried for a long time, again he was on a work trip and nobody knew how to contact him or when he would be back. I asked Tayna to wait until I could at least speak to his father, but he didn't want to stay anymore and went anyway, he was only eleven years old.

God only knows how hard it was for me to let them go, knowing how often their father was late to pick them up from school. How many times had he forgotten appointments altogether? How many times had he given the boys the wrong medicine, brought home the wrong groceries? How many times had he gone on a business trip without leaving enough money?

When the news broke in the family that I had sent the boys to their father, they said I had gone mad. My father commented a few times that this new guy must have been really good for me to desert my children for him! I have never been able to reply to my father's comment; it hurt too much. No one knew exactly what had happened. No one asked. Everyone just made their own conclusions. The truth is that I never, ever, thought of deserting the kids.

When they decided to go back to Brazil, I was soon to finish my studies and go back to Brazil to sort out the whole situation.

I was so confused, so unsure about my future and my life, so lost. I couldn't let the Aussie go, because he was my hope for a new happy life. I thought I had found my second half. I saw so much of me in him. I was going to sort out my life and everything in Brazil; we were going to prove everybody wrong, we would build an organic farm and live off it, we would build a little paradise on Earth, just for us and then the boys and I would be all together and happy again.

I didn't know then, but I was never again to be reunited with my sons and only God knows the torture it has always been to me and the pain I've endured through all the years that followed; all the years they spent in Paraty, knowing that they were not being looked after properly, not being able to be there when they needed me and the phone always out of order. How many times did I burst into tears because I missed them so much and was unable to see them? When I did manage to get close to them, their father was always there to humiliate and hurt me.

I arrived in Brazil in 1992, about five months after Tayna's departure. The Aussie arrived from Australia six months later. The boys' father, unbelievably enough, expected us to get back together as if nothing had ever happened.

If, in our long, sad story, he had just once said, "Let's sort this out, let's understand what's happening with us, let's see how we can fix this", I think I would probably have stayed. But his reaction was always the same; pretend that there was nothing wrong. I was the one who went to a shrink, I was the one always reading books, trying to understand the way I felt, I was the one always thinking there was something wrong with me. He never saw anything in him that needed to change, he had no flaws, there has never been anything wrong with him...

The Aussie and I got married six months after his arrival, so that he didn't have to cross the border any more and I found myself trying to achieve the impossible: set up a farm in a remote area accessible only on horseback, without any previous farming experience; be with the boys in town as much as I could, while maneuvering to avoid their father, manage a shop of natural food and products and baby-sit the Aussie who, after two years in the country, was still not able to go to town to buy his own cigarettes. It was a great deal more than I could handle.

By October 1994, I had to return to Holland to complete one subject I had left unfinished, or else I would have to pay back the scholarship I'd received from the Brazilian government.

On my own in Holland, I did a lot of thinking. Things had to change. I thought it would probably be better if the Aussie went back to Australia. I contacted his family, hoping for some help but all I got was a cold shoulder. Even though, it became clear to me that the relationship wouldn't go anywhere, I still cherished the dream of the farm and I thought he did, too. I expected us to talk things over and sort something out when I got back. I still had strong feelings for him, whatever they were. What I really wanted was for him to get real. Instead, he simply sold the shop or, more accurately, gave it away, and vanished back to Australia after borrowing the money for the ticket from my parents with promises to pay it back. He never did. My parents were so glad to see his back that they would probably have given him twice that amount, without expecting anything back.

I learned of his plans less than a week before he left through my father, who was quite surprised I knew nothing about it!

I did speak to him before he left: "Is that it? Is this the end of everything?"

"I may come back", was all he said. Apart from that, not another word, not even goodbye. He left Brazil two days before my arrival from Holland.

I called him in Australia, a few weeks after I've got back in Brazil and he already had another girlfriend.

That relationship was never anything more than a chaotic and pathetic entanglement. I was thirty-two; he was twenty-one. He never really felt to me anything more than a 6.2 feet ball and chain. His inexperience and clumsiness made sure sex never felt anything more than an awkward experience, and yet I had never been so attracted to a man as I was to him, but I would make sure I never would again!

So, in 1995, I arrived back in Brazil from Holland to start a life from scratch, deeply humiliated: no farm, no work, no shop and no money. I was absolutely broke. I spent my entire life's savings on that dream and everything was reduced to nothing, wasted.

I didn't even have any happy moments to remember from that relationship. I risked everything and I lost it all.

What hurt the most was the fact that I truly saw many qualities in him, qualities that nobody else saw. Everybody just saw an immature and insecure young man looking for someone to take care of him, everybody... but me. I really believed that I could help him become the wonderful man I thought he was, but I didn't. Why couldn't I see him for what he really was and understand the obvious, that I couldn't have possibly expected any support from him? He couldn't even take care of himself. My explanation today is that after my separation, I was so frightened by the idea of having to sort my entire life out from scratch on my own that I needed to invent this perfect man who would help and save me.

Whatever sense I make out of it all today, it won't change the fact that the deep wounds of this period in my life took a very long time to heal.

Maybe it's not meant to be
Too many oceans maybe
Too many inches and years
Too many dreams apart
Too much fear and so many tears

I need so to understand
An obsession, maybe
The magic everywhere
The beauty and the emptiness
In your eyes, your hands
All the losses, bleeding wounds
Too real and so very here

I still miss you so much
Yet I know, you are out of reach
You are lost in your cage
I'm trapped in my rage

Seeing just what I want to see
Feeling not what I want to feel
Easy, though it all would be
Yet, there's the way of reality

Loosing mind and my life
By the ocean embraced
Kissing death deep underneath
Waterfalls and so much peace
Pulling me down so strong
Why did it all go wrong?

Maybe one day I will
Hope's in my heart still
Joy and life always to be
Or just madness maybe?

Your two broken wings
And your freedom dreams
The blood in my hands
And the wounds, they scream

Silence makes strength free
For time's a healing breeze
Patiently awaiting
The growth of our souls

Irene, March 1996

Looking back at all this mess is almost unbearable. It almost makes me feel sick. How can we mess our lives up that much?
I look back at all the suffering and I have to wonder if it wouldn't have been better and less painful for all of us if I had just swallowed my pride, embraced my unhappiness and stayed in my first marriage, for my children. Maybe a dysfunctional family might have been better than no family at all.

From those around me, I only got criticism, judgment, anger, mockery and despise for the mistakes I've made in my life.
I had lost hope of ever finding someone with a little bit of understanding.
I know I have hurt people, people whom I love a great deal, people who loved me, but I also know that I never ever intended to hurt anyone, no matter how much people judge me or think I knew exactly what I was doing. I got hurt more than anyone else.
A person who is drowning can kill the one who tries to help him, but it doesn't make his suffering any less. I know the wounds from the past are not completely healed for any of us. I feel compassion for all of us, for all my sons had to go through, for all I had to go through.

It's easy to look back today and say I could have kicked that messed-up Aussie out of my life as soon as the boys started to complain or that I could have stayed in Holland with and for my kids, with or without their father, but at the time, I was unable to listen to my kids, to see their suffering, to understand their needs. I absolutely didn't know any better.
The truth is, that for many of us, the only way to learn life's lessons is to keep making mistakes, over and over again, until we learn whatever we are supposed to learn. As pathetic, tragic and senseless as this may sound, the fact is, some of us get so little from our upbringing to help us cope with the real world, that we will have to suffer a lot before we can gain some sort of balance and some sense of happiness in our lives, matter of fact, some never do.

To this day, the boys' father still maintains that fidelity is nonsense and he has never had a lasting relationship with anyone since we broke up, but I understand today that he doesn't know any better either and that in his own way he did love me, as did the Dutch and the Aussie guy.
No one can give more than one's got to give.
I know for sure that, had I been able to find appropriate

counseling when my marriage problems started, I would have been able to sort myself out in a much better way than I did. Someone with a clear mind could have helped us transform that entanglement into something more functional and fulfilling and even if that marriage was never meant to be, we could at least have parted in a much less painful way.

I never knew help was available. In my loneliness, unhappiness and despair I decided that there was no cure; it was all wrong from the start, there was no other way out, but to leave.

Taking this a bit further, my whole life could have been very different had I received the support I needed way back in my teenage years, when life started to become kind of a struggle for me.

Anyway, I did learn a thing or two in the process and I will take this wisdom with me wherever I go. I hope everybody else has learned something as well.

೮೩೧೮೩೧೮೩

I'm sorry for the long sidetrack, but I needed to give you my version of the events Tayna had mentioned in his e-mail. I still couldn't understand why his father was telling the boys I would abandon them if they came to Australia, though. Was it revenge?

I was starting to get anxious about Raoni not going after his papers. What an agony. I often cried when I thought about the possibility of the boys not coming. Greg was always sweet, but I don't think he really understood my whole issue with the boys. For me, the possibility of being here without them didn't exist; it didn't make any sense to me. I had an unfinished business as a mother that needed closure.

In the beginning of November, I seriously hurt my back. It was during a yoga stretch. Something clicked in my lower back and the pain was really bad. I stopped jogging and took it very easy. The pain slowly eased over a few weeks, but then, I had another twitch while running down the stairs and this time the pain was far worse than the first time. I became completely crooked for weeks and this time the pain didn't ease. I never completely recovered from it. Greg got me a special chair, but it was not much help. From the doctor I got a box of extra strong painkillers. He never found anything. If doctors can't cut you open or if they cannot fix it with drugs, they are lost, there's nothing they can do. I stopped using the pills after a few days, they didn't help anyway. The next year those pills were banned.

In the middle of the month, I had to be at the Family Court in Brisbane again. The divorce from the Aussie guy had, finally, gone through. I was so nervous, all by myself in an Australian Court, having to address a judge, not knowing if they would understand my English or I theirs, but all went well.
Still, it would take another month before I would get the final divorce papers.
From the Court we went to the Immigration Department to get the confirmation that the best thing for us to do was to get married. I couldn't see any reason for not doing it. We set the date for the 18th of December. Greg was so happy and I was, too.

Raoni had gone on holidays again and nobody knew where he was exactly. Talk about being a chip off the old block!
The closer the end of the year came, the more anxious I became, the more I urged Tayna to chase his brother and sort out all the papers. It annoyed him enormously and he became really pissed off with it all. It might have contributed to a serious stomach problem he got at about that same time. He was not really motivated to come, but the idea of their coming gave me great relief. I missed them so much.
Finally all the worries, the hassles of sending money over, their uncertain future, the anguish of unanswered e-mails, crashed computers and out-of-order-phones, the agony of not being able to communicate with them properly, not knowing exactly what was going on, what they were up to, the feeling of powerlessness, trying to help them from such a distance, the frustration convincing them to come over, their doubts and mistrust about coming, all of this would soon come to an end.

By mid December, Greg and I had bought the wedding rings and we still didn't have half the documents we needed to lodge our residency application. We made an appointment at DIAC for the 19th of January. They said I could lodge the application with the documents I had, but they would process it only when all documents were delivered - whenever that might be.

A few days before our marriage, I got a letter from my brother.
"Dear sister,
I've heard from Mum that you are going to do another stupidity. I was afraid that would happen again.
I'm not talking about Greg as I don't know him and have never

spoken to him. In fact, I believe he must be a great guy, but you are marrying only to get your situation in Australia sorted out.

I think you don't even know exactly what you feel about him. You are putting him in your plans too hastily. You will be sharing all your wishes and desires.

Seven months ago, you left Brazil with the idea to try a new life, work and also have fun in a wonderful country that seemed ideal for you to achieve your goals, right? You also left behind your sons and their need to be close to you. You thought they were big and could take care of themselves, right?

This for me is logic. You wanted something and you went for it. That's kind of acceptable. But now you come with this marriage stuff. Again? Do you know this is your third marriage? Are you prepared to have more kids?

How well do you know Greg? Are you in love? What does he want; can you see yourselves together in ten years time? If you don't know, don't marry. Maybe Australia's not worth it. Maybe it's not as good as you thought. The best place for us is where we are accepted without having to do inconsequential things. It just proves that a place alone doesn't make anyone happy. Putting your own ideals at stake is one thing but sharing in the ideals of someone else may be even worse.

Think more. Don't let time decide things for you.

Love
Paulo"

My answer to his letter was:

"Wow, little brother, why so much worry? A load of bull... to be honest.

To start with, why do you say my marriage is a stupidity? What's the assumption based on?

I'll try and explain things to you, even though I don't believe we will ever manage to really understand each other.

Okay, I would probably not marry now if that wouldn't make my situation here easier and yes, I do have doubts at times about this, as I have doubts about the existence of God and reincarnation, but I do have certainties too.

I know better that anyone how hard my life has been all these years in Brazil. I'm sure Brazil has got nothing to offer me. Not that I don't like or don't believe in my country, but only because one has to be much tougher than I am to make a living there.

I have lived in Holland for seven years and I also know exactly what that country has to offer me and I would go there if I had no alternative although I would whine and gripe about the weather all the time.

I have done a lot of thinking in the five years I stayed in Brazil, especially about relationships and what went wrong with mine. I wish I could live alone and not have to put up with all the frustration and all the bull... that comes along as extras in relationships, but the fact is that I'm not meant to live life alone.

If I were very successful in all other areas of my life, I would still need someone to share it with.

Why do you put that as something negative, risky or dubious? How different is your relationship with Adriana from mine with Greg? In fact, sharing our dreams, wishes and ideals is great, not only with your husband or spouse, but also with friends and family.

I remember well, my last day in São Paulo when we went to eat that pizza together and you said Greg could only be a sexual maniac and maybe worse. Where does all this mistrust towards people come from? Why all the fear?

I think it's great I can share my ideas and dreams with him. Actually, he's the only one helping me to make them come true.

All big steps in life involve risk. Maybe I take risks too easily, but that's how I am. I won't wait for certainties that may take a lifetime to show up. Were you absolutely sure when you married Adriana? How many people believed they had all the certainties in the world and one single event, a disease, a death, a change of heart knocks down all those carefully detailed plans?

You put serious questions about love and passion. To be honest I don't think you yourself know exactly what they mean. I have fallen deeply in love a few times and every time it ended in nothing. The good thing is, you get over your pain, get stronger, and learn about yourself and people.

Love... What do you understand by it? I wish I had your answer before I give you mine, but for me to love is to feel respect and tenderness for someone, to feel good when you are together. I feel all that for Greg and I have not spoken about sex yet, which is great too, by the way.

He's not rich, not super interesting nor handsome, but I feel good and safe with him and I haven't had that with anyone before. He gives me the certainty he'll always be there for me. Of course, he's got his limitations as well. I'm not blind: he smokes too much, he can be slack at times and he can see things too simplistically. Who's perfect?

You are right about the goals I had when I came here. I need someone by my side to achieve them.

As to leaving my sons behind, I have extensively spoken to them about my plans before I came. I have thoroughly sorted out the possibilities for them here. If they hadn't agreed to come, I wouldn't have come. I have never told you or anyone that I thought they could take care of themselves, have I? Only I and Greg know how much I worry about these boys. It has always been my plan that they would come too.

Yes, it's my third marriage. I know how to count to three. That's a joke compared to Liz Taylor ☺. As to having more kids, Greg's just getting over his vasectomy. He never wanted kids. We thoroughly discussed this issue, while I was still in Brazil.

Do I know Greg well...? How many times did you sleep with Adriana before you marry her? I've been living with Greg for seven months, seven days a week, 24 hours a day. You must learn something about a person, wouldn't you say? Enough for me to know that there's nothing in his character or personality that goes against any of my moral or ethical values, nothing that irritates me too much.

All Greg wants is for us to be together till the end of time. He hasn't got any major ambitions but to have enough money for the bills and a relatively easy life.

I'm the one with all the ambitions; I'm the one with all the ideas and plans and I'm not giving anything up and I have made this clear to Greg from the start. If I will get there, I don't know. I will try, that's for sure.

I'm expecting heavy artillery ahead with the boys coming over. It's going to be a huge expense. I need to work; I need to help them with the English, with finding a direction in life. How can I be happy if I'm not sure they are happy? Only when they are safe and sound on their paths I will feel free to follow mine.

In the seven months I've been here, I haven't seen anything that tells me I shouldn't be here or that there is no future for me here. The family received me very well. I don't feel worse here than in any other places I've been. I don't believe I'm being inconsequent. I don't think I'll find a better person to share a life with.

Hope you enjoy the visit of the oldies over there and have lots of fun. We marry on the 18th of December. On the 19th of January, we have an appointment with the immigration dept. Then we will have to wait for a while and only then, I can say my life will really start.

I hope to have clarified things in your head a bit. You did make me think it all over again and that was good.

Big hug

Irene"

His reply was short. "Okay, happy marriage and don't kill Greg!"

Our marriage at the Court House in Stanthorpe, 30 minutes from Wallangarra, was very simple; Mumboy in crutches because of her knee, Dadboy and one witness, Peter, a friend of Greg who also served as the photographer. Never heard of him after that.

I was happy. I had a strong feeling things would finally start happening for us. On that moment, I didn't have doubts about anything. The Freshwaters already felt as my family, getting married to Greg, wouldn't add much to that. At home, Mumboy had bought a nice cake, so as to not let the day pass completely unnoticed. We got a bread maker from the oldies, seeing that I was enjoying the fresh bread so much and I started experiencing different recipes straight away.

Then Christmas arrived. I was still shocked with the seven kilos I had put on from all that great fresh, hot bread and tons of chocolate and home-baked cookies.

The folks in Brazil, as usual, got all together at the oldies farm. My mother had a bad accident and needed twelve stitches on her head, so, the rest of the family didn't let her travel to Paulo as they had planned; a 2,000 km trip to central Brazil.

In The Garra, I met Greg oldest brother, Russ and partner Kay (Chookie), his oldest son, Clinton and his girlfriend.

We had a cold dinner, typical for Aussie Christmas, so I was told.

It was a very hot summer and I'd been in the sun scorching myself and getting sunburned.

Dadboy was larking around, as usual and although everybody was nice to me, I felt terribly out of place, with all those new faces around. I don't know if I would have survived it if Greg didn't stay by my side all the time.

I remember the big clean up we had before the family arrived. I gave particular attention to the veranda, cleaning and dusting every nook and cranny. So I was pleased when it was there that everyone would stay the most, enjoying the breeze on those hot summer days.

Reality check

On the 19th of January 2001, as planned, we went to our appointment at DIAC in Brisbane. Four hours to the north. My back was awful; I wasn't even able to walk straight. Sitting for that long in the car was an absolute torture, but I was full of hope and expectations and I had all my plans sorted out.

But, we found out pretty soon that things were not at all as I was expecting. It was all going to be much more complicated.

The officer at DIAC explained to us that if the boys weren't in Australia when I filed the papers, different procedures and regulations applied. Their application would have to go through DIAC in Chile, the only Immigration Department office in the whole of South America at the time and it would take at least eight months.

I panicked. My head started to spin: I was sure it was going to take more than that; the boys would never manage to sort out the infinity of papers and documents necessary for the whole process; they had already lost their birth certificates three or four times; I couldn't ask my mother or my sister to go through that whole bureaucratic process with them. It would also cost me about three times more than it was to process the papers here and I started to get very upset.

Then she said that I could lodge my process alone and then wait two to three years to get my residency and only then apply for a family reunion visa or something like that. I burst into tears and couldn't stop, everything got blurred and the woman kept talking like a robot, emotionless and that upset me even more. I was sobbing so much I couldn't even talk and everything she said made no sense to me.

I couldn't understand. It all seemed so absurd. I had called them before, they didn't tell me any of that, the information I had was so completely different from what she was telling me. I checked their website out while I was still in Brazil. It didn't seem to be that complicated.

After a while, she came up with the third alternative, which was to wait for the boys to come over so that we could apply together in the same process. That would be cheaper and faster but it also meant that I wouldn't be able to work before the boys arrived and she proceeded to explain the documents and requirements I would have to present for the boys to be accepted as my dependents. I couldn't think straight any more.

We had to make an appointment for the next day.

In the hotel that night, I couldn't sleep properly because of my back. Greg did everything he could to cheer me up and show me the brighter side of things, but I was inconsolable, I stayed up and cried most of the night. All I had planned and had been dreaming about in the last few months had just been reduced to nothing.

The next day the immigration clerk told me something about them not needing me any more and that there was no need for them to come to stay with me. Among other things, I had to prove that I had an emotional bond with the kids.

When I asked what exactly she meant by that she said something like, "You have to prove that you love them and that they love you." When I asked how I was supposed to prove that, she said that it was my problem not hers! For days, I worried about how I was going to prove that. By showing pictures, letters? Does that prove that there is love?

I couldn't understand why everything was so complicated. It felt as if I had already been found guilty of a crime and now I had to go through a very difficult trial to prove I was innocent. At some stage, she showed surprise with my Dutch passport. I guess I didn't fit her "poor-bugger-trying-to-rip-the-country-off" profile. I hated that woman, but I knew she was doing exactly what she had been told to do.

Why does it have to be like this? Why do they have to follow procedures so blindly, without trying to understand people's different circumstances? Why do they always have to go and ask a superior if you ask a question? If only they listened to people and tried to understand their difficulties and needs, they could then try and find out what regulations to apply and how things could be sorted out the best way. If they only had a slight idea of the unnecessary suffering, confusion and anxiety, they cause to people.

I concluded that the Immigration Department is not there to help people in the process of immigration. I've got a strong feeling that they are interested only in making sure you are not a criminal and won't get away with anything without giving the government its share. All the questions they ask are for that end and are not designed to help immigrants in any way. Everyone is a potential enemy of the state and that's how you will be treated. You'll get your visa when they are satisfied you pose no threat, no matter how long it takes and no matter how much you suffer.

In 2005, a report about Immigration practices came out,

following some incredible blunders from the Department. It said that there is a racist and discriminatory culture in the Department and that their procedures often do not follow official regulations. I'm absolutely convinced that if you are not coming to this country to generate a profit for someone, you are not welcome, not even when they are obliged to allow someone in to honor agreements and treaties. In all the years I've been here, I haven't seen any evidence to the contrary.

What's wrong with wanting to make a life in another country because we believe we will have a better life there? I bet there are a lot of Australians who would like to live somewhere else. I bet there is a lot who do. I bet they didn't have to go through this torture.

Anyway, the whole interview made me very weary and worried. Basically, I had to prove that the boys were dependent on me.

The sense Greg and I made from all the information was that we needed to get the boys over here as quick as possible. I had hoped I would have time to work to get the money, but that was not going to happen. This meant that we had to ask the oldies for money for the tickets and probably also to rent a place. Greg was already sending money every month to the boys and the oldies here couldn't help either. To finish everything off, I had to cross the border again. My Visa was going to expire at the end of the month and we wouldn't get the boys over before that. After I came back, I would be in the last three months of my Visa. It would expire in the beginning of May. If my situation wasn't sorted out by then I would have to leave the country for good.

We made another appointment for March and hoped that by then the boys and all the papers to lodge our visa applications would be here. From that day on getting prepared for the boys was all I could think about.

Several times after that meeting with DIAC, I burst into tears when I thought about the possibility of the boys not coming. I wrote to my sister Ursula, asking her for her thoughts on kids and all the emotional and physical stress that goes with it, but as usual, she didn't reply.

Asking my parents for that money was a soap opera apart.

I gave my mother a call and explained the situation. She was very reluctant and made it really hard for me. She was very businesslike, her voice hesitant. She usually talks like a machine gun, but this time every word was thought, long pauses in between. She said she would talk to my father and told me to call back a few days later, when they would be at the farm for the weekend. She even gave me an exact time to call. Something she had never done before. It felt no different from asking money to a bank. Not exactly what I was looking for after the episode at DIAC. When I called back a few days later, my father spoke to me as he always does. He didn't see any problems. I think my mother thought it had all gone wrong again.

I thought it would be easier and cheaper to get the tickets here, but my mother decided she was going to take care of everything. She had been told that sending money over would cost her 5% of the amount sent, plus taxes, fees and a double exchange rate as the money had to be converted first into US dollars and then into Australian dollars.

My lovely sis Ursula sent me a furious e-mail a few days later, giving me a really hard time for asking my parents for money again. "When are you going to take care of your own life? How dare you annoy them with your problems? I never tell them about any of my problems, they already have more problems than they deserve and they have done more than they needed for us."

I answered that I was feeling bad enough without her preaching and that I hoped to pay the money back in three months time.

I also told her that as a mother I would prefer to know when my children are in trouble. In our many afternoon teas in the kitchen, while I still lived there, my mother had often complained about us never telling her anything?

I told my sister I was sure we were all doing the best we could with our lives. I had all the intentions to pay that money back as soon as I could, I didn't know that wasn't going to happen for a long time. When, after a few years, I finally had the money and wanted to pay my mother back, she said she never expected me to and that I didn't have to. Thinking about it today, I probably could have asked for a personal loan at the bank. It would have avoided all this family humiliation again.

My mother bought the tickets from a Tourist Agent who made sure to sell her the most expensive tickets he had.

After wracking my brain trying to figure out how I was going to prove the bond and my love for my sons to the immigration Department, I thought of a letter written by their father, telling about my relationship with the boys and how we shared the costs of raising them. I was really worried he wouldn't, so it was a relief when he didn't create any problems.

If they were still little, things would have been so much easier, but they were over eighteen and that complicated things considerably. At twenty-five, it's all over.

When I was not stressing out about papers or trying to get in contact with the boys, I missed cultural life a bit, there was absolutely nothing to do in Wallangarra. But all in all I was happy with Greg and Australia was relaxed and sunny. We made plans to live in Lismore, a bigger city about one-and-a-half hours from Byron Bay, until the boys decided where to study.

Greg worked from home, for an electronic engineering company in Melbourne, so there was also a possibility that we would end up there.

My wish to write and sell books over the net was becoming stronger and stronger, but I was aware that a lot had to happen before that could ever become a reality.

Now and then, I would hear news from Raoni. He started to work as a cameraman on a schooner in Paraty, taking tourists on sailing trips. He would film the tourists and then sell them the videos, getting a percentage of the sale. He was proud of the money he was making and the sound system he had bought. In one of the few e-mails I got from him, he told me how he and a group of friends went to visit my little farm in the hills in Paraty. No one had been there for many months. The vegetation had overgrown the tracks and they had to cut their way through with machetes. The recently opened road had overtaken part of the track we used to take and they got lost, like I did when I last went there. A torrential summer rain caught them and because they were high in the mountains, the lightning was striking fairly close. Raoni said they were all shivering from cold and fear. They managed to find the track back and just when they started to despair again, Raoni saw the top of the roof of the shack on the farm and they ran towards it, soaking wet. They lit the fire on the wood stove and made a barbecue. Raoni had even brought his newly acquired sound system wrapped in a plastic bag. Miraculously, it didn't get wet. He said the shack was in a fairly good shape and it didn't look as if anyone had been in there.

They didn't stay overnight, but Raoni said he would love to fix that wonderful place.

There's a spot on the track from where one can see the entire Paraty-mirim bay. The sun was shining on it while it was still raining in the hills, making the scenery all the more beautiful.

He was also looking forward to our reunion and missed me heaps. As I finished reading the e-mail, my eyes were filled with tears.

Between the end of January and beginning of February, I went for my third journey to Vanuatu. I was starting to get sick of Vanuatu by then. This time I went back to the first hotel Greg and I stayed in, with its beautiful sandy beaches. I didn't need to go anywhere else.

Back in Australia, I got caught by customs again. The officer checked on the computer and then she looked at me in surprise: "You are in the system already!" My entire life history was there. I rolled my eyes and thought, "Oh, really?" I was dismissed in five minutes after a couple of questions.

When another customs officer asked me where I was going and I said Wallangarra, he said it was a mess over there. I didn't pay much attention, but was surprised that someone in an international airport would know of Wallangarra. As soon as I got home, I understood why. Cyclone-like winds had hit the region between NSW and Queensland. The destruction was visible. Entire trees were uprooted. Lismore was under water.

Soon after I came back, I went to an Oral History workshop in Tenterfield, the first town over the border into New South Wales, south of Wallangarra. This is how I got to know the Writers' Ink group there and became a member. As a new member of the group, I was asked to write a little story about joining the group and something about my background, to put in their newsletter.

"Writing has always been one of my best subjects in school. It just happens, I just have to start and then it's hard to stop. I write better than I speak. I think people are too complicated or I'm too complicated, maybe both. I say more than people want to hear and words once spoken can't be taken back. Writing is easier: you can read it again, think about it.

Words are powerful, they can make you laugh, they can make you sad, they can inspire, they can hurt and they can make you think. But can you earn a living from it? It takes years for an immigrant, like me, to get things a little stabilized financially. There are no social securities... It's going to be tough for a while and I don't know how much time there is going to be left for writing. Now I need to find my ground and settle in this country, but I will not give up."

Back in Brazil, Tayna didn't have a cent again. The problems with sending money never stopped and he was spending a lot with medicines for his stomach problem. I had to get in contact with the Embassy, as he didn't understand how to get the visas there, he was still worried with the fact that I hadn't sorted out my life, and feared things would get more complicated with their coming. His e-mails became less frequent and I told him that he had to see his coming here as a holiday, just to check things out. The first year he didn't have to think of anything too seriously. They would only study English - something he always wanted to do anyway - only in the second year, we would try to define a path for the future. Meanwhile he could always go back to Brazil if he really didn't like it here.

Raoni also started to look into his documents, which gave me some relief, but he was still having problems getting his University papers. So I contacted both their Universities to try to speed up things a bit. I also needed police clearances from Holland and I didn't have a clue of how to get them.

I tried to explain the immigration process and the regulations to the boys and why they had to be here before the beginning of May, but, when I read back all those e-mails I sent them, they look so confusing, a never-ending rigmarole about documents from school and consulate, translations, payments, all those whats, wheres and hows. It's actually a miracle that they came anyway.

At that stage, my lawyer asked for documents about an employment case that had been going on for a few years. I didn't have them with me and I was sure I had already given him the documents he was asking for. I had already won this case, but the employer appealed. If I won the appeal I would get about R$ 6,000. That would have come in very handy, but no one bothered answering the many e-mails and letters I sent, the lawyer included and I never knew how it all ended.

In the beginning of February, the company Greg worked for wanted him in Melbourne for a few days and I could go with him. They even paid my tickets and hotel. He was supposed to stay three days; we ended up staying eight. I loved it. After being in Wallangarra for so long, being in a big city looked great.

I visited Museums, I fell in love with the Victoria market and I especially loved the Botanic gardens, where I sat for hours almost every day.

I thought of my father, as there was a special dahlia garden and he has acres of them planted in the farm. We were even able to use the boss' car. How nice is that?

On the weekend, we took an excursion down the Great Ocean Road to the Twelve Apostles and some parks. Unfortunately, the weather wasn't fantastic, but it was still very beautiful. No, I wouldn't have any problems living there, that was for sure.

The one thing that caught my attention the most while down there was a protest I saw in the middle of town, in front of the State Library. Friends and family of people that had committed suicide where demanding the attention of the Government for the issue.

There were white wreaths everywhere, thousands of them, spread all over the stairs and the lawns, one for each person who had committed suicide the year before. I walked around looking at the wreaths. Most had a picture and a little something about the person. Many of the pictures were of young beautiful smiling people. I couldn't understand it. I came to know that Australia had been for many years during the 90's the number one country for juvenile suicide and that it had also one of the highest percentages in the world for adult suicide. Due to a strong campaign of some NGO's the numbers went down a bit, but Australia still continues to have one of the highest rates of suicide in the world. Something must be terribly wrong for this to be happening...

Back in The Garra, many issues were waiting for me. The boys' departure was getting closer and they still didn't have their visas. I started a frantic e-mail exchange with the Australian Embassy in São Paulo. They said they would send the visa by express post to São Paulo on the 16th of February. They didn't. I asked them to send it via fax. They replied they would, they didn't. The same had happened with my visa when I left Brazil and I asked them if that was the norm. Two different clerks told me the situation was rather unusual as they rarely have any delays in the delivery of ETA visas. I needed the visas to know if they contained any restrictions that might have some negative influence on the visa applications here. I had also sent a parcel a long time before with presents, a check and many documents to be signed and sent back and they hadn't arrived either. The clock was ticking and we had no tickets, no visas, and no documents. My adrenaline was going up exponentially.

Only in mid March did the visas and my package arrive, just days before the boys' departure.

Customs in Brazil had opened my package but they didn't see the check. I can only imagine the hassle if it had been stolen. Even though the check bore a name and would require the bearer to show identification for it to be cashed, I realize today that it was not the wisest thing to do.

Tayna's visa had a Mrs. instead of a Mr. on it and I worried. So I had to call the Embassy again and try to fix that. His mistaken gender is a very common event in Brazil and it pissed him off a lot when he was younger. We had hopes the problem would end when he came here, but then they mistook his name for Tanya. Tayna, as the Indian name that it is, is gender neutral. It's the name given by the Carajás Indians from Central Brazil, to the evening star, or Venus. Indians also call blond kids Taina, because they are light like the star, irrespective of whether they are boys or girls. The legend about the origin of the Carajás says that the evening star descended to Earth to become a courageous warrior and a wise elder who married the most beautiful young Indian in the tribe and taught the Indians all they know about crops and nature. I read the story in the library of a primary school where I taught for a few months in the Amazon. Tayna would be born in the Amazon, so I thought the name was thoroughly appropriate. The name was unheard of amongst white people back in 1979. It's only white people who have decided it is a girl's name. I like to think that, by calling my son Tayna, I haven't changed the original meaning the name had for the Indians. The "y" in the name was his father's invention, because his name's got a "y" as well. But I do see today, how all this doesn't mean anything for a young boy getting teased at school because he has a funny name.

At some stage, I got a phone from the boys. Raoni wanted to fax me the documents he had managed to get from school. With those papers and the ones I had already with me, a second translation marathon began. But this time it would be different. I had learned my lesson with the government translation services. After my nightmarish experiences with them, I couldn't believe there wasn't a better way to have translations done in this country. I searched the net and stumbled upon the address of the National Translators and Interpreters Accreditation Authority (NAATI). They have a directory with all accredited translators and interpreters in the country. Through them, I met a

Portuguese translator, Ana, who has done so many translations for me since that we have developed a friendship. Because I used to be a translator too, we ended up helping each other many times in our translations. Services are more personal, faster and cheaper. I realized that TIS was just a totally unnecessary intermediary agent, making things much more complicated and expensive for no good reason. They make use of the same NAATI directory!

Once we got through that round, I had enough papers to lodge the visa applications. It was countdown from then on.

Two days before the boys' departure I received a phone call. They weren't coming!

They had gone on a holiday north of Rio with some friends, to surf and were stopped on the road by a police blitz. They had some stuff surfers usually have on them when they go together on holidays. The Police officer said that one of the boys had to assume the responsibility, otherwise they would be charged with gang formation. Everybody backed off, so Raoni assumed responsibility although he wasn't the real culprit. He would have to await judgment and trial and couldn't leave the country. It would take months before they would set a trial date and it could be a year before they would be allowed to leave the country.

A few hours after that phone call, I was supposed to have a practical driving test. I was feeling like a zombie. My mind was raving. I didn't hear what the examiner in the car said after he told me to pull over. I had gone through a crossing without looking! I didn't need to ask him if I had passed the test.

I cried for days. I called their father many times to find out what we could do, but he didn't seem worried at all and didn't see the need to do anything about it. I postponed our new appointment with DIAC to the last day of my visa, second of May. If the boys weren't there by then everything would be lost. I would have to leave the country the next day. The feeling of frustration was overwhelming. All my effort to get them over here and the bastards were over there just having fun and being irresponsible! Sometimes I wanted to kill them, but then I remembered my own juvenile stupidity. They didn't really understand what was at stake. The agony lasted for weeks.

Mum, who never knew exactly what happened told me to let them go, to just live my life. I told her I knew they didn't value what I was trying to do for them, but I didn't need any recognition, I just felt I had to do it.

All I thought about was that if they were here everything would eventually be all right.

Meanwhile, an atmosphere of Easter started to fill the air. Greg had to go to Melbourne again. I could go again but I preferred to stay. With the boys' situation, I wanted to be on stand-by 24/7. I was also in savings mode. In one of Greg's calls from Melbourne, I asked him if he missed me. "Like a hole in my head". In the few seconds while I thought of a good reply, he said, "a hole like my mouth, or my nose, or my ear, babe..."

I got a call from Tayna a few days later, saying he would come and leave Raoni behind and I got really pissed off. I was shocked at his selfishness and lack of loyalty to his brother, leaving him alone to sort out the mess they had got into together.

One day I had a moment of enlightenment and called my lawyer in Brazil. After explaining the situation, he told me what I could do. It didn't seem completely right to me, but I was desperate. I called their father and together with the lawyer, they managed to get the boys out. I also managed to make a deal with their father. He would deposit about A$ 300 for the boys every month in my mother's account. I told her to keep that money for the tickets and chase him if he didn't pay. That was less than the expenses he normally had with the boys, less than what Greg was sending them and a lot less than the expenses we would have with them here.

My mother had to pay another fee to the travel agent for postponing the departure date, but at last, they would finally come... or so I thought.

I few days later I got to hear that the airline they were to travel with was on strike. Actually, the whole of Argentina was a mess. Their departure was again uncertain. More anxious and painful days followed, but finally it seemed things were about to happen. A new departure time was set for the end of April.

I gave the boys a call and told my mother I would call her as soon as the boys arrived here. She told me not to as they would be at my brother's and she didn't know exactly when they would be home. She would also send me an e-mail with the exact arrival time. She and my father would take them to the airport, a one and a half hour trip outside São Paulo on a good day.

To complicate things, they had a bunch of visitors from Holland staying at the time and mum was also sick with a heavy cold. When they arrived back home from a trip with the Dutch folks over the long Easter weekend, they found the boys and their father anxiously waiting for them.

On our way up to Brisbane's Airport we got caught up in a traffic jam and were running late but, because of the strikes, it was not until just before the boys left that they knew which flight they would catch and the exact arrival date and time. The time my mother sent me wasn't correct and at the end Greg and I arrived at Brisbane Airport a day too early. Well, better a day early than a day late, I guess.

I heard later on from the boys that it wasn't even certain if they would travel that day. There was a heated negotiation at the airline desk in São Paulo and my father slipped some money under the counter to make sure the boys would travel that day, otherwise that whole soap opera could have dragged on for many more days. It was finally decided they would go through an American airline, via California. They had to spend a lot of time at the stop over, and decided to see the beaches of St Monica. But it was too bloody cold they said!

Finally, on the 29th of April, I embraced my sons again.

I had prepared the van for them that Greg had borrowed from his good friend, Craig. The nights were pretty cold already, which was a shock for them, coming straight from the stinking heat in Rio.

It's only when I checked my e-mails after we arrived back home, that I received Tayna's last e-mail with the correct time he had sent just hours before he left. I knew everyone in Brazil would be dying to know they arrived well, but then I got a bug in my computer and didn't manage to send e-mails for two days. Greg was so busy with his work, I didn't want to annoy him with fixing my computer and I had my hands full with the boys.

As soon as they woke up the next day, we started to sort out the things we needed for the visa applications. First of all, the medical tests. Off we went to the doctor for the chest x-rays. The next day, blood samples for AIDS tests. Both almost fainted when the nurse couldn't find their veins and had to try several times. Then it was back to Brisbane to lodge the papers. I became upset with that immigration clerk again. To prove that I financially provided for Raoni I had all the invoices for the five years' school fees and many other expenses I had with him. A pile of about 70 pieces of paper! The woman said I had to translate everything. I asked her if she was out of her mind. She got pissed off. I told her it costs A$ 25 to translate each one of them. She said she couldn't read Portuguese. I told her to go look for someone who did, because I was not going to translate the damned papers. Off she went to talk to her superiors. Tayna gave me a black look. I shouldn't talk to her like that. After we paid the A$ 1,700 visa fee and lodged the papers, we could go, but they wouldn't look into it until they received all the missing papers.

When I got home, I received another furious e-mail from my sis Ursula, giving me a hard time because I didn't call the oldies as soon the boys arrived. How could I be so inconsiderate and selfish, after all they've done for me? She said they were outraged! No, I will never get it right with this family. That's my and their karma, I suppose. Why the hell did my mother tell me not to call? She's probably forgot what she said, like she often does. It really upset me. My mother had called one or two days after their arrival and complained about me not calling, but it didn't feel that she was all that pissed off. Anyway, I sent them a long e-mail asking them to forgive me and saying how much I appreciated all they had done.

My consolation was an e-mail I've got from a friend from the GIS office. He was a tiny young fellow, very religious. We used to get along pretty well. He wrote:

...Irene, I wanted to say that I appreciate your friendship, even though you are so far away. I don't know why I decided to say this only now, but before I lose too much time, here it goes:

I admire you a lot! You are such a life lesson for many! May God bless you today, tomorrow and always.

A big hug from your friend Vaguinho.

I printed that out, and stuck it onto my computer. So I see it every day. Especially when it seems everyone is against me, I look at it and remember that there are people out there that do appreciate me! Thanks Vaguinho!

Tayna had caught my mother's cold and passed it on to me. I spent the next few days in The Garra, running around like a headless chicken trying to keep everyone from treading on each other's toes.

The boys were bored out of their minds, complaining of the cold, sending e-mails to friends and dreaming of the surf in Byron Bay. In a week, we headed with the caravan to Byron Bay, where the boys and I would stay until I found a house. We took both cars. Greg towed the caravan with the oldies' car and I was behind him with the old Nissan. The caravan swung all the way down.

I had been sensing a rivalry between the boys for years: things they said about each other, contempt, criticism and easy judgments.

In the van, I had the opportunity to experience just how deep and how strong that rivalry really was. There was so much anger. I don't know how many fights and really bad arguments they had in the time we were together, and I can only imagine how awful that all must have been to Greg, but in some weird way, I was happy that I could finally be a part of it. I talked a lot to them. I don't believe I did much, but I thought that just giving them the chance to express their feelings would go a long way.

One day, in the van, the boys had an awful fight. It all started with something Raoni had written about Tayna in a post card he was sending to a friend. Tayna ripped the post card; Raoni hit him in the face with the towel. Tayna lost his mind and destroyed Raoni's sound equipment. I tried to stop him, but trying to stop almost six feet of pure rage was impossible. I felt so sorry for Raoni. That sound equipment was his pride and joy. He worked so hard to buy it; he had taken the trouble to bring it all the way to Australia.

My cold was getting worse and I felt pretty miserable and feverish. Yet, I had to keep the boys apart and look for a house. I contacted real estate agents, there wasn't anything available in Byron and all I could find were a few very expensive, two-bedroom units. So I decided to look in Ballina, a town twenty minutes to the south. One day I found a gorgeous house, within walking distance of the beach. It was a hot day, I had been in the car for a long time and my fever was killing me, so I decided to go to the real estate office the next day. Next day, I took Raoni with me, he also loved the house. I remembered to bring my mobile this time and called the office from there. The house had been rented a few minutes earlier.

It took us another eight days to find something decent and I spent those days in the van in Byron, mainly trying to keep my sanity and preventing the boys from killing each other.

Eventually, we settled in Ballina, in a nice townhouse overlooking the Richmond River. It had three big bedrooms and three toilets and the backyard opened to the river and a park.

We found out pretty soon that going to any of the many beaches in town by bus was a real hassle, there were very few buses and only then, did we fully realized what we had lost with that house at the beach.

Greg came over to help us move in, bringing some stuff and we both went back to The Garra to take the caravan back. We came back the next day with a few more things and Dadboy and a friend of his came a few days later under a pouring rain with a big Ute and a trailer with the furniture. Light and telephone connected, life could begin. We had to install an extra phone line for Greg's broadband connection, as there was some technicality that with the existing phone wiring that wasn't right.

The garage was quite narrow. Soon Greg's car got scratched on both sides and I wasn't impressed with the cockroaches that showed up later. I thought I had left them behind, in Brazil. Not so. I was in coastal New South Wales!

I didn't have a washing machine and I had to go twice a week to the Laundromat. We didn't have a decent fridge either. I had hopes that soon we would be able to buy one, but we never did. We used Craig's little fridge from the caravan for years. Even today, after we bought our fridge and washing machine, Greg still says he can't understand how I managed to put all the groceries for a week for an entire family into that little space.

It was good to discover ABC and SBS. They always have something on worth watching, so much better than the commercial television channels. Until then I had mostly watched satellite TV.

I found the rental system here in Australia so weird, those inspections every three months and they always send you a lovely letter in advance saying that if you can't attend their inspection they will get in anyway, because they've got a spare key. One day the real estate agent complained because the boys' surfboards were against the wall. When you leave the house, they want the carpets cleaned professionally. There are so many rules. It's claustrophobic.

In Holland or in Brazil tenants can do whatever they like with carpets and wallpapers, they could leave it as it was or paint or renew everything, without having to ask anyone and there are no inspections.

I found the letters I got from the real estate agents so threatening that I was convinced that I was going to lose my bond for the smallest of things. I spent a lot of time cleaning the place.

I always left the houses we rented squeaky clean, even though

Greg would roll his eyes and tell me it didn't have to be so perfect.

As the rush of moving in and getting settled was over and life calmed down a bit, the boys started to feel terribly bored. They had such a busy life in Brazil, so many friends popping in all the time, so many things to do and places to go. We couldn't do anything because we hadn't received our visas yet. Without the papers from DIAC, we couldn't work or study.

Despite that, our new life routine started to set in. Tayna had ventured out alone at night, only to find that there was precious little for young people to do. We found out that Ballina is a retirement town, populated with old people or young families. The town is dead after 7 p.m.; it's an awfully boring place for young people to live.

Greg set up a computer for the boys and they spent hours ICQing friends. There were always arguments about how long one had used it and who should use it first. They were always arguing about the dishes as well. "It's your turn!", "No, it's yours, I did it yesterday!"

Greg thought I spoiled the boys and was often annoyed. Nonetheless, they were going along pretty well. The boys liked him and respected him. He did better with Tayna; I think they have more in common. I tried to hide from Greg the things I knew he wouldn't appreciate and thank goodness, he couldn't understand the cursing and the swearing.

I started taking the boys to the beaches around. We didn't really know what the situation was with driver's licenses, so Greg didn't want the boys to drive before they had their Australian licenses.

In a car park at Broken Head, one day, there was a van parked there with some young guys in it and they were using heroine. Raoni got pretty shocked; he couldn't understand why they were doing that in that wonderful place at 10 o'clock in the morning. He later told Chica he felt blessed he had such open-minded parents who made him aware of all that, so that he never got into it.

They loved Lennox Head. Raoni surfed his legs off, and they were both drooling with the perfect waves. Tayna was amazed by all the lorikeets and surprised that people didn't catch them. Public toilets everywhere at the beaches was also new for them.

Raoni decided one day to come back from one of the beaches on foot. He thought it would be a piece of cake, but he walked for over two hours, got home when it was already dark and found me freaking out, imagining all sorts of things had happened to him.

Tayna joined the local soccer club and I was disappointed when he decided to pull out just two months later. Despite my protests and arguments with the club, we lost a whole year's membership plus insurance. Soon after that, he hurt his back and couldn't surf for quite a while.

I continued taking Raoni to the beaches every day, but he soon realized the fun thing about surfing was sticking around with the friends on the beach. Being alone was no fun at all. They fell into a vacuum, a limbo with nothing to do, nowhere to go, no one to talk to.

Communication with other young people was difficult, they didn't really understand the jokes and the slang and felt left out most of the time. They felt terribly lonely. Both were missing Brazil like crazy. At home they spent long hours in their rooms looking at pictures of friends and girlfriends, thinking of the good times in Brazil.

Raoni was so in love with Chica when he left, but I wondered if she was the right girl for him. I only remembered her as a child, from when I lived in Paraty.

He would get so anxious waiting for the papers.

I caught them crying in their bedrooms many times and when I looked at them down, sad and depressed, I thought of how happy they were in Paraty and I felt terribly guilty. Since then I've asked myself a thousand times if I had done the right thing by bringing them to Australia.

At least I had Greg and my hope for the future and the maturity to wait for things to get better. They didn't. When I look back at those difficult times, my heart fills with so much love and pride for them, they have been so brave!

Not long after we moved in, their father wrote them an e-mail, advising them to be aware of the cultural differences, things that are acceptable for us in Brazil and that might be frowned upon over here. He missed them and was rooting for them, hoping that they would make good use of the opportunity to help them become more independent and telling them not to be afraid to overcome obstacles. He'd like me to clarify the possibilities here and immigration regulations and ended with a list of explanations as to why he didn't have any money to send.

We went to the local TAFE (Technical and Further Education) to check it out and inquire about English courses. TAFE is a low-cost, very broad and common Education System here. Most of the courses are of good quality. We met a very nice teacher there, Julie, who helped us enormously: first she arranged for the long distance English course for immigrants, a government initiative; then, when we got our temporary visas, she helped them with the enrolments in the technical courses and finally she was an invaluable support with all the paper work needed for their advanced courses. She advised us of every scheme she knew for immigrants, something DIAC never bothered doing. She even arranged, under one of those schemes, a reimbursement of some of the fees we had paid. If everybody were helpful like her, what a wonderful world this would be!

The Government program was very useful for the boys, but it only takes students to a certain level. It was of no use to me. So, I borrowed some books from the Library and studied on my own.

We also went to the University in Lismore to enquire about the possibilities for the boys. If their English continued to improve, we could try and get them into Uni in the new study year in 2002.

It was explained that as immigrants, we wouldn't receive any help from the Government until our resident visas were through. That could take years. As people on a temporary visa, we had to pay full international student fees. They are much higher than the already very high fees Australians or residents pay. On average between 15 and 30 thousand dollars a year, and then there are books, transport, food, and several other compulsory fees and memberships. Recently the Liberal-National Government has also allowed an increase in fees of 25%, and it's getting worse.

So far, so good, I knew that part and I was prepared for it. They would have to study part time and work part time. With my salary included, we would be able to meet the study expenses. You would think there's nothing wrong with that, wouldn't you?

Well, the government thinks there is. People on a temporary visa couldn't study part-time, they must study full time. That means that on the one hand the education costs are the highest possible and on the other hand, the time left to work (so that you can pay for those costs) is the least possible.

Why they have to make life so difficult for those who want to pursue tertiary education is beyond my understanding, especially in a country with a gross deficit in skilled labor. Do they think all international students get support from elsewhere? Is education a business for profit like any other? From what I've seen so far, most students haven't got any other source of income, but from the menial odd jobs they manage to get. I heard plenty of criticism about immigrants that continue unemployed and don't mix in after years of being here. With this kind of support how can they?

Years later, when I got involved with the refugees issues I learned that they, in turn, are not allowed to study full time. What's the logic behind these rules? Is there any?

I wanted to enquire further about their study possibilities, but Raoni said he didn't need to get into Uni straight away. He was happy enough with a diploma from TAFE for the time being, and Tayna told me not to bother. He looked so disappointed. He was already unhappy, and this was the last blow for him, for all of us. With a few hours left to work each week, we wouldn't be able to make the money necessary for the fees. Tayna was silent for the rest of the day.

Like at DIAC in the beginning of the year, all the plans I had and was living for, turned out to have been built on misinformation and again I was floored to the ground.

When things go wrong, we are often accused of not asking around for information beforehand. But, I have learned that a lot has got to do with luck, with stumbling upon the right person in the right mood, at the right time.

I asked myself again what the hell I was doing here. Was this country really worth it? But I had gone too far already. The boys were here. I had Greg and we were married.

That same evening, Tayna informed me of his decision: if he couldn't continue Uni here, he was going back to Brazil. He missed the fun of Brazil, the friends. He felt too lonely.

He had been here for two months. I couldn't accept his decision. It was too much for me. I told him I wouldn't pay for his ticket back. He looked at me with fuming eyes and went to his bedroom, slamming the door behind him.

Later that night Greg told me I couldn't do that. If he wanted to go, I had to let him go. (I had promised him I would, before he came, anyway. I had to keep my word). Tayna's decision came a few days after their tickets had expired.

I could have exchanged the return part of his ticket for a new one and get a considerable discount if he had told me that a week earlier. I had to buy an entire new ticket.

By mid June, the boys started to drive and Greg felt confident enough to let them take the car now and then. They started going to Byron in the weekends and that was great for them. They met many Brazilians, discovered a capoeira school and they enrolled immediately. Not long after, our temporary visas arrived. From then on, we could work and study.

Raoni started a maritime operations course and together we started an English course for University preparation. Sitting in the same classroom with my younger son was a very peculiar experience. He was quite positive. He started looking for work and I didn't have to tell him to study.

I think the certainty that he was going back to Brazil at the end of the year, gave Tayna new motivation to put in the effort to do his Tourism course, though he never stopped complaining about missing his friends and the boredom of Australia. He wasn't very enthusiastic about anything and it was frustrating trying to understand and help him.

We bought them bikes. Raoni started to use his straight away to go to school, two blocks from home, but Tayna had to travel 30-40 minutes by bus to get to his. The hassle in the beginning eased when he found another student who would give him a hike, but often, their times didn't match.

Public transport outside the big cities is minimal in Australia. Most people don't bother using it. Cars are fairly cheap and more convenient. Looking back today, I think I should have made an effort and bought the boys a car, even if we had to hit the credit card again, which was at that time already in the red.

With the boys studying, I had a little more time for myself; I could start looking for work. And man, have I tried!

I had hopes of finding something as a biologist because my diploma was accepted here. Dozens of applications went out. I contacted former teachers, acquaintances and bosses for references. That was a big accomplishment in itself. Finding people from so long ago, e-mail addresses that had changed, people, who had moved or retired. I even looked into the possibilities of a PhD. I really hoped I would get a good job and finally make use of my Diplomas, which had cost me so many tears and so much effort.

But, all I got was letters that started with "we are sorry to inform…".

The more letters I received, the more I looked into websites, writing and publishing.

July arrived and we were still struggling.
Above all, I hated being dependent and having to ask for money for everything. I remembered that the boys still had a father and that we had made a deal. I sent him a short e-mail reminding him of our agreement and the money he was supposed to send. He hadn't sent any yet. I told him I had new expenses with the courses, fees and books and that it was quite difficult to bear it all alone.
I don't remember my exact words, but he sent back a furious e-mail, recalling facts from ages ago. He wanted to send the money directly to the boys; I didn't need to know of his dealings with them. If I managed to always send money to the boys in Brazil that was only because I was a spoiled, rich-daddy bitch and had always lived off my parents. I had abandoned my sons all those years and didn't have the right to talk about priorities nor charge him. It was my own fault if I was having financial problems, I should have thought about that before letting the boys come over, my fault I didn't plan things well enough, my fault I didn't have a job. It was about time I took over the financial responsibility of the boys, because he had been the only one responsible since our marriage. About time I stopped depending on Greg and thinking I was special and too good to do just any work.
I sent him an e-mail back reminding him of how much my parents helped us during the time we were married, from furniture to dental treatment for him, which of course he conveniently erased from his memory. My mother did received 500.00 Brazilian reais that month and 400.00 the next. But that's all I have ever received from him in all the years the boys have been in Australia.

It was very frustrating not finding a job and watching Greg cope alone with all the expenses. I came to know later that the region we were in was one the worst in Australia in terms of employment. It didn't look as if a job as a biologist would become a reality, so I took a job as a door saleswoman for some company that sold household stuff door to door. I absolutely hated it.
Raoni helped me many times. Because of my back problems, I thought the walking would do me good. It didn't.
An advert for a volunteer telephone counselor for Lifeline caught

my attention and I enrolled. It included attendance of an evening training course of two months.

In one of those night classes, my car got broken into. I couldn't deliver some of the goods that day, as people weren't home. The stuff was stolen and it wasn't cheap, either. At first, they told me I had to pay for it all, but after much negotiation, I ended up paying for half of it. Weeks of work were reduced to nothing.

After a lot of thinking, Raoni finally decided to study naval architecture in Sydney and Tayna, finally, started to put more effort into his course. Taking into consideration the level of his English and the amount of subjects he was doing, he wasn't doing badly at all and I was proud of him.

Life went on in my new and busy routine; cooking and cleaning turned into a real job, I couldn't expect much help from anyone. The boys' bedrooms were always a mess.

Greg didn't know half of what went on, as most of the arguments went on in Portuguese.

He's the kind of guy who will hide or run away to avoid an argument or a confrontation, so he never said anything. But the emotions were there and had to go somewhere. He started having serious problems with his stomach and vomiting on a regular basis. Don't know how many times he threw up his dinner before he finished it. He would say it was only temporary and that it would pass, but when I found blood in the toilet, I summoned him to go see a doctor. The symptoms eased with several different pills a day.

We were nearing the end of August when we finally paid off Greg's credit card debt; we had paid all the costs of the immigration process, moving and settling down in Ballina with it. With a little pay increase Greg got at that time, we could breathe again, but only just.

I did manage to get myself the new pair of glasses I needed for a long time and I started belly dance classes, a project I had been cherishing for years as well. I wasn't sure if it was doing my back any good, though.

At the dance class, I was reminded again of my awkwardness amongst people. Something in the air didn't feel comfortable. Some of the girls there had even less talent and coordination than I have. One of them was having trouble with a quite simple exercise. When she asked the teacher, instead of encouraging her, the teacher said, "I don't know what your problem is with this." Another student just did the exercise in front of her and said, "Look it's so simple!" Giggles could be heard here and there. I came very close to going up to her to try and explain how it was supposed to go, even though I didn't really understand it myself, but I worried about the teacher's position, so I didn't do anything.

That woman didn't come to the next class. She never came back.

I kept thinking of her. Maybe that class meant a lot to her, a hope of doing something creative with herself. Who knows what she had already put herself through just to be there? I felt so sorry for her and I felt a bit guilty. I should have done something. From that day on, I would never let an opportunity go by to help a fellow student, if I thought the teacher wasn't doing enough. I wouldn't care about the teacher's position anymore. If they didn't want to have their authority undermined, they had better do what they were supposed to do. I did it on several occasions after that, in other classes. It has always been so that as soon as the teacher saw me explaining or doing something with another student she would come and try to do it herself.

I also went to see a physiotherapist. She had the nerve to charge me A$ 500 bucks, which wasn't covered by Medicare, for a few visits that didn't help me in any way whatsoever, and sent me away with a few Xeroxed pictures of exercises she didn't even bother explaining. How do these people sleep at night? I tried those few exercises anyway and I also started doing a bit of yoga again every day.

When August bit the dust and my job seeking was still going nowhere, I tried different Government programs designed to help skilled immigrants and mature people. At the mature age program, I only argued with people and the whole thing ended up being a very frustrating exercise. All they could do for me was to put a few bells and whistles on my CV, and I even had to travel to another town for that, another one of those great, useless Government initiatives. The only people getting a job out of that were the people supposed to help others get a job. At least someone's getting something out of it! Maybe that's how the Government sees it.

The boys were busy with their courses but arguments and fights continued on a regular basis. Raoni started to put together his application form for the Naval Architecture course in Sydney. He got immeasurable help from his teacher at TAFE. He needed lots of documents from Brazil and again I had to count on his father's good will to help us out in getting them.

We all took our driving tests, written and practical and to my shame, the boys got their driving licenses with no problems whatsoever. It amazed me how easy it all seemed to them; it's as if they had always driven on that side of the road. I failed again in the practical test! I got messed up with different rules for NSW and QLD about the use of the blinker on roundabouts.

On the morning of 12 September I was looking through the front window when the lady next door passed by.

"Have you seen what happened?" she asked.

"No, what?"

"A huge attack in the US. Maybe terrorists..."

"Yeah, sure. I bet it's another one of their freaks blowing up a building..."

"No, no. they are probably from the Middle East... It's all over the TV..." She replied without stopping.

I turned the TV on and as I saw the images repeating again and again I slowly sat down dumbfounded... This can't be really happening! What a horrifying sight, so many dead people... The repercussions here were enormous. At the counseling course, we prayed a lot for peace. Some thought they had lost friends there.

As a Latin American at heart, I don't easily see America as a victim of anything, I'm perfectly aware of the atrocities and nauseating games America is always playing to defend its economic interests, but no one deserves to die like that. It was unacceptable, absurd. It's awful that in the twenty-first century people cannot talk to settle their differences.

John Howard, the Australian prime minister then, was in the US the day it happened and immediately offered total support. Heavy artillery was sent from here to the Middle East straight away. I thought that could end up very fishy for Australia. I worried. War, retaliation, lots of innocent people dying, more refugees spread all over the world. Was there not enough suffering and chaos in the world already?

I couldn't stop asking myself "why? Why did this happen?" What had the US done to get so much hatred thrown back at them? I came to the conclusion that they have been messing around in the Middle East far too long. Their support for Israel, the occupation of Palestinian territories, secret deals with oil magnates and God only knows what else, not at all for the benefit

of the majority of people; so many mistakes, known and unknown, being made for too long. And I also reckoned that the loyalty of Australia to the US is based on the fear of not being able to defend itself from some imaginary super enemy.
Always this bloody fear!

Ilona sent an e-mail telling me she believed I would be pretty safe here. I said I wasn't that sure.
She had started a screenwriting course and I told her I couldn't write between a dish washing and an argument with the boys. I needed peace of mind to think. I told her I would probably get serious with writing in a few years, but it did make me think about it. Until then my writing was irregular and inconsistent. From then on, I started to write my journal more regularly, trying to keep track of events and thoughts.

With terrorists or without them, my life had to go on. I worried about the extra expenses we would soon have with Raoni in Sydney. I don't know how many hours I spent looking for jobs on the net and in newspapers searching the classifieds, entire days writing applications, only to be told that the position had been taken already. I hated it!
Greg explained to me, that often they already had someone for a position; putting out an ad is only a mechanism to comply with transparency regulations.
To clean toilets or fry fish, they wanted someone experienced, someone who had been doing it for donkeys. Why do they want to damn people to do this kind of work their whole lives? Nobody should do this kind of work for long. With every "no" I got upset, no matter how stupid the job, no matter how insignificant. I needed the bloody money.

I decided to get out on the streets. Ask around. I followed several leads, a hospital, the Local Environment department, but again, it was all useless, all time and effort, for nothing.
Mum kept asking about my job prospects and insisted I continue looking and doing my best. So I had to find explanations as to why I still didn't have one. For the better jobs, I was told I lacked the experience. For the stupid jobs, I was often told I was over qualified and although they never said it to my face, I don't think being over forty is of any help when you're looking for your first job in a foreign country. Then there weren't a lot of jobs around anyway. Not knowing anyone didn't help either. I guess

everybody gets some sort of help for a first job from an acquaintance or a relative. I had no one here. Then I had the boys to worry about, too; they needed a lot of my time and someone had to do the house chores. Looking for work had to be done between one thing and another. When I think about it today, I realize I couldn't have possibly found a decent job under those circumstances. My role then, was to be the backbone, to make sure life continued, that food was on the table and the house was kept in relatively good order.

Mum told us to start something for ourselves.
Often I thought about starting my own biz, writing, a website, but the more I looked into all that it involved, the more I felt overwhelmed: tax law, publishing law, writers contracts, finances and management, website building, research, editing and translating work, technical aspects, electronic media, marketing, advertising and what have you. Where was I going to find time to do everything? I also wanted to do something with counseling, but didn't know exactly what or how. I often had to push all these ideas away from my mind, to be able to concentrate on the issues of the day.

The oldies finally sold the house in São Paulo and that made me a bit sad. The house in which we had spent so many years of our lives, the house dad designed and built himself. He used to say they would need a lot of dynamite to get that house down. I wished so much we could have kept the house in the family. Those walls had witnessed so much of our lives. Those walls were a part of our lives. So many memories... You don't sell your memories.
But it was such a big house for only two oldies. My mother had to pay someone merely to keep it clean. She'd had enough of it. Fair enough. Rates and other costs were also an unnecessary burden. Coincidentally the Filets, Ilona's parents and my parents' best friends, also sold their house at the same time.
Mum started to pack and I can only imagine going through the junk one gathers in more than thirty years, so much to throw away, so much to pack. Johanna again helped with the packing. All my stuff was still there as well. Ji was so kind to take care of that. They had plans to move to the farm before Christmas.

In October, Dadboy had to have a major surgery. They found cancer in his lungs. We went to visit him in the hospital in

Brisbane. He had a huge cut in his back. They took 2/3 of his left lung. Over 50 years of smoking had taken its toll, even though he had quit years ago.

But he reacted very well to it and, in no time, he was the same larky old chap he'd always been.

Being all the time, in the middle of the crossfire between the boys and a buffer zone between them and Greg was at times more then I could handle. With summer getting closer, the heat and the discomfort increasing, I often felt stressed out, tired and sad. I didn't feel a lot of support from Greg; he didn't seem to understand that I couldn't change the boys overnight; he was often pissed off with their attitudes and behavior. I often felt terribly alone in all this. We were still struggling financially. Helping out the boys in their many difficulties and needs, fixing crashed computers, looking for work in vain, running the household, etc... It all looked so useless, at times.

It was in one of those hot days, when the boys were being particularly difficult and I had been looking for jobs in vain for most of the day that I seriously thought of giving everything up and going to Holland. The thoughts of leaving raved in my head for days, until one day Greg and I talked it all over. Again, I got his reassurance and support. He loved me, in spite of everything, in spite of all the mess. We would get through it all, together. He would always be there for me.

The only thing I had to console me in those days was the telephone counseling training course. It was very interesting and I was excited about it. Not that the job possibilities were so good, but because of the many interesting and nice people I'd started to meet and it was great to learn how to help people. Pity I couldn't help myself!

Not every single day was chaos and tears, though. There were days when everything seemed magical, even if it was for a short time only. I remember a warm morning. I used to take the old bread to the riverbank to feed the seagulls, ibises and other birds. I didn't mean to stay long but the sun felt so nice and warm that I decided to sit for a while on the embankment. The tide was high; my feet could touch the water. I looked at the intense blue of the Australian sky.

As I started throwing the bread pieces to the seagulls, a pair of eagles, or something like it, came from I don't know where.

One of them caught a fish from the water, very close to me. They were little and brown, with a white head and neck. It was great to observe how it plunged down towards the water, stopping suddenly, just a few centimeters above it to make a rather intricate man oeuvre and get the fish.

While I watched it fly away, a huge pelican came flying slowly and majestically, low over the surface of the water. In wonder, I watched as it too, flew away. Looking at the deep green of the vegetation on the other side of the river and the blue sky behind it, hearing the ripples going up and down on the sand I thanked God for being there and I felt blessed. When I got home, the telephone was ringing. It was my English teacher telling me I had missed the class that had just finished...

November arrived and the heat was becoming unbearable. I was dragging myself around with no energy for anything. I kept my household duties to the strictly essential, but I kept looking for work and into publishing, website and writing issues.

The arguments between the boys and between me and them didn't seem to lessen either. I was either too soft or too hard with them and often felt guilty about it afterwards, always those arguments about the dishes, always their trying to get away with it. Man, I hated finding all the dirty dishes from the night before still on the sink first thing in the morning. Greg too, got really annoyed. I usually ended up getting much more upset and saying a lot more than I wanted to.

At least their courses were coming to an end. Tayna had done exceptionally well. He finished second best in his class. I was really proud of him, but he didn't think of it as a big deal. He still didn't feel anything for Uni. "Too difficult!" he said. I tried to convince him to the contrary, but to no avail. I still strongly believe he would have had no problems whatsoever.

When the news that Tayna was going back hit the folks in Brazil, they said it was a mad decision. Tell me about it. The oldies told me to let him pay for it, but how could I? They told me to let him care for himself in Brazil. Again, how could I do that? They felt sorry for Greg, putting up with all the mess and all the expenses. They told me I was acting out of guilt. I told them they might be right, but I didn't know where the magic button was that I had to press for everything to be as it should. I wish people keep their mouths shut, when all they can do is criticize, when they are not interested in understanding all the issues involved.

The days in which I felt completely overwhelmed were so many that when I saw a leaflet offering a free relaxation course at the medical centre in town, I enrolled immediately.

A whole new world of meditation, Buddhism and the books of Thich Nhat Hanh opened up for me. I started doing meditation every day, even though it has always been very hard for me. I just don't manage to get my mind still for more than two minutes in a row; no matter how much I try, I just can't tame that pack of wild horses running free inside my head! Yet, I kept trying, believing it was all a matter of perseverance.

As the end of the year approached things went from bad to worse. By mid December, I had a few days straight out of hell. The boys had a Homeric fight again.

It was a stinking hot day. They got home from the beach late in the afternoon. A heated argument started as soon as they arrived. I had to get between them to avoid them from attacking each other (I have received a few punches in my life in this process). Amongst the screams, the shouts and the swearing I tried to make sense of what had happened, while Greg kept asking for translation as he watched the whole thing going on in Portuguese.

Raoni was in the water when Tayna signaled from the beach, pointing to the next beach. Tayna was telling him that he was going to have a look at the next beach. Raoni got out of the water half an hour later and saw no car, no food, no clothes, no Tayna. He thought Tayna had left him behind, as he had done before and started walking back home, bare feet on the melting asphalt, under the scorching sun. Tayna catches up with him somewhere on the way and stops the car. As he gets out, Raoni throws the surfboard at him. They screamed and shouted at each other. The result was a bruised arm, a cut eyebrow and two destroyed surfboards.

I had given them some money for clothes a few days before, so I told them they would have to use that money to fix the boards and they didn't like that.

Half an hour later, all was peace and quiet, as if nothing had happened. Tayna went to see some girlfriends nearby, Raoni went to his room and I ran to the computer to write and try to make sense of it all.

Before they arrived home and the tornado hit the house, I was cheerfully telling Greg how I thought I'd finally found out what I really wanted to do with my life. After all the screaming and throwing of things I didn't want anything any more.

I wasn't completely recovered from that day, when a few days later Tayna handed me his ticket reservation to Brazil. He had changed it again on his way back from school. Since I had made his reservation four months earlier, he had changed it more than ten times. The guy from the travel agency, who dealt with Tayna from the beginning, had left the office, leaving a very confusing file behind for the other agents.

What it all came down to was that the reservation Tayna showed me was much more expensive than the one I had originally made. He was now travelling at the "high season" price. That was the last straw for me. Screaming I told him that I wasn't going to pay one cent more for the ticket and that it was up to him to find a ticket as cheap as the one I had previously given him, even if he had to stay for another six months.

But I couldn't trust him. I worried I would end up losing the whole ticket if I left it up to him, so the next day I went to the travel agency where I tried, very politely at first, to explain the situation, still in the belief that it was all a simple misunderstanding. As the agent tried to convince me more and more, that there was nothing she could do, I ended up screaming and having a huge argument with her.

I went home feeling depressed. Why does it always have to come to this point to get something done?

When I was younger, I used to argue with everyone, from the guy in the bus who didn't give me the correct change to the teacher who didn't give me the right mark on the test to the grocery guy, because the ice cream was too expensive. I didn't think much about it then. It was just so natural to me. I don't know where I got all that energy from. But since I had come here, I only got upset; I hadn't come here to argue.

Two hours later the agent called me at home to say that she managed to get the original, cheaper ticket back. So, a few screams and a good scene do help after all?

I spent the rest of that day and the next ones trying to figure out why it is that since I got the boys, I always felt so bogged, as if my entire life had been put on hold, every little thing, even my thoughts. Never knowing what to do. I couldn't understand why motherhood was so difficult for me.

Writing at the computer with my eyes still red from all the crying of that day, I was interrupted by Tayna, burping behind me as he stand at the door. Looking at me as if nothing had happened that day, he asked, "What do you think, would it be better if I changed the ticket and postponed it for another week?"

A tsunami of rage went through my veins, my whole body trembled. I don't know what held me back from attacking him at that moment. Instead, calmly I told him, "After everything that happened today, you want to change the ticket again? You listen: I don't want to hear one word about tickets any more. Get one thing in your head and don't forget it: if you mess up and lose this ticket you will sort it out yourself." He smiled and said he was embarrassed to go back there anyway, after what happened.

Thinking of that whole episode at the travel agency in a calmer mood some time later I came to the conclusion it was Tayna's fault after all, as in his last change, he didn't check the fares and flights.

That same evening I started organizing things for dinner in the kitchen and Raoni started to bombard me with questions. He was writing to people in his search for a place to stay in Sydney and didn't know what to say.

Impatiently, I told him to use his head, instead of making stupid questions and he started to swear and scream at me... F... you, F... this, F... that...

Yeah, yeah... I know. I should have known better. He was anxious about going to Sydney, the time for him to leave was fast approaching and he was only asking me very normal questions. He didn't have the faintest idea of what had happened that day and couldn't read my state of mind at that moment. I know that he really needed me then and like I did so many times before, I was too overwhelmed to help him.

Not long after, their father sent an e-mail demanding a report on Tayna. What had he done over here? Why was he going back? I wanted to tell him to go to hell and send me the freaking money he was supposed to have sent. Instead, very politely, I gave him a thorough account of all Tayna had done and his feelings and thoughts about going back. He ended the e-mail saying his financial situation was very bad (surprise, surprise!) and that Tayna would have to work to help make ends meet if he went back. It would not be easy for him.

Very naïvely, I asked him to talk to Tayna and try to convince him to stay, but his reply was that Tayna was big enough to make his own decisions.

It was only much later that I understood his reaction. He already had a complete explanation in his mind for the reason why Tayna was going back. I must have done something terrible again; Greg could only be another loser, like my other Australian husband and we had traumatized Tayna again.

As his departure date approached, Tayna looked more and more confused. One day he said he would stay if we could pay for him to stay on the Gold Coast. We couldn't afford to pay three rents. If he wanted to stay, he had to go live with Raoni in Sydney. There were courses for him in Sydney, but there weren't courses for Raoni on the Gold Coast. Then he said he would stay if he got a job. He tried a bit, walked a lot, spreading his résumé around, but to no avail, especially at that time of the year. Until the day of his departure, he often looked lost. He had such a childish look in his eyes. I wished so much I could do something to change everything... But, as always, I didn't know how.

It was now countdown for Tayna's departure and the thought of his going back made me terribly sad. Letting them go felt like being on a rescue boat in a stormy sea, holding their hands, while they kicked and screamed for me to set them free, to let them jump into the water, knowing they didn't have a clue of how treacherous the waters were, knowing they couldn't swim that well, that they weren't wearing life-saving jackets, aware that they could even drawn. Okay, physically they were not children anymore, but for me, in their heads they were!

The only things Tayna could think about were his friends and the good times they had together in Brazil. He had never worked in Brazil, never dealt with bosses ripping him off, the poor salaries, the lack of respect. I knew he was making decisions that were based on a lack of experience of life.

I worried that he would soon realize his mistake. He would want to come back and I wouldn't have the money to get him back here. I worried about his visa. I believed that if he wasn't here by the time our residencies came out, he would lose it. I worried about where he was going to stay in Brazil, now that the oldies had sold the house. How was he going to go to school? Where? I asked the oldies about the spare car I used to use, but they had sold it as well. He was expecting to find everything as it was before he left, but everything had changed.

I knew Tayna would have a tough time in Brazil, that he wasn't aware of the difficulties he would face.

I knew no one would be there for him.

My mother asked me why I was making such a fuss about Tayna, why I worried so much. She kept saying that I had done all I could, that he wasn't a child anymore; he had made his choices and he had to accept the consequences. I agreed, but it didn't stop me from worrying about him. I won't have complete peace of mind until the day I see that they are where they are supposed to be, until I am convinced that they have become the people they are meant to be or at least, that they are going in that direction.

I had so many good intentions when I brought them here, but they didn't understand it and they didn't even want it.

It seemed that everything had gone down the drain, all the effort for nothing. It felt like death to me, like something lost forever.

I had this strong feeling that I wasn't finished with them. I saw so many issues in them that I thought needed to be addressed before they were ready to go; I really believed I could still give them something more.

Tayna made a few friends and life in Ballina was just starting to happen for him. His English had improved so much. All that made it even harder for me to accept that he was going back.

I had used all my powers to convince him to stay. I had done everything I could to offer him the possibility of a better future and he decided to throw the opportunity away.

It hurt like hell, I spent a long time trying to understand what I had done wrong, but I knew answers wouldn't come easily.

From the day they arrived, every new argument told me clearly of my inadequacy as a mother. Day after day I understood that all the things I had neglected during their upbringing where being thrown back in my face, quite literally.

Their father and I had been rivals instead of spouses. That's the lessons the boys received and that's how they understood people are supposed to deal with their differences. The same judgment, rivalry, resentment, frustration and anger that made up our marriage was reflected in their relationship; that was all they knew. They have never had a chance to work that out. Since the separation, when they were ten and twelve, they had been practically on their own. There had never been an adult around to help them sort themselves out and to guide them through their disputes and into maturity. They never learned to compromise, to share, to respect each other and to communicate. We were too busy with our own pain and our own mess.

It took me a long time to learn that we don't teach our kids to live by telling them about life, but by living our lives the best we can with them so they can learn to live theirs the best way they can.

I didn't realize how deep their concerns were.

Tayna had been giving out signals while he was still in Brazil.

Even before it was certain that they would come, my brother Ji, mentioned that it would be better if they came with a few months difference, so as to make adaptation better. He told me I had to consider the possibility of them not adapting.

While they were en route, I got an e-mail from Mari (Ji's wife), telling me to take it easy, because the boys looked very apprehensive in their last days there, but again, I missed to pick the clues.

Occasionally I felt more resigned, "Maybe it's good they go their own ways: Raoni to Sydney, Tayna to Brazil. Everybody would probably be happier this way". All the fighting, the arguments would be over.

Now and then, I thought it would be a good lesson for them to assume the consequences of their decisions.

There was nothing I could do any more but hope everything worked out fine for them.

Another e-mail from his father by the end of the year put me more at ease. He had arranged a traineeship for Tayna in a big hotel in Paraty and he would study in Ubatuba, a nearby town, where a new University had opened. That made it easier for me to let him go. I thought of how often he had been so sad and I hoped he would be happier there.

I made a promise to myself: I would do everything for them, until our residency was sorted out, but after that, it would be up to them. On that day, I would declare my financial responsibility for them as a parent terminated.

To keep my sanity and my worries at bay, I started designing websites.

Raoni managed to arrange a stay in a student's flat and had his trip booked for the end of January. I didn't think his English was good enough. I didn't think he was ready to go. Just the thought of him alone in Sydney, worried me, but Greg wouldn't even consider living there.

I knew it would be hard for him. He often went to his room and stayed there for hours very quietly, deep in thought, something sad over him and I never knew what to do or what to say. We did talk a few times and I hugged him whenever I could, but I knew he needed so much more than that. I know that there's so much more going on in his head than what he shows and I felt I had no permission to enter there and it hurt me. Was it just a boy's thing or a lack of trust? Nonetheless, he worried me less than Tayna.

Then Christmas and New Year arrived. Tayna didn't want to go to The Garra and I didn't want the family to be apart at Christmas, so I decided to stay the night of the 24th. I bought a nice piece of meat; I wanted to make something special. So I made an Indonesian dish called gado-gado (vegetables with peanut sauce) and roasted the meat. I finished cooking and wanted to have a shower so that I could at least, be fresh at my special Christmas dinner, but everyone started to whine and gripe that they were hungry and wanted to eat. So, I put the food on the table and sat, sweaty and tired, just like any other day. There was no point in getting out the nice dinner set and the Christmas tablecloth.

"Was this the reason why you didn't go to Wallangarra? You could have gone." Tayna said at the table.

"Don't you think it's a special dinner?"

They all agreed that it was a very ordinary dinner.

After it, everybody took off as usual, to their TV's, their computers, their telephones and I was left alone to clean up the leftovers of my special Christmas dinner and the mess in the kitchen.

In my room later that night, trying to keep away the tears, I thought of the Christmas nights at home, so long ago, the big Christmas trees beautifully decorated, lots of presents under it, candles and dimmed lights, the huge table and the whole family together. I usually got disappointed with my presents and was always critical about the rest of the family, but I looked back at that time with so much tenderness. We never really realize the preciousness of what we've got, until it's gone forever, never to come back.

I looked around me and all I could think of was, "What a screwed up family I've got, what a loser and how stupid I am". It seemed I kept making mistakes in my life over and over again, a never-ending story. Every new trial to fix a previous messed up situation just threw me into a bigger chaos. Like the one I was in then. In a strange country, grabbing the coins around the house to make ends meet, owing money to my parents and others, powerless in relation to everything that had to do with the boys. No matter what I did or how hard I tried, it just felt like a drop of water in a furnace.

Why does everything have to be so difficult, so complicated? Why couldn't life unfold naturally, without so much effort?

The struggle took away the pleasure and joy from everything, made everything seem so meaningless. Why do I feel I'm always swimming against the flow, speeding on the opposite direction?

My plan to come to Australia and start a new life for me and the boys was so much simpler in my head. Things have turned out so different from how I had planned. I wanted to have a nice house, in a good location before they arrived, so that we could receive the boys in our own house, not having to disrupt the oldies' lives in The Garra, but we ended up in a caravan where they almost killed each other. I wanted everything to happen smoothly, but the boys ended up getting over here in the most chaotic way possible. My worst nightmares had come true. Not being able to help them in their transition into an independent life, not getting a job.

The nice words in the Christmas cards that arrived from friends and family cheered me up a bit, but not really.

I guess you never know how bad the poop smells until you start poking into it!

Later that night, I remembered I had left a tin of Coke in the freezer and I still had a bit or rum, somewhere. I thought, "Okay. That's going to be my consolation, my own private Christmas celebration, seeing that no one cares..."

When I got down to the kitchen, there was Coke everywhere, all over the floor, on the clean dishes, on the bench.

"What the hell happened here?"

"Dunno, mum, the Coke exploded!" Raoni said.

"You are going to clean up this mess, right now!"

"But I did, already!"

In Wallangarra for Christmas, Raoni was bored out of his mind and I tried to hide from Mumboy the food he hadn't finished.

Back in Ballina, we finally paid off Tayna's ticket, but the soap opera was doomed to last forever: another problem had shown up. They had booked a domestic flight that allowed only 20 kg of luggage but the international part from Sydney to Brazil allowed 60 kg and Tayna had a lot more stuff to take back with him than he had when he arrived. In a call to the travel agency, the clerk started yelling at me (she started this time!) but said she would see what she could do. I had left it over to Tayna to sort it out the next day. I just couldn't find the energy to look into it, anymore. Temperatures soared to over 40°C and it was very muggy. The summer fires were sweeping through Australia again. A hundred and fifty homes had burnt down to ashes by then and there were no signs of rain.

I'm not sure if it's just my need to see something positive in that difficult year, but I want to believe that the boys had, in all that turmoil, matured towards a greater understanding and acceptance of each other. They had grown closer and a lot of the rivalry was gone. When Tayna called back a few days after he arrived in Brazil he said Raoni made him mad sometimes, but he really loved him and always would. For years after the fights in the van in Byron Bay, Tayna would still excuse himself for having broken Raoni's equipment. He promised to give him a new one as soon as he could and he actually did offer him a new sound system, a few years later, but Raoni didn't need it anymore. I knew there was still a long way to go, but there was no doubt that their relationship had improved.

Raoni had defined a path for his future and was excited about it. That was much better than the lack of direction he showed when he was in Brazil. Deep inside I'm still not sure if he's really following his true destiny and I guess I'll have to wait and see.

I had managed to do many things I always wanted to and I was spending more time reading and writing; I had discovered meditation and Thich Nhat Hanh, I had become a telephone counselor and, last but not least, all the stress and turmoil had helped me lose most of the weight I had gained as a zombie in the Limbo of Wallangarra.

Greg and I had grown yet closer and the certainty that my place was next to him and the hope that things would happen for me in this country, one day, didn't fade with all the mess.

Mushrooms & Tears

An angry e-mail from Johanna caught me completely by surprise, a few days before Tayna's departure. She had never asked me to do anything for her kids; she had been so kind to help me out so many times, but all she got was ingratitude.

The boys' father had asked her to sort out Tayna's documents for his enrolment at Uni. Very diligently she had run to get it all done, paid all the expenses, sent everything up to him and he never replied, never paid her back, did not even call back to say thanks. I didn't know any of that, so it hit me like a brick out of the blue. I thanked her for her effort and told Tayna to pay her from the money I had given him. He wasn't very happy with that, he already had other plans for the money. Tayna got there with a present for her and the money just in time. She was getting angrier and angrier.

The present was an Exuma album. That's a band we used to listen to in our younger days, especially their first records from 1970. We didn't really follow them after that. She and Rubinho just loved it and I was very glad for them and for me.

On the 7th of January, 4 o'clock in the morning we were getting ready to go to the Ballina airport. The plane to Sydney would depart at 5 a.m. Greg drove us there, half asleep, after a quick breakfast. Raoni was so quiet, so serious. The boys hugged each other and wished each other good luck, then I hugged Tayna and he passed through the metal detector, then through the small departure lounge and to the exit door. As he walked to the small plane, he looked back and waved but I don't think he saw us. With tears falling freely through my face we watched the plain until it disappeared into the clouds and we all walked back to the car in silence.

Back home Greg crashed in bed and slept most of the morning, I cried most of the day. I went into Tayna's room, skimmed through the things he left behind: his books, little drawings, textbooks and other small things. I held his picture in my hands, one in which he's standing at the lighthouse in Ballina, with the sun in his squinty eyes. He looks so humble, in his worn out T-shirt from high school, his hands closed in a half fist like he often does, as if there's always some tension, as if he's never completely relaxed. I looked over his bedroom, the big picture of his soccer team, Flamengo, still on the wall.

Will he ever realize how much I love him?

I thought of how complicated our relationship had always been, our communication problems. We just didn't seem to be able to understand each other. All I could think of was "What a pathetic and lousy mother I've been" and the awareness that it was all over just made it all the more painful.

I put everything carefully into a shoebox and cleaned the room. I told Raoni to move in there the same day. I couldn't bear to see that room empty. Greg moved his office into Raoni's room the next day. Until then, his office had been a 1,5 by 2 meters walk-through wardrobe, which became an oven when the sun came through the window.

The sadness lasted for days. The days looked so beautiful, so peaceful, especially at dusk. I was so distant, life didn't seem real. I would just sit there at my desk and look at the river through my window, digesting my pain.

Writing in those days was almost impossible. The tears fell freely down my face making it hard to see the keys on the board.

There was nothing else for me to do but to accept the bitter truth about all the mistakes made in their upbringing, the realization of what a disaster of a parent I had been; the truth that my relationship with the boys had been wrong for a long time, that it had been deteriorating over the years and I never noticed!

I had to accept that my belief that everything between us would be just fine, as soon as we were together again, had been just an illusion. A change of country doesn't magically change things overnight.

I had to digest the truth that I had my chance with the boys and I missed it. I thought of all the things I should or shouldn't have done while Tayna was younger. I hate to think of all the times I've been impatient; all the times I was too busy to listen to him, to try to understand him; of all the times I argued with him, all the opportunities I missed to love him for who he was, to accept his limitations, to look beyond them and tenderly guide him in the right direction. Parenting for me, was over and it had been over for quite a while. I wasn't in parenting mode anymore; I was in damage control mode.

The fact that Raoni stayed, gave me so much consolation. He too, would go in a few days, but he would still be in Australia and I would be able to talk to him on the phone any day without having to spend a fortune and I could visit him whenever I wanted to.

I spoke to Tayna the night he arrived in Brazil. He sounded all right. He had a nice, relaxed trip with no hassles. He said he loved me and I told him I loved him very much, too. There was nothing else I could do. He wanted to finish his studies in Brazil. So be it. I could only hope that one day, here or in Brazil, he too would find his destiny.

By the end of the month, it was Raoni's time to go.
Students travel cheaply by train; it's not comfortable, almost claustrophobic, but I guess young people can put up with a lot more than I do these days.
As I expected, it wasn't as heartbreaking as Tayna's departure, maybe because I didn't even have the time to say goodbye properly. He had so much stuff in his hands, three bags and the computer box, apart from the luggage that had already gone to the luggage car. He was going to find his seat and put his stuff away in the train and then come back to give us a hug, but the doors of the train locked before he even found his seat. I had given him a kiss before in the car and on our way to the station I held his hand for a while. Maybe it was better that it was all over so quickly.
I worried about him, as well. I think he's so much like me in many ways. So proud... he also tries too hard to sort everything out by himself before he cries out for help, if he ever does. I needed to keep a close eye on him.
We spoke a lot on the phone the next few days and the transition into his new life went without any problems. Everything seemed all right at school and the people he went to live with seemed to be okay too.

It was hard getting used to the silence in the house. It was so big, so empty, but I didn't have too much trouble finding what to do in the extra time I had on my hands. I kept looking for jobs, belly dancing, writing, designing websites and learning about e-commerce. Occasionally I went to the beach. I kept counseling at Lifeline, but it was pretty hard at times. I would get very upset with some of the cases I had to deal with, I would get shocked with the apathy and often, not really know what to say, overwhelmed with all the suffering in this world. But when I did manage to say the right thing, to bring some light into someone's dark moment it felt great.
I decided to look more seriously into my back problems. I turned Raoni's room into an exercise/meditation room.
It upset me when I thought that I had spent so much money with

those physiotherapists and that they hadn't told me anything nor done anything and that all I know about my back I found out by myself, by doing my own research and my own exercises.

I decided to venture going to church again. It had been ages. But it didn't do anything for me. I only got annoyed with the screaming and crying children. The senile priest seemed to be more in another world than on this one and when I did manage to hear him, it all sounded so superficial and obvious. After a few times I decided that reading a good book was a great deal more helpful to me.

I still felt bad about not having a job, so I intensified my search for work. I thought moving to Lismore would be a good thing to do, but Greg talked me out of it in no time. We would spend a lot of money with Raoni's study and maintenance in Sydney and Tayna's ticket had created a new hole in the budget. Moving was an extra expense we didn't really need at that point in time.

I dreamt about the things I would love doing: develop innovative schools for stranded and strayed young people, revolutionize the entire educational system, for that matter, implement nature conservation projects, small scale pilot projects in which we could prove that it's possible to achieve a perfect balance between men's needs and the preservation of nature, provided we are willing to challenge our beliefs about what we really need to live. Then, there's always the cozy little house near the mountains and the ocean that Greg and I always dream about.

A few weeks had passed since Raoni had left and I felt the need to give him some encouragement:
"Hi sweetie.
I'm writing just to tell you that I love you and that you are my brave little guy. And you had to be, because Raoni means "dangerous panther" :-) (Raoni is also an Indian name. Literally, it means panther with cubs. Indians were especially fearful of panthers when they had cubs, because they become a lot more aggressive)
I'm so proud of you because you went out there to fight for what you believe in. You gave up your easy life to seek for something better, to grow as a human being. I don't think everyone needs to do that and it's not for everyone either. There are leaders and there are followers. We need both in this world.
So many chose to hide in their pseudo-security, in what's already

known. If they are happy like that, good on them, but I think it's the courageous ones, the adventurers, the ones that go search for answers, the ones that believe that life's more than the eye can see, the ones that give up comfort and friends for the unknown: they are the ones who find the answers for themselves and others, the ones that truly bring innovation to this world.

You are so much like me, always looking for something better. Puppy, I want to tell you also that this road is not the easiest, it can get very lonely sometimes and often we feel lost and cornered. In these moments, never forget that only God can love you more than I do, that I will always be here for you, till the day I die; but more important than that is for you to remember that you are able to sort out your own problems, to overcome obstacles, physical, mental, financial, whatever. Giving up is just a choice one decides to make.

Never ever stop believing in yourself, in your value and in your potential. We are all unique and we all have a special place reserved for us in this world. Never ever let anyone tell you that something is not for you. Decide for yourself, experiment, try, make mistakes and learn. Never beg for love or attention from anyone. Never do anything against your values and nature just to please someone or for money.

If someone cannot see your value, if someone doesn't respect you or accept you for what you are that person doesn't deserve your friendship. Give them a gentle goodbye and continue to follow your own way, let no one get you down. Believe always that your day will come, your place under the sun, the right person to share your life with. All you need to be very happy is already waiting for you and above all else, never feel less than anyone. We are all different, not more, not less than anyone else.

We have the right to be respected and to be happy. Never stop believing, never stop searching and never stop learning. Don't be afraid to love, or suffer, or cry.

Love you.

Irene"

He replied:

"Hi Mum,

I've got your letter and I liked it so much. You said I'm courageous because I left the good and known behind and to go for something even better. Yes, I'm courageous, I love challenges and I need to know my limits. In the water, I'm always looking for the best wave, when I started fixing boards I wanted to know if I could shape them as well. That was just the beginning.

We are what we experienced. Like myself, only my picture!

All the past experiences and all information we gather during our life make us unique and defines how we think. I inherited my courage from you.

You have always risked yourself to make your dreams come true. They may not always have worked out as expected, but they were real for as long as they lasted.

I remember when you were in doubt about coming to Australia. Everybody telling you this cyberdating thing was absurd. And look today. Greg's a great guy, so attentive and he loves you a lot. And all you've done for me and Tayna... This whole Australian story reaffirmed to me who we are, where we came from and where we are heading.

I have learned to be simple and humble with my friends in Paraty, but we are all different.

You know, I have never paid attention to religion. It had never been a part of my life. I rarely see people thanking God for what they've got, they only remember him when they need or want something. But I know He exists (whatever that may be) and I thank him from the depths of my heart for the parents he has given me.

This letter's getting too long, but I still wanted to say that I'm following my way in peace and alone and I'm making all this sacrifice because I need to know if I can do more than shape surfboards in my backyard. It's not about money, I don't care about it and I don't like materialistic people.

I love you so much. I left home not because I didn't like you, very much the contrary. I want you to be proud of your son and be very happy. One day we are going to go on a sailing trip on a boat designed by myself!

Love, Raoni"

It filled my eyes with tears. It reached me on the exact day I had been talking to Greg about how miserable I felt about my role as a mother, feeling that I could have done so much more. I read the letter to Greg and he said:

"See? You haven't been such a bad mother". But I wondered...

I wrote my mother about all this and asked her if she had had similar feelings when we left home. I also told her about the difficulties in our relationship, but again, she didn't answer.

Again, I had the feeling I was talking to a wall or speaking an unknown language.

The world around me was quite upsetting. The treatment of refugees had become something completely inhumane. They were picking people from boats that were sinking and throwing them straight into detention centers behind razor wire, where they aren't allowed to talk to anyone. It often happens that they send legitimate refugees back to their countries to be murdered because they failed to ask for the right forms. How are they supposed to know what forms to ask for if they neither speak the language nor have any kind of legal assistance? Shame on all those responsible for this!

They kept saying that they were doing it for Australia and it was refreshing to see banners go up in protest saying, "Not in my name!"

Is there any group of people needier than refugees? How can anyone see these people as threatening?

The fear that they will take away jobs, bring in diseases or become a burden to the government is so sickening. Always that bloody fear...

To put in place xenophobic laws, the government used edited footage from rescue operations of refugees at sea, giving the population the idea that the refugees were drowning their own children to save themselves. So many people went: "Oh my God, these people are monsters; we don't want any of them in our country!" It took the media a few years to find out the truth, but by then the laws were well in place.

Meanwhile for Raoni reality also started to bite. Disappointment with flat mates, the pace of life, the travel distances to school... but he was excited about the first classes and overall enjoying being on his own. He was exasperated with my worries and would tell me to try and do the things I always wanted and let him live his life. He was being so brave!

I had just started to settle into my new life and routine, when Greg lost his job. That was mid February. I saw it as a lesson in faith and patience and I didn't fret. I saw new opportunities. I thought maybe Greg could get some new work in Sydney; we could be closer to Raoni...

I got an e-mail from Ilona with something about the death of Cassia Eller, a blues singer in Brazil. She died in 2001, I don't know how exactly, probably from a drug overdose.

I liked her very much, her very intense style of singing, but there were times, in interviews, where she came over to me as a mess of a person, a way of talking and looking that was kind of insane. That's more or less how I always felt about Kurt Kobain as well. I feel so sorry for these people. They have got fame and money and yet – maybe because of it – they seem so confused. Have they finally found peace?

An e-mail from Ursula told me the postcards for Christmas I had sent her arrived two months late. They had become managers of a small hotel they had taken over from friends in the centre of Cancun. She was sick of staying home. I knew exactly what she was talking about, but I told her how I wished so much I had spent more time with the boys when they were little. I knew too, that my words would go into one ear and straight out the other, like they did to me when the boys were young and I thought that being a mother wasn't glamorous enough and my restlessness too big to be able to listen to anyone.

March arrived and with it the time to pack and go back to The Garra.
2001 had been a difficult year, but at least, I had my own house. Even if it was only for ten months and as chaotic as it may have been during that time, going back to Greg's parents seemed more difficult than ever. Yet, I had to be thankful that we still had a place to go.
It didn't take me long to get work. A couple of days after I filled in a few forms at the employment agency in Tenterfield, I was called at the meatworks in Wallangarra. The dole they would pay Greg was less than what I was earning. It was very hard work and such a strange place. It was my first experience with the Australian labor class, my first experience with any labor class for that matter. I later heard alcoholism and suicide were quite high in the region. The uniforms and boots they gave me were at least five sizes too big. The apron dangled on the floor.
I was shocked with the robotic way of working. Everything had to be done very quickly, the pace dictated by the machines. It was dirty, smelly and noisy. From time to time, we had a five-minute break, apparently for people to have a smoke. I don't smoke any more, but I do have to go to the toilet often. We had to clean ourselves before and after getting out and back into the working area. There were a lot of people working there and only a few taps and hoses available. By the time I got to a hose and managed to clean myself from all the blood and fat, it was past the time to come back.

I had been called to fill in for the sick, so I wasn't even getting any training, just given the worst jobs available, the ones no one else wanted to do. I was given a sort of huge vacuum cleaner that sucks vestiges of fur from the carcasses. The metal hose was very hot and in no time, my arm was covered with little burns and blisters.

Another thing I was told to do at the meatworks was to rip fat from the inside of the carcasses - not with a knife but with my bare hands, I had to grab tightly and pull at a fast pace for hours on end. I had cramps in my hands and they ached for days. I know I'm a bit of a wuss, but I think no one should be expected to be a robot like that, work that requires performing the same things on a fast tempo all day long. It's inhumane.

I don't understand how anyone can freely choose to do this as a profession for life. The employment agent had said they preferred young guys and there were indeed a few of them who seemed to be having fun in there, but they were two or three amongst dozens of sad looking creatures. It was a surreal world.

A few meters before me were the guys who were cutting the heads off the carcasses. If they found anything wrong with it, it was thrown out in a ditch, together with everything that was to be burned or cooked in the furnaces: blood, fat, skin, suspicious parts, etc. The ditch passed right in front of my feet and I often looked at the heads of the sheep that passed by. Their eyes looked so alive. Were they really dead? Had they ever been alive?

Worst of all, was the standing for five to eight hours non-stop on the concrete with cheap plastic gumboots. After two hours standing there my feet already started to ache and it would only get worse and worse. The last few hours of the day were an absolute torture. I couldn't think anymore. All I wanted was for the bell to go announcing the end of the shift. I bought expensive insoles, but they didn't help. I was told that in time, I would get used to it, but I never did.

After ripping fat from meat for a few days, they sent me to the debunking room. It was cold like a fridge, 5°C. No one mentioned gloves. For days, I had frozen hands handling the meat, until someone remembered to tell me that there were gloves I could use. The gloves were big enough for me to put thin woolen gloves inside to keep my hands warm.

Still, I was optimistic and looking on the bright side. The pay was reasonable.

I had worked 2 weeks and had made about A\$ 700.00, which

went straight to Raoni to pay for his dentist. His wisdom teeth had become a problem and had to be extracted. He was costing us A\$ 300 a week for living expenses alone. But if I worked hard, I could even pay the tickets back to mum in a few months. I kept telling myself I wouldn't be doing that all my life and that everyone has to start somewhere.

Greg thought of opening a computer shop in Stanthorpe and I thought of a restaurant in Byron Bay.
What an ironic situation! First, I didn't get a job when I desperately needed one. Then I became the sole provider, although for a brief period, with a job I could not have imagined in my worst nightmares!
A month or so later, the employment agency contacted me for work at a mushroom farm nearby. I went to the introduction day and they said they needed people on a full time basis. I made my calculations and decided that it would be a better thing to do. The pay was less but with more hours, I would end up getting decent money and I thought anything would be better than the meatworks. I couldn't bear to do that work any longer. At the meatworks, I was told I would regret leaving. There were rumors about bad employment conditions on that mushroom farm.
I hated the fact that both were casual jobs with no fixed working times. I never knew how much I would earn. I couldn't make plans. Life was getting more and more unpredictable. Actually, "casualisation" of employment has increased a lot in the last years in Australia. This way bosses don't have to pay employees anything they normally would on a permanent job, like holidays or sick leave. Although legislation to give employees some rights has been passed, employers will always find a way around it. If they don't resort to casualisation they will resort to getting specific work, agreements approved. Either way, it's the workers who lose. "Welcome to the real world", Greg said.
I had discovered an Australia that even Australians don't care to know about.
Not long after that, he got some contract work from his former employer. That would keep us going for a few more months, but life was still very uncertain.

Meanwhile Raoni moved out of the flat he was in and went to a house where he soon came to know that one of the guys was a drug dealer, so he got out of there as soon as he could and moved in with an Indonesian student and his uncle in Maroubra.

He loved the fact that he was close to the beach, but the uncle was neurotic and gave the boys a hard time most of the time.

In Brazil, schools had started for Tayna and he was having problems getting to Uni. There was no public transport. His father didn't have a car. There was a van that went on a regular basis, but the times didn't match. He always missed the first class and had to leave before the last class was finished.

I tried to get him a car, but everyone in Brazil said I was spoiling him. For a few months, I was writing and calling my father and brother to help find him a car. Tayna had a look around, but prices weren't too good. I didn't have the money for a decent car. Greg didn't like the idea at all. At the end, we decided he wouldn't be able to pay the maintenance and all the others costs anyway. Everybody was giving him a hard time, as they thought he had to find a way himself to sort out his problem. I could understand how the difficulty in getting to school would discourage him. I would be discouraged as well.

And a problem he had with his eye in Ballina got a lot worse and I had to send him medicine from here.

In The Garra, Dadboy had recovered from his lung operation and had been well for several months but he had started coughing again and people were worried. Mumboy's knee was becoming a bigger problem as well.

At some stage, Greg suggested I try again for a driving license. I wasn't in the mood for it, but ended up making another appointment. As I failed for the third time, I told Greg, I wouldn't do any more tests. I did have a serious look into the matter again and found out that one only has to have an Australian driver's license within three months after getting residence, not three months from getting into the country. It would be a long time before that happened.

As weeks passed by, I began receiving e-mails from Tayna's father. Tayna was missing too many classes and teachers were warning he would fail the year for lack of attendance. His study achievements were going from bad to worse and his motivation dropped to almost zero. He wanted to quit Uni all together. He had a new job but the older staff often gave him a hard time. His father ranted that he was much slacker than before, didn't want anything and behaved as if he was sixteen. He wanted to send him to the army! He had come back from Australia worse than he was before and it must have been something I had done to him.

I told him Tayna was his responsibility now. When I asked him to support me to convince Tayna to stay, he couldn't care less.

He was the one that was there. He was the one that had to fix him and get some help somewhere else if needs be.

I started to worry about Tayna like crazy and all I could do was send e-mails…What else could I do?

"What do you think you are doing with your life? Why are you quitting? Wasn't that the reason why you went back to Brazil? Stop messing around; life is tough for everyone, stop dreaming about an ideal job and an ideal life, that don't exist. Life's hard, that's the reality. The sooner you accept that, the better everything will be for you. It's when we overcome our difficulties that we grow confidence in ourselves, that we gain respect and get further in life. Don't quit a job at the first adversity, stay as long as it takes for you to appreciate it. You'll feel bad about yourself if you keep quitting. You'll feel great when you earn your own money and don't have to depend on anyone."

I knew it was all going into one ear and straight out the other, I don't know how many e-mails I sent knowing he couldn't care less. I heard from his father that he wasn't even reading my e-mails.

Tayna's writing became more irregular.

His father was writing more often than he ever did, getting more and more worried about Tayna, knowing nothing else to do but to threaten and put pressure on him.

I would receive an e-mail from him with bad news and then not hear anything for long periods; not knowing what was going on.

After every e-mail, I desperately tried to call them, but usually, I wouldn't get through. I would get a fax or an internet noise or the phone would be cut off or out of order. I could only send e-mails and hope they would read it, or even receive it, as I knew their computer was out of order most of the time.

Agonizing periods of silence, in which I could do nothing but worry and anxiously wait for the next e-mail.

When I read back those e-mails today, I must admit that I have not always been fair with his father. It hurt me a lot when he misunderstood my words and distorted them, but I guess I often did the same. I think there were times he was being honest, but I didn't believe it. I guess we have hurt each other too much for too long.

In Maroubra, Raoni was starting to have difficulties with some of the more technical subjects and he managed to find yet another place to live. He was now sharing a nice little apartment with two other students, within walking distance of the beach and away from the crazy Indonesian uncle. He had found out he also had gambling problems, which made him understand why he was always trying to rip him off. He even started to charge him every time he sat to watch TV! He had finished his dentist treatment, but now he needed a new pair of glasses.

A flu epidemic had broken out in Sydney and Raoni missed a test at school because he was feeling too bad to get out of bed and it had been pouring down for three days. In school next day, he gets to hear that to get a chance for another test; he should have brought a doctor's certificate. This is the logic: if you are so sick and miserable that you can't drag yourself out of bed to go to school, you need to drag yourself into the rain with high fever to see a doctor and ask him for a bloody certificate!

I was often late with sending him his money (I found it hard to ask Greg every time); so he sent me a note to stick on my desktop: "I've got a son in Sydney and he needs money to be able to survive".

It didn't take me long to get disappointed with the mushroom farm. The full time job promised at the intro day, had become a few hours a day and on a totally unpredictable basis.

Nonetheless, I did my best. It had gone well for three weeks but then they started to put a lot of pressure on me to pick more and faster.

The temperature was dropping. The work was so frustrating, so unrewarding, so depressing, much like the dark, damp, manure smelling rooms we worked in.

I really believe that every human being has got a special calling and that only when we do what we are meant to do, can we really make a better life for ourselves and a better world.

Maybe it's my inability to understand how people can do the same kind of mechanical work day in, day out, year in, year out; I found them so indifferent, so negative about everything, about life; always those rough jokes, the bullying, maybe it's because they don't see me as being one of them, but no matter what I said or did, those workers didn't seem to trust me. I was always looked at with suspicion and left on my own, looking at the walls. How many times did I come home from that farm to burst out in tears and cry for hours? It felt as if I couldn't get any lower, but

deep inside I knew things can always get worse!
I had hit the lowest point in this whole cybernetic adventure. All the magic was gone. Reality had struck like lightning. I thought Greg was being slack in getting us out of that situation when, in fact, he knew better.
Nothing made sense. What the hell was I doing here?
I looked at the reality I was in and the dreams and expectations I had in my head when I decided to come to this country. Living with a family that didn't put up with half of what my own family used to put up with me, not feeling at home in the only "home" I had; not being understood nor understanding anybody around me; not having any money...

There were days I desperately needed to be alone with myself, but I didn't even have that, there was always someone around.
I felt so stupid, I felt as if I'd always been chasing dreams that will never come true. I needed to make sense of life so strongly and I would run to the computer to write. Writing does this amazing thing for me. It opens up my mind, sometimes I get an answer or an insight; sometimes it just calms me down.
I wrote, "Sometimes I wish I could give up all my dreams and wishes, give up my aspirations entirely, like the saints have done. I'm not supposed to worry about the future, about money, about anything. But the thought of giving up all my dreams makes me so sad; it feels like death to me. And yet, I know that it's exactly the non realization of those dreams that makes me so sad, so frustrated, and so restless.
When people ask me what I want in life I always answer that I want to leave something behind when I die. Something that's going to continue and is going to make a difference in this crazy world, something that's going to contribute somehow to make this planet a more human and happier place.
I want to look back at my life when I'm on my death bed and have the feeling that my life wasn't spent uselessly, that my work was good and will continue.
It all sounds good and right, but problems arise when these ideals are mixed with selfish and vain desires for respect and praise from people.
This is when sadness, frustration and anxiety creep in, feelings that get in the way of a happy, satisfied and peaceful mind, which is necessary if I want to help others to be happier."

It was also on one of those days that I had my first and only argument with Mumboy. We were back at the corner of the living room. On that particular day, the TV was kept on and louder for longer than usual. I was so tired and so depressed. I just wanted to sleep and I couldn't. I waited in vain for hours for the TV to be turned off. I got sick of it. I got out of my bed and started to pack. I was going to move to the van outside then and there.

Mumboy got upset.

"What are you doing?"

"I'm moving out"

"Why?"

"'Cause I can't sleep when the TV's so loud!"

"Why didn't you ask me to turn it down?"

"This is your house and I'm not going to tell you what to do in your own house".

I had asked them twice before, in other occasions to turn the TV down. I didn't think I had to keep asking for it over and over.

I kept racing around... She grabbed me by the arm and I felt waves of rage go through my body.

"You're not going out there at this time."

"You watch"

Greg told me afterwards that she had got really pissed off and had come very close to kicking us out that night. I couldn't care less. It was bitterly cold in that van at times but my regained privacy was more than worth it.

Thinking about the incident afterwards I wrote in my journal: "I must accept that I have a huge communication problem. Why can I not just tell people what I want and need? Why do I expect them to know what I need? Why is this submission and acceptance so difficult to me? Why does every cell of my being revolt against the submission to people? Why can I not be like everybody else and find ways around the things I don't like? Why can I not be humble and just do what I'm told without having to ask the whys and hows? Why can I never get it my way? Why do I always get stuck with people that are not at all interested in change, evolution or improvement, but cling fiercely to the belief that the best way to do things is the way things have always been done?"

It was in my little new domain that I read "The dark night of the soul". When things seem darkest, the stars shine the most. That's to remind us that the darkest time is just before dawn, that when things seem really dark, we might in fact be very close to a breakthrough! And I read Rabindranath Tagore, "When the bird won't sing we know it has lost faith in the great continuum of things, faith that all things change, all wounds heal. Things get better, as sure as the rising sun..."

Truth is, my soul was darker than night and beautiful words didn't really make the darkness go away. Although, now and then I would hear a weak voice, deep inside, telling me that life's not meant to be easy, especially if you have so many dreams, if you want so much, nothing will come for free.

It was at this time that I started subscribing to several cyber action newsletters: Greenpeace, WWF, Amnesty and others. Maybe an attempt to keep my mind away from all the problems with Tayna and the mushroom farm. I found it such a great way for people to participate and have a voice in important issues in the world, without having to make any effort but to press a few keys on the keyboard, without having to leave the comfort of our house (or van!) Social activism for slack-asses! What a great idea!

I would often go through old e-mails I sent the boys and one of them vividly brought back the memory of my last days in Brazil when I had an ugly argument with Tayna. I had to write to him:

"I was extremely stressed out, those last days in Brazil and there were lots of problems that I had to sort out. I also had so much work to do, just days before coming here. Then the toilet seat was broken and I fell off the toilet, then you didn't buy the things we needed for the house, do you remember all this? We had a huge argument and you got really pissed off with me, do you remember?"

What I want to say is that I realize now how difficult it must have been for you and probably still is, to have a mother like me. I'm such a complicated person and difficult to understand and my mind's always speeding and I want so many things in life and I've got such a big mouth at times and I hurt people I love.

I missed so many opportunities to listen to you, to just sit with you and your brother. Can you forgive me? Can you understand and do you believe me when I say that although I didn't manage to show it as I would like to, I do love you more than anything else in this world? In everything I ever did; I have never ever forgotten you and Raoni. I know I didn't do many things properly and I should have thought much more before I did many of the things that I did, but I always thought I was doing the right thing for the three of us, that we would be happier."

"Yeah Mum, I can imagine what was going through your head then. You are what you are and I love you, too."
He ordered a new surfboard and didn't have the money to pay for it. Again, I had to go through the nightmare of sending money over. Again, the oldies had to advance some cash before the money arrived.

One day, in autumn, he sent me an e-mail telling me he had gone to Camburi. At that time of the year, Paraty is so beautiful; everything looks so crisp: the sea, the hills. There grew a wild yellow flower, marcela in Portuguese, that covered the steep hill and when the sun shined on it in the afternoons, the whole hill turned into gold. I used to pick them and make pillows with them. I was told they had a relaxing effect.
Tayna said he was sitting on the beach looking at the flowers on the hill when he remembered my picking the flowers and the days we spent there together, just the three of us, with no one else on the beach and he said he missed me so much.
For a moment, I didn't feel the cold in the van, completely absorbed in the memories of those happy days in Brazil. Imagining him going up that hill…

In time, the contract work Greg was doing and the money from the mushroom farm made it possible for us to look for a place to rent. There was nothing in The Garra, so we went to Stanthorpe. We moved to a nice little unit a few days before my birthday. It took me a week to get it looking cozy and nice. It was much smaller than the Ballina house and most of my pot plants had died with the cold, but I was so glad to have my own place again.
The manager of the units block was an old sour, cranky lady who lived alone in one of the flats. One day, Mumboy and Dadboy came for a visit. As they always do, they had the three little dogs with them. They were still parking the car when the old lady ran to our place to tell us that the dogs couldn't come in. Dadboy got so pissed off with her that he screamed at her: "I bet your mother had a hard time conceiving you!"
On another occasion, Mumboy went to her, to apologize for Dadboy's comments.

Payback time came months later when, towards the end of the year, Mumboy had to stay in hospital for a few days because of her knee and we had to baby-sit the dogs. Hiding the three of them in the house was quite a chore, but it also gave me some sort of satisfaction.

She used to peep through her window all day, policing everyone and every movement on the block.

Every time we passed with the car, we could see her watching, hidden behind the curtain.

One day, I put all my pot plants on a tiny strip of grass in front of our unit. It was a rainy day and I thought the plants would love it. A few hours later, when I went to get them back, they were dry and piled close together against my front door. I was flabbergasted. Until today, I don't understand what went on in that woman's mind to do that. I didn't know how to say what I wanted to say, without saying more than I should; again, I had so swallow my frustration and didn't say a word.

The soccer world cup gave me something to get excited about. SBS was going to show all the games. I would not have survived that period without SBS. It's such a shame that they have become more commercial and have a lot more ads and a lot more stuff that is vulgar on these days.

Yep, Cyndi Lauper's right: *"Money changes everything..." (She's so unusual, 1984)*

I had great hopes for Brazil. Greg couldn't care less. In those days, he felt for soccer as much as I felt for cricket or rugby.

I screamed, jumped, and whistled all by myself through the games. Brazil was having one spectacular game after another, until they finally, won the Cup. I was proud of Brazil. The team remained humble, respecting each new opponent in every game.

But I had no one to share my excitement with. At the mushroom farm, no one was interested. Not in Soccer, not in Brazil, not in me. I felt terribly lonely then. I missed having friends so much.

It seems so difficult to make friends in this country. People seem so indifferent and suspicious. It seems that once people make their little circle of friends, that's it. No one gets out; no one gets in. I felt the same in Holland and I wonder: Is it me? Is this exactly what being a foreigner feels like? It feels like there's something strange in the air, something wrong.

Is it a cultural thing? The difference between developed and developing countries? It seems to me that in developed countries, people are expected to take care of themselves and not expect anything from anyone. Maybe richer countries are richer exactly because of that. I think people have accepted the responsibility that everyone has to contribute and that's okay, but the other side of the coin seems to be that people have got this attitude of "I did my bit, now I want my share" and "I've done my share, don't expect me to help you with yours." I'm not saying everybody's like that, but as an immigrant it feels like there is an awful lot of people who think like that.

Rich countries are well-organized, fairly functional societies where people are polite, but the politeness doesn't feel spontaneous. I see a lot of stress, loneliness, depression, anger, greed and materialism. People also seem to worry more with external appearances. Social interaction is reduced to the bare minimum and everybody keeps a "professional" distance. It seems to me that a lot of the joy that can be derived from human interaction is replaced by possessions, by the comfort that things can provide.

In poorer countries, people rely a lot more on each other, there's more sharing and no one is ashamed of being broke. People are a lot more social and love being together. On the other hand, people don't really respect the public good, they actually mock it and avoid contributing to it. The result is a messy and chaotic society, but people seem to take life the way it comes and have a lot more fun on the way!

Sure, there must be a balance somewhere and I think the balance is to be found in the dialogue between the two worlds. There's much they need to learn from each other.

In time, I found another Belly Dance group. It all felt a bit awkward again and once more, I felt out of place. Again, it seemed no one dared to ask questions. Why would I go to a class if I knew everything? Nonetheless, it was good to dance again. Soon we had public presentations and I started practicing everyday for at least 2 hours. I spent the rest of my days looking into publishing, websites, writing, worrying about the boys and doing things around the house.

By this time, Tayna's e-mails started to sound more and more negative. He had missed too many classes and couldn't cope with the difficulties anymore. He still didn't know how to go to Uni and he complained about the lack of money, about his father threats to stop paying for his study if he failed. He was going to become a laborer. He wasn't sure if Tourism was what he wanted. He said something about physical education, which, in my opinion, has always been one of his major strengths. So, I looked for courses here and sent him the information. It was good he found consolation in reading Paulo Coelho, but each e-mail upset me more and more.

I spent the coldest days of winter working at the mushroom farm. Temperatures dropped to −18°C. Work started before 7 a.m. Our working tools stayed outside so, they had a layer of ice on them when we grabbed them. Some workers didn't have gloves.

I was still very upset with the whole situation. Again, I came very close to leaving Australia. It was Raoni in Sydney who made me stay, this time. I couldn't do that to him. Greg always maintained that I had a choice, that I didn't have to do that work, but I never saw that I had any other choices.

There was an Iranian mother - a refugee - and her daughter working at the farm as well. The father was a graduate optician who was feeling quite depressed at not being able to work (he wouldn't stoop so low as to work at the farm). I went to some lengths to try to help them, inquiring around about work possibilities for the man. I found out that he could do a traineeship and get his diploma here without having to do the whole course again. I gave them addresses and phone numbers, but I don't think they have ever followed it through.

In August, I decided to do something about the Mushroom farm. I wrote a letter to the boss to suggest several simple changes that would make work for everyone so much better. I had thought long about it. I showed Greg the letter and he didn't see anything wrong with it, someone told me he may even promote me and I did have a bit of hope of that happening somehow.

Often employees got upset there and they went to authorities anonymously to lay complaints on that farm. I didn't like that. I thought the right thing to do was to talk to the boss directly and so I did. People had warned me that I would lose my job, that I didn't know the kind of person he really was. So, I decided that if he didn't do anything about the problems, I would look for someone who did. As a precaution, I gathered addresses and secretly took pictures of the place, before I sent him the letter:

08/08/02
"Dear ...
After having worked here for four months, I feel a strong need to express my concern regarding the working conditions in this farm. I have only taken the time to write this letter because I

truly believe in your good intention to run this farm as well as you can. I want you to see me as an ally in pursuing this goal. I'm positive that if some things are not working as they should that's only because there are too many issues requiring your attention. I don't have any intentions of upsetting you, may that unintentionally happen. All I want is to find answers to ease my concerns, to offer a contribution to enhance the working conditions for everybody and help increase the future viability of the farm. Co-operation and trust are fundamental in any venture.

I'm finding it very hard to cope with the way we are expected to do our work here. During the training period we are treated mildly and with flexibility but as soon as a few weeks pass by, the tone becomes harsher and less and less regard is shown towards our feelings and discerning ability. To put it bluntly, I feel treated like an object, a working animal with no brains and no feelings. I'm absolutely convinced that I'm not alone in this. It's the talks of the streets. There is a reputation of unfavorable working conditions for this farm in the region. I have heard it from employment agencies in Stanthorpe and from managers at the Meatworks in Wallangarra. And these are professional people. I've seen pickers abandon their work and go home totally upset by the way they had been treated. The high turnover of personnel is a clear indicator that something is not functioning as it should. I have heard complaints enough from actual and former pickers to believe that there is a general feeling of disrespect towards them as human beings and employees. I truly believe that that is not how you would like your farm to be seen by others and I'm sure you did not choose to implement a working system that upsets your employees, but that is what is happening. I believe there are possible alternatives available to change this situation.

I'd like to make it clear at once that this is not a complaint towards the supervisors or team leaders. I see them as being in the same situation as us, working, sometimes, under even more stressful conditions than we are. Actually, they can be very patient and human in those days when the stress seems to relent a bit. And I believe they are doing what they can within their possibilities.

I'm not a top picker. I know that. I know my picking rate is often under average, I know my clumsiness has earned me two warnings for unintentionally bumping into other pickers. And I'm thankful from the deepest of my heart for still being here. I need this job as much as you need your business, more than anyone else. I'm a new immigrant with no rights to any government support, my husband was made redundant beginning this year and I have two studying sons away from home that totally depend on my financial support...

I have two degrees, one from the Wageningen Agricultural University in Holland and I have also undertaken training as a counselor and worked with Lifeline for several months... I believe that I'm able to contribute in many ways to improve the conditions in this farm.

I would like to look at some of the major factors I believe are contributing to the negative work atmosphere. The first one refers to the picking system: ...What I want to point out here is that the ideal situation: all sizes and quality level perfectly separated is impossible to achieve under the present conditions.

Currently, there's a never-ending feeling of frustration, for being constantly reprimanded, for being always wrong and one always will because what one's expected to do cannot be done. There's no human being on earth that likes to be harshly reprimanded all the time. One does not have to be a genius to conclude what these feelings will do for the workforce's morale in the short run and for the productivity of the farm in the long run. No one feels motivated to do their best, if they are always wrong no matter what.

Secondly... trolleys are very unstable and almost all of them have wheels that do not roll properly over unleveled floors and at the same time we are expected to pick as fast as possible. The stress that this situation creates is directly proportional to the amount of people working in the rooms.

Probably the major problem that I see is not receiving clear instructions and having to change what we are doing all the time. I have expressed this concern to you before, to which I received a reply that something would be done, but it didn't. Actually, it seems that this particular problem has worsened instead. It does not help us to do our job properly, it's anti-productive and because it's so annoying, it generates tension and lack of motivation.

I have some suggestions in this regard that I would like to discuss with you.

Furthermore, I don't believe there is any justification for the unavailability of cleaning products and proper cleaning tools for the toilets, or the lack of water to wash one's hands or rubber gloves for the pickers.

Finally, I need to say that I'm deeply concerned and disturbed by the large amount of mice and probably rats on the mushroom beds and in the rooms. Some pickers have found mice in their lunch bags and had to throw their lunches away. Others are afraid of being bitten by them on the beds. It's so disturbing to me because selling food (that's often eaten raw) that has been visited by mice and rats or that grows on feces and urine of these animals is totally against my moral and ethical values.

I look forward to discussing these issues with you at any time of your convenience. I assure you that I have not spoken to any one about this letter or its content and I rely on your judiciousness to see me as someone that's trying to help, because I truly believe that it's possible to have employees feel satisfied and proud of their job and willing to do everything they can for the best interest of the farm, if they feel respected and are given proper working conditions.

Sincerely,

Irene Elizabeth Schardijn"

It took him a week to give me feedback on that. I was called at his office one day in mid August, after work. His sister was also there. With my letter in his hands, he looked at me, furious. His face and his eyes were red; he looked possessed; he started to scream. He screamed for about five minutes. I was a horrible person. No one in the farm liked me. I was one of the lousiest and worst employees they had ever had. He punched the table a few times. I felt physically threatened. I think that is what he wanted. I was so completely shocked that I couldn't talk. I couldn't think properly for a few days, actually. That reaction was so absurd to me, that I had difficulty making sense of it. I never knew if he had previous knowledge of my letter and just acted out that whole scene or if he had read it just then. I did manage to ask him if that was his definitive answer to the issues I had raised in the letter. When he barked back a 'yes' at me I told him I would complain to the relevant authorities about the irregularities I had seen. Still screaming, he told me to do as I wished, to pack my stuff and to leave immediately.

"What about my pay", I asked.

"When do you want it?"

"Tomorrow."

He agreed and the next day, as usual, I was there before seven o'clock in the morning. The manager didn't have a clue of what had happened the day before, so I briefed her.

CRCRCRCR

There was something peculiar about that manager. Most of the people there hated her. She could be really rough at times; they called her "the whip". Somehow and I cannot explain why, she liked me. I think it must have been to do with the day when I burst into tears there and couldn't stop. I had been there for about a month or so. Until then, all I got was praise for my care in handling the mushrooms. My boxes where always graded "A". But then, quite suddenly, they told me I had to pick more. I had to pick faster or I would be fired. There is when I started to get clumsy and stressed out. They started to put a lot of pressure on me. They wouldn't leave me alone for a moment. All the time there was someone next to me, telling me what to do and what not. One day the manager and one of the team leaders were one on each side of me talking to me at the same time: "Do this, do that. Don't do this, don't do that. Stop doing that. Come on faster, faster!" I did everything I could to pretend I was a machine and do what they were telling me, but nothing I did was right. I was getting so confused I didn't know who to listen to first or what to do. I started to cry and then sob without control. The manager took me to another room, but I couldn't stop crying. She started saying that they had to follow procedures and that their system was the best in the world and that she had to guarantee that things went as they should.

I wondered if she had ever been abroad and told her I was doing absolutely all I could. I didn't know what else I could do to improve myself. I told her about Greg's redundancy, about the boys and my worries about not being able to help them. I explained the situation with new immigrants. She told me to go home and come back the next day, promising me I wouldn't be fired if I didn't meet the picking rate. From that day on, she took it a bit easier on me. I actually gave her a big mouth several times after that and she always ignored it. She had been really nice to me on several occasions, but the pressure to pick more never really ended. She could be as cold as a hangman and a real bitch at times, other times she would be kind and warm as a saint. That farm was her life. Her father had worked there before her. She gave it all she had. And yet, so many times, I saw that farmer treat her like a dog. Why do people put up with being treated like that?

I have never despised or thought less of any of these workers; I even felt true tenderness for some of them. I could see qualities in them that they themselves couldn't see. There were some young people that were there to avoid school. I tried to talk to them that working there forever wouldn't make them happy. There was this young girl, she was seventeen. I got a real motherly attachment to her. She was so cute. She was so slim and supple and she loved dancing. I could see a great dancer in her. If only she believed in it and went to a dance school and got out of that dead end life. But she wouldn't go to school. She would rather stay at the farm, because her family knew the boss' family; her father had worked there. Why leave what's so familiar? Then there were the boys: the twenty-year-old one, who already had to support a five-year-old kid. I could see his struggle with himself, not knowing how to get out of that trap he was in. He was cranky and complained about everything all the time; there was the one with the long hair and tattoos, who used to play the guitar in a band and had been a cook in the Whitsunday's. He had something so sad about him. What was his story? Why did he end up in that dump? It hurt me when someone told me he didn't like me and there was a very young guy there to do all the little - and sometimes bigger - odd jobs. He was the underdog of the underdogs. One day I saw him building a wall, mixing the cement with his bare hands. I grabbed a bunch of our thin medical rubber gloves and gave it to him, knowing they wouldn't be of much help anyway. I told him he would get cuts all over his hands if he continued doing that. He gave me a smile I'll never forget.

Some of the older ladies there were so funny. They were like sunrays in that dark gloomy place. How would I have survived it without them? Others seemed too intelligent to be there. Why would they deliberately choose to stay on that job for so long? There were histories of domestic violence. There were alcoholism problems. They seem to believe they are not made for something bigger. It's a vicious circle. They probably have done stupid things; some may even have been in jail. They seem crushed under a punishment that was thrown upon them. That comes in very handy for employers looking for human machines to help them fill their pockets, so that they can buy their imported cars and look respectable.

I felt so sorry for the way they were treated and screamed at in that place. Each one of those workers was dear to me in one way or another. And yet, I have never managed to gain one faint sign of friendship. Several times, they went to complain about me to the manager. When I did something clumsy, they thought I did it on purpose. Some of the team leaders had great fun mocking me and sometimes they wouldn't wait for me to leave before they started talking about me. Some never looked me in the eyes and some were outright hostile. How many times did I break my head trying to understand what I had done wrong, but I never managed; making it therefore all the more painful.

Lonely days, indeed...

ରଙ୍ଗରଙ୍ଗରଙ୍ଗ

As the manager finished listening to my report of the events, she called the farmer out of his bed (they lived nearby) and in no time, he was there with his sister in their French cars. He asked me if I was okay, probably feeling bad about the previous day. I was cold as a stone, every cell of my body was overflowing with disdain for him, but politely I told him I was just fine.

He paid me my money and I was out of there. Knowing I was leaving that place, never to come back, was comforting. I felt relieved. I was starting to really hate that place, but I worried about our situation. I needed to find something else soon; otherwise, we would be in trouble. I was a bit sad too. This world's so full of stupid and ignorant people. But, there I was, back at ground zero again, penniless and unemployed. Luckily, our tax return wouldn't take too long to arrive.

I had difficulties accepting the way I had been treated. I didn't think that was possible in a developed country. I had learned from reading the farm's rules and regulations that to be fired, one had to receive three warnings in a certain period of time. I didn't, so I thought I had been unfairly dismissed. I called Unions, workers associations, government and even political parties, only to learn that casual workers have no rights whatsoever unless they have been in the same job for over a year. Before that, employers can do whatever they like with them. Casuals are supposed to earn considerably more than full time employees to make up for their not receiving any of the work benefits such as sick leave, holidays, maternity, etc. We were receiving less than the agreed award for Queensland for the work category, because that farm had a special award agreement approved by the authorities and there was nothing we could do about it. That was the reality and changing the situation was a lifetime commitment. It would require years and years of political lobby. Did I want that? No! I've got better things to do! So, after a while I resigned myself to the fact that Australia didn't differ much from Brazil in that respect after all

When I began to get upset with the Mushroom farm I contacted an employment agency to look for other jobs and ended up becoming good friends with the agent there. She told me she'd heard many complaints about that farm. One day she called me and told me that the farmer's sister had gone there and spoken about me. She wanted to make sure that other employers knew what kind of person I was: I didn't want to comply with their health and safety regulations; I was a true troublemaker, someone not to be trusted. I was hated by everyone on that farm, she said. She had also gone with the same story to other employment agencies in town. That upset me so much. How was I going to get another job with her spreading around those lies about me?

The employment agency lady was rather shocked with the farmer's sister and very sympathetic with my situation and got me a job at a winery. There are many in the region. The work atmosphere was quite nice. People were so much more educated and nicer than at the mushroom farm, but I had to bend forward a lot to put wine bottles in boxes on the floor and after a week, my back was so painful that I had to quit. I actually had to go to the chiropractor every week for two months after that.

As I had planned and told the farmer, my next step was to contact the authorities to tell them about the irregularities I had seen in that farm. Besides the working conditions I described in my letter to the farmer, there were also some serious health and safety issues I worried about. Most of the workers there were on some kind of disability pension, some had problems with their legs or feet, some were considerably overweight, some were pensioners or nearly so. It worried me because we had to go up high platforms to pick mushroom. Most of the platforms needed maintenance. I worried someone would get really hurt one day. It had happened before.

There was a tiny sixty four year old with a pierced nose. She was so funny; she made me laugh so many times. She must have been a wild little thing in her younger days. She easily felt dizzy and had blood pressure problems, which she didn't report for fear of losing her job. After I left the farm, I heard from a worker that she had fallen from the platform and would not come back to work. I have always known that would happen one day. There were so many serious accidents just waiting to happen in that place.

When I contacted the authorities I made sure I told them every little thing I saw there. The slippery concrete covered with a thick layer of ice workers had to walk on carrying huge metal frames for the platforms, wires hanging from the roof, the disgusting situation of the smoko rooms, rubbish and wrecks spread all over the place, the bullying... It was really hard to believe you were somewhere in a developed country. Certainly not the Australia you see in the tourist brochures - And I've been told, it can get much worse. From the first officials I spoke to, I got answers like, "It's not our responsibility to look into these issues" or "that area's not under our jurisdiction." I started to believe everything they did was perfectly right and accepted by the authorities.

It was the lady at the employment agency again, who told me to talk to Industrial Relations. The senior officer I dealt with was very sympathetic to my situation and was well acquainted with that farm. He had received many complaints before and knew the owner, whom he considered a very "volatile" person. From referral to referral, I ended at the local Council. They too told me that farm was well known to them. They also had a long record of complaints. With my insistence and after an inspection, the farm was ordered to make several changes. I heard from a worker that the improvements would cost the farm over 40 thousand dollars.

The workers would get new smoko rooms and toilets; he had to clean up the place and keep it that way and he had to set in place a new drainage system.

As to the Industrial Relations, in spite of their original support, I was rather disappointed. All they did was tell the farmer to put in place an anti-bullying policy. I had expected more than that, yet, I guess that's better than nothing.

Last but not least, I contacted the international firm that had given the farmer a certificate of quality for their mushrooms several years before. Every mushroom box that left that farm had a big stamp on it: "certified quality". I wrote them a letter telling them about the mice and the situation I encountered there, my worries about public health issues, reminding them of their reputation. I was informed, two weeks later that the firm's general manager for the entire South East Asia region himself had taken a plane and made a visit to the farm. I heard he wasn't pleased at all, but I never got an official reply.

One day a young worker from the farm stumbled into me in town. Excited, she told me how things were getting better at the farm. "We are going to get this... and we are going to get that..." And I just smiled. She didn't know and I didn't tell her why that was happening.

As we often passed in front of the farm in our way to the oldies, we could see the progress of the improvements being made and I felt good. I thought, "I lost my job, still don't know how I'm going to pay next month's bills, but it was worth it". It just shows how much one person can do, how powerful we can be, if only we have the will to do something and I felt proud I did it all by myself. Not even Greg helped me in any way. If a poor 5.2 ft immigrant without a clue of legislation, without a clue about anything, can get so much done, imagine what those workers could achieve if they organized themselves!

I still wasn't satisfied with the way I had been treated and dismissed, though. I still thought it wasn't right and I didn't get any closure to that matter, but all in all, I thought the result was good and I put it all behind me. Life must go on.

As I got back to my internet surfing, I stumbled upon the address of my cousin Georgy in Holland whom I had lost touch with for at least ten years. Since that random cybernetic encounter, we never lost contact. What an amazing thing the Internet is!

My cyber-action activities landed me on the website of The Community of St Egydio, a Christian NGO that does a lot of great work in many social areas. The area that interested me the most was their campaign against the death penalty. They have a pen pal program where you can write to inmates on death row. They gave me the name of someone in San Quentin, California and I have been exchanging letters with him ever since.

I started to get a bit of an insight of what it is to be on death row. My pen pal seemed so resigned. He didn't really want to fight for his life anymore. He had been in prison for more than twenty years. I believed he could even get out of there, one day. I tried to convince him to fight, but he was sure he wouldn't get out of there alive. I realized it was another one of those issues in which a mass change of heart will take a generation or more to happen. I managed to find a former attorney who worked on his case and he also told me that the way the system works doesn't leave anyone with much hope.

I sent my pen pall all the letters I had exchanged with the attorney and he was astonished. He himself couldn't get in contact with them when he needed to.

It's amazing how the overwhelming majority of people on death row has a history of (severe) abuse or come from dysfunctional families or has mental problems. And it's always the guys who can't afford to defend themselves that end up there. A lawyer advocating against the death penalty said on TV that it's called capital punishment because it punishes those who have no capital! I don't know of any rich person getting the death penalty. And yet, politicians keep killing these people. Because the people who vote for them believe that they will be safer if criminals are killed. I truly believe many of them should be given another chance. How can killing have a corrective effect? How does it diminish crime? How can someone not change at all after so many years in prison? My pen pal seemed to be such a decent guy and I came to the conclusion that the system ends up killing good men.

I think the Justice system should jump into action only when the disputing parties cannot come to an agreement, don't manage to solve their differences. I have seen many cases where victims have forgiven their attackers, in a wonderful display of the greatness of the human soul, but the State cannot let it go. They have to kill a man who has been already forgiven by those he hurt and by God. It's beyond me. It just proves that we live in a mad society, but I know one thing: God shows as much mercy to us as we show to others. I can only pray that these people, when they go, find peace and are free from all the miseries of this world. I need to believe that there's another Justice, besides this crooked one we have here on Earth, that they will have another chance somewhere else, somehow.

In Brazil, Tayna finally gave up Uni, overwhelmed by the difficulties with the subjects he had missed. One day he called to ask again about the possibilities of my sending some money for a car. Minutes after I put the phone down, I got a phone from Raoni. I thought both calling on the same day in such a short time from one another was quite a coincidence. He too, wanted to know if I could help out with a car he saw and wanted to buy.

I don't know if I will have food in the fridge tomorrow, or light or the telephone, I still owed my parents money, but both my sons wanted cars!

We had a belly dance presentation at the new piazza the Council had build in town. It was windy but sunny on the day and the presentation was great. I had practiced a lot and I was happy with the results. A second presentation that same day was a fiasco. The sound broke down half way through and we couldn't hear the music. I got frustrated and annoyed. In another presentation a few months later, the stage was too small, we had to dance on the lawn, with drunks bumping into us, and they just remembered to turn the amplifier on half way through the first music, so that we all got completely lost. What's wrong with a little bit of planning? Why couldn't we spend a few minutes in advance checking the place and sound? It seems that whatever I try to do is always seen as unimportant to everybody else, no matter how much effort I put into it.

My consolation was the kids that came running to us afterwards, asking when we would come back. God bless the children.

As September came to an end and our situation hadn't improved, I decided to go to Airlie Beach, where Russ and Kay lived. They had come over for a weekend and Chookie had told me that job prospects there would be better for me. I think they were shocked when I accepted the invitation to spend some time there. For a while, I dreamt of making it a nice little holiday with Raoni and Greg coming up as well later on, during school holidays, but soon the reality of being penniless set in.

Raoni, very sensibly, decided to use the holiday to look for work. He asked me how he was supposed to find a job. I told him to walk around the neighborhood, looking for signs for positions on windows of shops, restaurants, etc... and if they didn't have anything on offer, he should leave his résumé anyway. And so he did. He got a job in a café in no time.

I can tell others how to get a job, but I can't get one myself!

He would do one of the worst jobs there is, kitchen hand, but he was filled with courage and optimism, he gave it everything. It hurts to see our own kids being exploited and ripped off. Guilt slipped in again. Maybe it's good that, at their young age, they are not completely aware of it.

Why couldn't I see things like Greg did? He thinks hard work will do them no harm; everyone had to go through it.

Is that really so?

Anyway, although it wasn't much, that little salary he earned was more than welcome.

In the world outside, Brazil was under the prospect of making Lula the new president, our first leftist president since the coupe organized by the Americans in 1964 to overthrow the directly and democratically elected leftist president then.

And it was the first anniversary of 11 September. I was getting annoyed with the bombardment of requests to remember the 3,000 people killed that day. One or two e-mails would have been enough, but I received over a dozen of them!

It was refreshing to receive an e-mail reminding us that we must remember *all* the innocent victims of aggression, not only those carrying an American passport.

How many died in Hiroshima and Nagasaki? Cambodia? Vietnam? The 1991 Gulf war? Palestine? Iran? Panama? Latin America? Kosovo? Afghanistan? How many millions of human souls died in wars initiated or supported by the US? Who will they attack next?

I reckoned that the ones who died straight away in the face of all this madness and terror were the lucky ones, because the survivors will carry the demons with them for as long as they live!

At the beginning of October, the girls from the Belly dance group came for a little farewell party before I took off to Airlie. They were the only friends I had made after years in this country. I had this hope I might find a decent job in the Whitsunday's and not come back any more, hence the party. Leah, one of the girls, who became very dear to me, told me she was going to miss me, especially because no one would ask questions anymore.

A few days later I was on a bus to Gladstone, were Russ was working. We overnighted there and the next day we drove another five hours to the north by car.

I had a good opportunity to get to know my sister in law better. Chookie was a sort of surrogate mother for some young people in Airlie. She always had some of them overnighting or staying for a while longer.

Even the wallabies came knocking on the door at night asking for the bread she baked especially for them. I wondered if she was happy, but we can't truly read someone's heart, unless they allow us in there.

I had good feelings about Airlie. The climate was much more like what I was used to in Brazil and it reminded me a lot of Paraty. Beaches were within walking distance. The warm breeze, the sound of the ripples on the coarse sand, the sun on my skin...

Wonderful. It would be great if we could make a living up there. I was very optimistic in the first weeks. I sent out lots of applications and visited all the employment agencies in town and around. Chookie helped me so much.

Positions had opened at KFC. Chookie knew the manager and she wanted a job too. So, off we went. Chookie got the job straight away and I was told that I was too qualified to work in the kitchen. Chookie convinced them to give me a chance, but after the interview, they continued to say no, saying that I looked disappointed with the wages and I wasn't bubbly enough. I didn't think 10 bucks an hour was great, but I thought that could eventually increase. I wasn't jumping for joy, but I truly wanted to give it a go, but they didn't want to know anything about it. I got really upset then, but today I'm so glad I didn't work there. Back then, I didn't know about the things exposed in animal protection websites such as kfccruelty and openrescue.

This reminds me of a joke I saw on TV one day: "The only thing missing for KFC to become a very dirty thing is U"

I tried everything, even a Polynesian dance position. I went to my appointment all excited. I had even practiced a bit, but the guy didn't even show up at the appointment, When I phoned him, he just said they had hired three new girls recently and wouldn't need anyone for a while. Couldn't he have told me that before making the appointment? It took me a whole afternoon to get there. It was out of town and the trains were few and far between.

I hated that job hunting and being judged in a few minutes by people who don't know anything about me. I felt so lost walking down the streets, spreading around my resume; I often got paralyzed in front of a place not knowing if I should go in or turn back and asking myself what the hell I was doing.

By the end of the second week, rejections started to come in and I felt more and more frustrated. After fifteen rejection letters, depression set in.

One of the kids who used to spend time at Chookie's place was a young guy with an IQ just below normal. One night, after receiving his salary he blew it all on grog with some mates and played havoc at the caravan park where he lived and worked. He was kicked out of the place a few days later.

He stayed with Chookie for a few days, but in no time he had another job and I had to ask myself why he could get a job and I couldn't? It didn't make any sense to me.

Most didn't give me any reasons. Can this people not understand that I don't get the dole? Does being over qualified means that I'm going to do the job worse than anyone else?

I had gone to Airlie Beach full of hope that something would happen in my life, but in that hot spring day, I was feeling a total loser. Forty-three years old and no job, no money, no life, no nothing. I had no energy whatsoever, I couldn't even write. My mind just wandered around.

When is life going to start happening for me? Why can't I just get a job like everybody else? Why does it always feel I'm paddling up stream, with a tennis racket for a paddle, in a boat full of holes?

I wrote to Greg:

"I'm going to regret this, but I have to get it out.

I'm trying to hide my tears, but I guess they will notice it at any time.

At the moment, I'm thinking about what the hell I'm doing here. I got some fifteen job rejections to date. From everything I've been applying for.

I'm so worried, about everything, about Raoni in Sydney: I don't want to let him down. Tayna needs a car next year. I still have all my stuff in Brazil. Probably a sign that I should never had left. What are we going to do when the money is finished? Don't expect me to ask for any money to my parents or to yours.

I think it was all a big mistake to have come to Australia.

I have nothing to do with your family, with the countryside. I probably have nothing to do with Australia. I don't think I belong here.

If I don't get a job by the end of the month, I'm going to go to Holland. I haven't seen you doing much to try and make some money and I don't think you will. That's your way, there's nothing I can do about it. I'm not going to press you. I'm not going to argue. You do what you think you should. I'd rather leave.

It was just another stupid dream of mine, like so many others that only ended in tears and disappointment.

I really liked this place and I really wished we could make a life here, but it will probably be like this forever. Always surrounded by people that have nothing to do with me, always doing something I don't like.

I'm trying to keep positive, I tell myself I haven't looked long enough, but this is how it went in Ballina and it lasted for ten months without any results. I try to tell myself not to worry about problems before they happen, that all this worrying is just because I'm like my mother. But I find it freaking hard to keep positive when there is only money in the bank for a few weeks, when I feel stuck and I feel like I'm alone to sort everything out by myself.

I don't know what to say anymore. I've got mixed feelings about everything and everyone. I think I must be really f... up in my head. That's why I'm here. I have no reason to write a book about a virtual relationship with a happy end. There is no happy end. There is only a stupid idiot that's always dreaming...

You better start preparing yourself, because I'll be off to Holland by the end of this month if a miracle doesn't happen. And I don't believe in miracles much these days. I guess I should have learned something by now. I came here because I thought we were going to start a life together. It's three years later and all I have done was live with your family.

Guess I end this and try to put my mind on something else.

Love

Irene"

That e-mail hit Greg at a moment he was feeling as depressed as I was. He was also asking himself why the heck he couldn't get himself together and get a job. And he only felt worse knowing how I was feeling. He even went to see a shrink, but, as one would expect, the shrink gave him a pat on the shoulder saying: "don't worry, you'll be all right!"

Chookie came in just when I finished writing; tears were rolling down my face. She tried to calm me down in vain. After she left the room, I heard her talking to Russ on the phone. She was determined to get me out of the house that night. She took me to the pub and we started to drink. I think we drank two bottles of white wine, maybe more; it was a long time ago since I had been that drunk. They told me I even had a few cigarettes. I was as sick as a mongrel dog. Back home, I crashed on the sofa with clothes and all, without brushing my teeth, without turning the lights off and after vomiting my guts out a few times. For two days, my head felt like it was going to explode and I couldn't eat anything.

I couldn't believe the e-mail I got from Tayna a few days later. He was as sick as a mongrel dog from a wine hangover. The laborers working at his father's umpteenth renovation had entered his room and robbed a few of his things. His father had gone, no one knew where to, leaving him to take care of everything, he didn't know where to get the will to go to work and he so badly wanted his own place... "At least you've got a job", I thought.

Days later, cured from the hangover, I could see things from a brighter perspective. Chookie told me that she and Russ had been through very rough times in their life too. Russ had to use his superannuation and there were times they lived on bread and vegemite. If they are Aussies and had to go through all that, I thought, I shouldn't be complaining so much. She also had an eighteen-year-old girl lodging at the time, who slaved in a kitchen for A\$ 4.50 an hour as an apprentice. I suppose life's hard for everyone...

I had gone up to Airlie with a hope to visit the islands somehow. But, every time I thought about it, all I could find were very expensive cruises. It must have been my confusion that didn't let me think of other possibilities. It was only three days before my departure that I learned of local ferries that go between the islands at a much cheaper rate. It was too late to go by then and the weather had changed as well. I thought, "maybe another time..."

Chook and Russ have since moved to Stanthorpe to be close to Mumboy. Staying in the Whitsunday's for free will not happen again.

By the end of the month I was back home. Sleeping on a couch for a month didn't particularly help my back. I started having problems with my leg. But I tried to see the positive in it all. It made me re-think many things. I learnt to appreciate what I had. My little house, my peaceful life, the normal everyday routine, (Never thought I would ever say this in my life) and Greg and I had grown yet another bit closer.

After being back in my normal routine for a while, I got an e-mail from an acquaintance, complaining I had sent him a virus that crashed his computer. I wracked my brain trying to understand where that came from. I hadn't had a virus in years. Since 2000 when we were plagued by viruses, Greg had always kept our anti-virus up to date, but after a while, I remembered I had sent some friends an e-mail:

You received VIRUS
We group of hackers want to much damage many computers.
We no have expertise, no money.

Please, delete all files from your hard disk.
Break all boot diskettes and CD's.
Ask friends to do same.
Thank you.

As the end of the year approached, Raoni decided to go to Brazil for holidays in 2003, which meant more expenses.

The situation between Tayna and his father was deteriorating rapidly. Tayna didn't have a clue about what he wanted: Uni or work. Paraty or Sydney. And his English was going backwards.

I continued applying for jobs in vain and finding the recruitment procedures more unbearable with each attempt. I had the feeling that for most jobs they were looking for someone with no brain and no feelings. Someone who can be bossed around and do as they are told. No questions asked. Nonetheless, I was still feeling guilty towards Greg and I still wanted a job. We had long talks about it and Greg always said it was all right, but I wasn't sure. I did know one thing for sure; I wouldn't do anything I didn't like, not ever and he said I didn't have to.

Good things cannot last forever, but the bright side of it is that nor can bad things. Not long after I returned, Dadboy got some work for Greg. They were going to work together. The pay wasn't bad either. They had to keep vegetation clear from electricity poles. Dadboy had done that most of his life.

Greg and Dadboy had the opportunity to get closer to each other like never before. They would leave very early in the morning on Mondays and be back on Fridays, covering large areas during the week and staying in small hotels along the way. Greg was able to fully experience just how much Dadboy loved that lifestyle: the early mornings, a good hard day's work and in the evening a drink with mates at the pub and a good night's sleep.

As Greg went for the week, all was peace and quiet in my life again. My back had worsened considerably, so I took my exercises more seriously and tried to do it twice a day and I continued trying hard with the meditation.

As days passed by, I had this funny feeling, one day. I thought, "Things have been so calm for a while, would this be the stillness before a storm?" A few days later, on the 12th of November, someone knocked on the door. I was practicing; I had my belly dance costume on and was covered in sweat. It was someone from the Court House in Stanthorpe. She handed me an envelope with a strange smile on her face and a receipt to sign.

I had to sit down when I saw that it was a summons to appear in court to answer for a claim of about A$ 300,000 (costs included) for damages to the Mushroom farm due to defamation.

Yep, there goes my peaceful and quiet life down the drain.

Greg wasn't home. I wasn't sure if I had understood the letter; I called Mumboy. She told me I had to talk to a lawyer and gave me the phone number of one. I explained the case. "Defamation cases are too complicated", he said. He needed to get a barrister. He wanted five thousand dollars on the table before anything else. I said thanks.

I called the officer I had spoken to at Industrial Relations. He thought the farmer was just bullying and not to worry, but I couldn't. The weekend arrived. Greg laughed when I showed him the letter. He said it was absurd. No rhyme no reason. The claim was based on the letter I had sent to authorities. How did he get a confidential letter from the authorities? That was when I realized that the summons mentioned that letter and referred to it as an attached copy, but there was no copy attached. Was it just bullying, indeed? I called the Court and asked for the copies. They hadn't received it either. I got in contact with the farmer's lawyer. From him I heard that the copies would be sent in a few days. Every time I asked, I got the same answer: in a few days. Two weeks went past and no copies arrived.

I wasn't going to sit and wait to see what happened. They didn't seem to be in a hurry to provide their evidence; I was going to make sure I had mine organized. I sent many pictures I had taken from the mushroom beds, with clear signs of mice to a forensic expert. Some pictures showed mushrooms gnawed by mice; others showed nests or tunnels made by them. He told me the pictures could very well be used in Court. I also had pictures from the mess around the farm, the disgusting toilets and smoko rooms.

I looked for affordable legal advice. I was sent from one referral to another. No one wanted to touch a defamation case. I started to worry I might not get help on this. When I asked people what would happen if I didn't get a lawyer to defend me, I was told that I would have to defend myself alone and I shook my head in disbelief. Lawyers were telling me that I had to defend myself on my own? When they themselves said defamation is complicated and needed to consult a barrister? Even in Brazil and everywhere else I know of, a person has a right to legal representation in Court, even if you are given a lawyer who doesn't give a damn. No one is allowed in Court in Brazil without a lawyer, unless they choose to. But apparently that was another thing I had to learn about Australia.

Meanwhile the date to appear in Court was approaching and when I inquired at the Court, they said the date would have to be postponed until that letter had been delivered.

The whole thing started to take much more of my time and my peace of mind than I wanted. I eventually, landed at the local legal aid office and the guy in charge on that day got sympathy for my case and made some effort to get me some help. A few referrals later I was put in contact with an organization called QPILCH, Queensland Public Interest Law Clearing House. They were really helpful. They found a law firm that wanted to take up my case. They told me they couldn't believe my luck. The law firm was one of the biggest in Australia; it even had offices overseas and was very strong in defamation cases. They were going to do it on a pro-bono basis. No win, no pay. Having the backing of a firm like that gave me a great deal of confidence. I reckoned that they had taken my case only because they had seen a possibility to win. When I told them about the missing papers, they said they would look after it and not to worry. From then on, I should leave the dealings with Court and lawyers to them. It was a great relief.

Meanwhile in Central Brazil, my brother Paulo lost his job. He had done so much to try and keep it. He had been working so hard, on weekends, sacrificing time with the family. I know how much that job meant to him. He thought he was going to lose his mind and he felt really miserable. I felt so sorry for him. I tried to cheer him up with messages of hope and wisdom, but I know from my own experience that when I'm really down I need to see something happen. Words don't help that much. Thoughts of self-doubt filled his mind. Pray, brother, pray.

In Paraty, Tayna had been threatened by armed guys in Camburi. The beach was empty and he was alone. As he didn't have anything of value on him, they pointed the gun at his head and punched him. This happened on our beautiful Camburi beach, our little paradise. Where is the violence in Brazil going to? It was a big scare, but it didn't help him to make up his mind as to what he wanted to do with his life.

The tension between him and his father wasn't improving either. His father had a girlfriend at the time, two years younger than Tayna. She was very abusive and hit Tayna twice. They argued a lot. By around that time he had a huge argument with her. She screamed at him that he wouldn't get anything from his father, that he would give everything he had to her! With tears in my eyes I heard Neia, their house cleaner of fourteen years, tell me the whole story. His father at first took her side, but Neia threatened to go away if he didn't let Tayna tell his side of the story. After that, he avoided bringing her home, but to this day, amongst other women, his father is still going on with her.

We lived close to Church in Stanthorpe. It was just around the corner and I thought it wouldn't hurt to go to the early mass for older people, no noisy kids. It went fine for a few weeks until I decided to ask for some advice from the priest about my difficulties with work and the court case. With regard to work, he told me to do unpaid work for a while and he had nothing to say about the court case, but he was very interested about two other issues: my private (sexual) life and the possibility of the archbishop of Perth becoming a cardinal.

"Have you heard about it? Don't you think it's exciting?" I looked at him. He didn't seem to be expecting any answer. I think he was just thinking aloud. I didn't answer, but thought to myself, "Who cares who's going to be the next cardinal?"

When he knew I and Greg were not married in the church, that we didn't want kids, and that I had divorced someone whom I had married in church, he said we were living sinfully and that I couldn't get the communion anymore. He told me I had to get an annulment from Church first and meanwhile I couldn't live with Greg. I told him I didn't think I was doing anything wrong with Greg and that I was not going to leave him.

I went there hoping for a hand to help me out of my hole, but instead he made the hole a lot deeper, instead of finding relief and a more peaceful state of mind, I was sent home with an even heavier load to carry. I felt bad about us and sad for days. I wanted to ignore it all and dismiss it as useless stuff from another era that had neither place nor use in this day and age, but, I don't know why, it bothered me. It kept coming back to my mind. The priest gave me many booklets and brochures to read about marriages and annulments. The more I read the more useless I found it. It all seemed to serve an agenda of power and control and I could not agree with any of it. At that time, coincidentally, the TV was full of child sexual abuse scandals in the Catholic and Anglican churches and I wondered if these people are concerned about anything other than sex and power? This was when I became interested in the Protestant church, when I felt sympathetic towards Martin Luther. I have never been to Church again; I don't think I ever will. But, I don't really know why, I decided to look into the annulment thing, anyway. I got in contact with the Catholic Tribunal, from whom I got forms and stuff to fill out. Not a little effort. I needed to find witnesses and dig out papers from long ago... I spent days putting my case together.

In mid December, I got a call from the law firm. As soon as they approached the mushroom farm's lawyer and asked him to send up the papers that were missing, he asked them to drop the case. The lawyer needed to know if I wanted to drop the case or not. He tried to explain the technicalities. He said defamation cases are very hard, time consuming and can last for a long time. He said I had to prepare myself, as it could be a very frustrating enterprise.

I had asked a few workers if they would testify in court. No one was willing. It would take a lot of effort to get them to overcome their fears, to tell what was going on at the farm. I have no doubt that the farmer would have made life sour for anyone who testified in my favor. The workers knew it. Not only would they lose their jobs, but his sister would go to employment agencies and other farms to make sure their search for another job would be as hard as possible. This was going to be a very tough fight indeed.

I asked him what would happen if I won, he said they would counter claim the farm; they would be hit with a bill of over a$ 600,000. In other words, the farm would go to hell. I told him that was not what I was looking for. All I wanted was to see some changes in the way things were done on that farm. He said no one could tell anyone how to run their business apart from making them comply with the regulations already in place.

I knew that farmer would have a hard time explaining how he got the letter I had sent to the authorities, I think he didn't even have it. So I reckoned there was a very good chance that farm would indeed go to hell.

He told me to think about it. And boy, did I think!

Was I supposed to teach that farmer a lesson for life, a lesson about respect for employees and human beings? Something he obviously hadn't learned in the long time that the farm had been in operation or during his studies. Was it my task to bring changes to the working conditions in that region? Is it right to push workers to their limits when bosses don't offer minimal working conditions? Am I being an arrogant bitch because I believe that employers who cannot offer their workers decent working conditions should probably not be in business at all? Do I have a problem with authority?

A few days later, I stumbled upon a little story about St Francis of Assisi: The story is told that Francis and Brother Leo were once on a journey to St. Mary of the Angels, Francis' headquarters outside Assisi, when Leo asked Francis what he thought perfect joy was. Perfect joy for him would be to arrive cold and hungry at St Mary's and be mistaken by the porter for thieves, beaten and driven back into the cold and rain. Francis said that if, for the love of God, he and Leo could endure such treatment without losing their patience and compassion, that would, for him, be perfect joy. That made me fall into a soul search that lasted many days. I wracked my conscience to find out what really motivated me to do what I did. Was it a need for revenge? Anger? Was I supposed to have accepted everything I saw in that farm, with a smile on my face? Am I just a rebellious person by nature? Am I doing this for the sake of the employees or just my own?

Is it wrong to stand up against injustice? Are Gandhi, Martin Luther King, Steven Biko, Mandela, Chico Mendes, Joan of Arc and all those great men and women who gave their lives for Justice and Human Rights, who have changed the face of this world, are they all wrong? I am not comparing myself to them, but the British government used to call Gandhi a troublemaker and Jesus was arrested for being a troublemaker as well! Are we all supposed to accept stupid circumstances around us, imposed by stupid people, without saying a word?

I don't think so. I think there are many different ways to serve the same God. He didn't bless only "those who mourn, the meek, the merciful, the pure at heart, the peacemakers and the persecuted", he also blessed "those who hunger and thirst for Justice".

I reckon that without these men and women we would still be living like pre-historic men, being ruled by the law of the strongest, like all other animals. Would workers have any rights? Wouldn't we all still be keeping slaves? I believe that the ultimate force behind the evolution of the human kind as a whole lies in the unselfish burning desire of a few for Justice.

And what about the wrong doers? If we are thankful to them for making our life hell and us more perfectly holy, what will happen to them? Would they not continue mistreating people unchallenged and become worse and worse? Are we not supposed to love our enemies too and help them become better people? I believe that by fighting injustice we do everybody a favor, as long as our fight for justice and better working conditions is free from hatred, anger, resentment, or a desire for revenge; as long as we care about the oppressors as much as we care about the oppressed, as long as we are able to understand and forgive those who wrong us, then I believe, we are doing the work of God as well.

The episode gave me a burning desire to be able to deal with unstable and volatile people like that farmer without feeling hurt, without getting upset. I wrote in my journal: "One day I shall have so much peace and wisdom in me that no one and nothing will be able to disturb the peace and joy in my heart or interfere with my purpose."

At the end of the day, I had to admit that a lot of what happened went mixed with feelings that shouldn't have been there. I was annoyed when I wrote that letter to the farmer. I had been naïve in believing that he was reasonable. I was angry and frustrated when I contacted the authorities. I thought I was able to sort out the situation when I wasn't, but I did have the good of the other workers in mind. I worried about what would happen to those workers if I proceeded with the case. I visited a few of them and I spoke to a few more on the phone. It would have been so great if I had managed to get a few of them sign a membership with the Union, so that the changes being made would remain and more improvements would follow. But, they were all too afraid of what would happen if the boss found out they were involved with the Union. It had become clear to me that I would need to be around if the case was to proceed and that could take years.

I needed to be in contact with the workers, convince them to come to court or be with them if the farm blew up. I wouldn't be able to live with the knowledge that any of them had become desperate or had killed themselves for losing their job.

As the end of December got closer, Greg got a call from his former employer. They wanted him in Melbourne for a big project. There was a strong possibility for further projects and the salary was very, very good. I called the law firm back and told them about the news and, in short, all I had been thinking about. The lawyer advised me to forget about everything and concentrate on building a new life in Melbourne. And so I did.

But not without learning my lessons: I should just have ignored the whole thing from the day I'd got that letter from the Court. Maybe I should have called the farmer and asked what the story was, even though the lawyer advised me not to. I had gone too far, tried too hard to understand the law and the whole situation. I shouldn't have let it worry me so much. I shouldn't have lodged a complaint about the way my case was handled by Industrial relations. Today, I'm convinced he was just bluffing and bullying. He thought abusing me, dismissing me in a time when my life was so difficult and slandering me to employment agencies wasn't enough punishment for writing him an honest letter. He succeeded in upsetting me a lot more. It kept me busy and worried for over a month. It disturbed my normal life and routine and I even lost a few nights of sleep.

People who need to hurt others like that are so small and pitiful.

I decided I would never again try to change job conditions. I learned these things don't change overnight. If I don't like a job, or someone I will just walk away.

If it was because he was broke and couldn't afford to comply with the improvements ordered by the Council or if he finally accepted the fact that he doesn't have what it takes to run a business, I don't know, but the farm changed hands a few months after we moved to Melbourne.

I've got a feeling that farmer might have learned something too. Chookie works there these days and she says the toilets and the smoko rooms still look great.

Raoni stayed with us for a few days around Christmas and we spent Christmas Eve with the oldies in The Garra. It was great to have Raoni around again, even if it was only for a few days. We managed to talk a bit about some issues. He still found Greg a bit difficult to read and was worried about me being unhappy. I think I managed to put him at ease. I think he'd been too lonely. I was still not sure if he was happy himself. Why do I keep thinking that? He seemed all right most of the time, but somehow, I don't know why, I think there's some sadness hidden inside him.

The house was chaotic for a week. I expected Raoni to be bored out of his mind during those days, so I had to find ways to keep him active. He then went to spent a few days with friends in Byron Bay and I was a bit sad after he left.

As the year approached its end Tayna made a balance of his year: he'd had his life threatened in Camburi, been bullied at work, had his stuff stolen at home, ended up in hospital due to an overdose of red wine, lived mostly in a mess at home due to his father's never-ending renovations and spent most of his time in arguments with him. He forgot to mention he had also abandoned Australia and Uni in Brazil.

I wouldn't bother making a balance of my year.

Demons

I entered the New Year excited about going to Melbourne and the prospects of a life change.

As soon as we got back from the Gold Coast, where Greg used to have a barbecue with his computer game group every year, I started to pack.

With the excitement, I couldn't get myself together to do any of the things I had intended to do on a regular basis: the meditation, back exercises, pranayamas and writing.

The belly dance girls came again for a little farewell, just before we emptied the house. We took everything to Wallangarra on the 13th of January and two days later, we hit the road.

In spite of my back and the 1,500 km under temperatures above 40° C, I was happy. Being on the road made me feel we were going somewhere. Everything we needed to start a new life was in the car and the trailer.

We took it easy and the trip went without any problems.

At arrival in Melbourne the next day, we went straight to Greg's work, where he met the boss and left the trailer, then straight to the caravan park in Williamstown, where I had previously reserved a self-contained cabin on the internet. It wasn't wonderful, the manager was cranky, but it was comfortable and it had everything we needed. I just didn't realize how far it was from the city.

We took everything out of the car and I set up the video recorder and TV so that I could record the Samuel Becket series being shown on SBS, for Rubinho. There's a reason why my nephew is called Samuel! Wires had to go across the kitchen, but I managed to record it. We stayed there for five days.

Priority number one was to find a house to rent. The one townhouse in Brunswick we both liked and had seen on the net when we were still in Queensland was still available. It looked even better inside. We loved it straight away. The neighborhood was quiet and the house cozy and spacious. The price was relatively good as well.

We were completely broke. The boss helped us out with the expenses of settling in, the oldies in The Garra helped us out to buy a fridge and after going through a lot of hassles to get all the paperwork sorted out for credit, we bought a washing machine on installments.

The carpet in the bedrooms was thick and clean, on top of it I put all the blankets we had. That would be our bed for the next 2 months.

While at the caravan park, searching the newspapers for a house, I also looked for jobs and I sent out applications for several of them. I was short listed for two and I was really interested in one of them. I was kind of proud that out of hundreds of people, I had made it to the last two people.

At the interview, I loved the place, the office and the boss. I thought I could really enjoy working there and I found everything he said very interesting. I left with big hopes that I would get the job. I had a feeling he liked me too. He said the job would be for only two years, which I thought was ideal as well. Still full of hopes and expectations I called back a few days later, only to hear that he was taking the other person. I got really upset for days. It would have solved so many problems. One after the other, from each one of the other applications I had sent I got a "no": the library officer position, GIS consultant, Court typist, Technical writer, Assistant / Trainee manager at the Body shop, Sales/customer operator at an Insurance company and the Photographer one.

Apart from that, we started to settle into our new home. I had been scrubbing, dusting, washing, sweeping and mopping for two weeks and I was about to sit back and enjoy my new house, when e-mails from Tayna and his father started to get in.

He didn't know what to do with Tayna anymore. He was fed up, sick of Tayna's lack of respect and slackness. He wanted to throw him out of the house and let him learn what life is all about the hard way. He couldn't let the opportunity pass to make clear it was all my fault; he had done everything he could as a father and he had done enough.

I panicked. I was convinced that Tayna needed to be in Uni to get his residency here and couldn't quit school.

After a lengthy conversation, Greg and I decided that Tayna had to come back. I was sure that here, he would, in time, find work and a direction in life. I had doubts that that would happen in Brazil. I begged his father to be patient and put up with Tayna for a few more months so that I could arrange for his return. It all seemed so unreasonable to me, really hard to believe.

But, Tayna didn't want to come. He didn't even want to think about it. He wanted to come back in a few years, only for his visa, but he wasn't going to stay.

With a fortune spent on phone calls and loads of e-mails, tempers cooled down a bit and Tayna decided he would continue his studies in Brazil. I wanted so much to have him here... but I resigned. All I could do was hope he would keep his promise, hope for a brand new attitude in his new study year, hope he would be positive. I urged him not to let doubts accumulate in class, to clarify them straight away, as soon as they showed up. I hoped he'd finally understand that nothing in life comes for free. I hoped a lot.

It didn't take long, though, for hope to turn into some kind of bad Sci-Fi movie, where one enters a time travel capsule, goes back in time and everything starts to repeat itself, like a big dejavu.

As classes started, exactly as the year before, the same problems with transportation started, as well: the van that didn't go at the right time, the classes he got late to or had to leave too early, the difficulties with the same subjects...

He sent me several desperate e-mails, asking me to help him with a car, a motorbike. But he never answered my questions. How much do you need? Can you pay in installments? When and how are you going to get a bike driver's license? How much would it cost? Classes, paperwork, insurance, registration, etc...

Nothing had changed; nothing had been done to change the situation since last year. It seemed they hoped the problems would all go away on their own.

Fires, as usual, were consuming huge areas of Australia and the TV was full of the prospect of war in Iraq. I couldn't have thought of a more appropriate background scenery for the situation with my son in Brazil.

One night, I fell asleep while I tried to understand why I wanted so much to have Tayna here and why he didn't want to come. The dream I had that night was still very fresh in my mind when I woke up the next day.

There were many people sleeping in a big place. It looked a bit like a big camp or something. My family was there and lots of other people. In the dream, I was sleeping. Ursula woke me up to ask me for my scissors. (I had bought a pair of little scissors the day before). Next thing, in the dream, I get up while everybody else was still asleep; I was kind of the leader in a group of people that was sleeping next to me. My group got up together with me. I had lots of plans for the day. Another group, my family amongst them, who were staying in another shed, came to us, still in pajamas asking what the hurry was.

Then, I don't know why, things started to go wrong. As I prepared myself to go, I started to lose things and look for them. Tayna was with me, he was about eleven years old. (Time his father and I separated). People started to leave. I got behind, things just kept going wrong. After a while, when we thought we would finally leave, I didn't have the car keys, which, I remembered, were together with the scissors that Ursula had got and she didn't put them back in my pocket. They were on a table (I had been looking for a table to buy).

Tayna was getting pretty annoyed by then. Last thing I remember I was going up a street in a hurry, Tayna was far behind, he couldn't cope with my pace. I was going to meet some people, who were going to build a boat for me, I was late. I looked back and saw Tayna far behind me and then I woke up.

I thought long about that dream and after a few days I understood it. That was exactly what happened between me and Tayna. I have been too busy in my chaos, he fell behind. I think many times he tried to catch up, but I was always a step ahead, always too busy and in a hurry. He waited a long time. He got tired of always running after me. He got tired of always being left behind, tired of the chaos. He gave up.

February 2003 started with my getting upset with being rejected in another job interview and wondering why I get so upset with so many little things and why I was so inadequate in my dealings with people, the constant feeling that people don't like me. Is it me? Is it the culture? Why am I always dissatisfied with all and everything? Questions and more questions that are never answered, circumstances that are never turned around...

But, slowly the new routine started to settle in. I did my meditation for the first time in over a month and bit by bit, I started to write and look into publishing issues again.

I had been annoyed with myself for not being able to stop my bad eating habits, the cravings for cookies, chocolate and the snacking between meals, always spoiling my appetite. I looked into macrobiotics and natural food, as a way of getting my eating habits sorted out, but it didn't go very far and my thoughts of becoming a vegetarian were quickly brushed off by Greg's telling me he wouldn't survive without meat.

I started to give more attention to the cooking, trying to find ways to keep both of us happy.

One night, I decided to make some pastry filled with mince and spinach, but I made the mistake of putting them straight onto the wire in the oven, instead of on a tray. As the dough got soft and sunk into the wire, it became impossible to turn them. The dough was very brittle, the pastries broke and the fillings fell out. I had crumbs everywhere in the kitchen and filling all over the sink. I burned my fingers and I wanted to scream, but I finally managed to salvage a few. At dinner later on Greg said,

"They are great. Interesting pattern on the dough! How did you do that?"

"You don't want to know".

Nonetheless, in spite of the mess, I got my taste for cooking back.

Back in Paraty, two brothers, who were Tayna's best buddies from Primary School in Holland, were going to visit him. It promised to be a big reunion.

Unfortunately, the younger one had gotten into drugs, lost it and was spending most of his time in a mental institution. His older brother took him to Brazil for a break. He was very paranoid at first, worrying about some conspiracy against him and making phone calls to Holland all the time and smoking one cigarette after the other.

Their mother had also lost it completely a long time ago and was in a mental institution as well. Tayna said he remembered how their house was always in a mess, cigarette butts and junk food leftovers everywhere. She smoked pot and screamed at them all day. I saw her now and then, during the kids' school activities. She looked a bit messed up. I knew she was having problems (who doesn't?) but never imagined it would be that bad. It was so sad to hear all that. It's amazing how involved we get in our own little lives, that we become blind to people's tragedies happening just next door.

As days passed in Paraty, the young man became more sociable. I reckon that seeing Tayna brought back good memories from childhood. He asked if he could stay a little longer, but Tayna's father categorically said no. What a pity. It could have made all the difference for this young man's life. Another victim of the deadly cocktail of drugs, chaos and messed up parents.

Back to his normal life, Tayna's problems continued. He quit work. His father, then, had the idea of renting a place in Ubatuba for him. He would only pay his study expenses if I paid the rent.

Otherwise, Tayna would have to sort it out himself. He had found a very nice place, a family house, where the kids had all left home. The lady was an English teacher. She was going to cook, clean and wash for Tayna. He only had to worry about his study. The place was also quite close to Uni. He just needed to get a part time job for his pocket money.

It all sounded very good, but Tayna himself was always elusive when I questioned him about the whole thing. I didn't see any real enthusiasm about his moving there. I sent many e-mails, but they were rarely answered.

Greg and I were already bearing all Raoni's study and living expenses, a lot more than he was spending on Tayna and now I was expected to help with Tayna's expenses as well. I was really pissed off, but with Tayna's attitude towards coming back, all I could do was accept the situation and try and support his father's effort. I tried to convince myself that it was a great solution. Ubatuba is also a great town, a bit bigger than Paraty, but with great beaches and less than an hour away from Paraty. He could still go every weekend to Paraty see his friends. His father even told him that he would pay a tutor to help him get over his difficulties. Anyone in Brazil, simply anyone that would sincerely want to study, would just have killed to be in the position Tayna was in.

Nonetheless, trying to support his father's efforts became harder as days passed by. I didn't like his top down approach, Tayna's insecurities made me doubt it was the best thing to do, he was feeling more and more lost. He wanted to quit Uni and travel. Freshen his mind. He wasn't sure at all about his career choice and wondered if he should change or continue with what he had started. I thought a lot of his problems were because he had never made a conscious decision about his career and study. He was always pushed into things either by me or his father.

I sent him some websites links about career counseling that I thought were good. He never looked into it. I told him to consider the option of living with me here in Melbourne. He wouldn't have to work; I could help him with his study. I told him that Melbourne is a great city with lots of things to do. There is even a planetarium, which he loves so much. Surfing beaches are a bit far but he could go there on the weekends. He could join a gym; there are all kinds of fitness and sports clubs one can imagine, anytime, any day. He would have nice food and a quiet, clean house all the time. And I was sure that with time he would make friends and start having his own life. He could spend some time deciding what he wanted to do for a career. Then, he could go to Sydney, if he wanted.

"Just think about it. Greg likes you very much and you know how happy I would be to have you with me again. But, again, I don't want you to come if you are not sure about it."

I told him to also see the possibilities in Ubatuba, to see that that solution was good too, if finishing Uni was what he wanted. I urged him to make a decision and stick to it.

My mother joined the team in the pressure against Tayna and I couldn't understand why they wanted so much to see Tayna pay for his own study. His father has never worked while he was in Uni nor did I. Why did they want to make it so hard for him? I didn't get it. I worried so much about him. What was going to become of my son? I didn't think pressure was the answer.

It was hard to try and make sense of what was really going on. I got only bits and pieces of the story. Either Tayna or his father only told me the part they wanted to tell. I even called my brother to have a look at the situation and he wrote to me:

Hi, little sis,

I wish I had something else to tell you but I think you and his father have given Tayna the best alternative possible and he doesn't want it. At twenty-four, I was married, responsible for a family and I worked very hard.

Tayna's in no condition to choose any more. If he really wanted to study, he would think his situation is excellent, he should be happy to be living away from his father and the arguments.

I'm sure his father loves him and is worried about him. A twenty four year old man that doesn't know what he wants is a problem for everyone.

I'm still shocked that he has let go the opportunity to live in Australia near his mum and brother. He has two options. He either gets into his study or gets himself some work.

Don't give him more options, don't be soft with him. He must understand that he's not at an age to be depending on anyone. He must become aware of the reality of life.

You have no idea how difficult life is over here. They are going to throw out a hundred and thirty managers at Volkswagen. Paul still hasn't found work with a family depending on him. Interest rates are sky high; there is no financing for second hand cars.

Giving him a car is the worst thing you could do. He hasn't even got the money for petrol. What about rego, maintenance, tickets, insurance,...?

Let him show he's got the responsibility to afford such a luxury.
Take care
Ji
What else can I say? I guess they are all right. It's my fault. I've spoiled him too much.

Meanwhile I signed every single petition that came up my way for peace in Iraq, but it was all in vain. The warmongers in power had their minds made up. I didn't go to the Peace rally and I felt guilty about it.
The government spent millions putting together a booklet on dealing with terrorism and sending it to each house in Australia. In protest against the war people sent it back, jamming the post offices!
They also set up a special free phone for everyone to alert the police of any suspicious terrorist behavior. One doesn't need to be very clever to see where this would lead. Hoaxes, some more absurd than others became commonplace. But, the general discrimination towards Muslims was and still isn't a hoax. About this, no one sees anything; no one does anything.

When we finally bought a mattress, my back and legs were worse than ever. A new attempt with a different chiropractor was, again, a fiasco, again a lot of wasted money. Greg, in turn, got a very bad ear infection. The heat was unbelievable. I had never seen anything like it. 43°C and a very hot wind that blew all the time, knocking down everything in its way, taking away every drop of energy I might have had in me. I dragged myself through the days, managing, only just, to get myself through the things that absolutely needed to be done.

I continued to apply for some really stupid jobs and I got interviews for a few of them.
One was with a greenie organization. Several things went wrong: first the girl I spoke on the 1800 phone number that was given in the newspaper ad was in Sydney and she didn't have a clue. She gave me the wrong time for the interview. When I got there, I thought I was late. As usual, I got lost on my way there, but in the end, I was two hours too early. She also didn't say anything about what to bring, so I was the only one that didn't have a résumé or a writing pad. The interview consisted of some role-play games. Again, I find myself in a situation where I felt totally out of place, were no one said anything that made any sense to me.

Everything seemed irrational and senseless. So, I wasn't surprised when one hour after I got home, they called me to say I didn't need to come to the next selection stage. I wasn't sure about going to that interview at all and I almost didn't go. I should have listened to my intuition. Nonetheless, it's always frustrating to get yet another no! And although I knew it was just a stupid job, I felt rejected again.

Another job appointment, with the Moreland council, as a School crossing supervisor, went okay, sort of. I got there more than an hour late. They have this thing here, of starting the numbering all over again on the same street as it changes neighborhoods. So, I ended up at the right street and at the right number, but three municipalities further away. I then had to wait 20 minutes for the next bus going back. I almost gave up at some stage, but I thought, "Oh well, let's go anyway and see what happens..."

After passing the first interview, I had to have a medical examination and another interview. Man, I had to give them a detailed account of my whole life. This is for a job of 7.5 hours per week and a weekly wage of 100 bucks before tax. Now, please tell me, how do people get motivated to work for someone else in this world?

To get to the doctor I had to take a tram, then a bus. I bought a two hours ticket in the tram; I didn't have to show the ticket to the bus driver because he wasn't there when I got in. When I looked for the ticket at the doctor, to see how much time I had left, I realized I had lost it. I didn't know how far I had travelled without any ticket. It must have fallen out of the shallow pocket of my jumper. I got a bit pissed off, but found consolation when the medical examination and interview took so long that the ticket wouldn't be valid anymore anyway. If I had bought the expensive ticket, valid for the whole day and lost it, I would have been even more pissed off. Finally, I found out that I had bought the wrong ticket to start with. Even if I hadn't lost it, if a controller had asked for it, I would have been in trouble anyway. Oh my... Life's so complicated!

One of the questions in the interview was, "Have you ever had an argument with a former employer of yours?" I don't know how to lie, so you can guess the end of the story.

I still got a few more rejections before I finally decided not to look for those stupid little jobs that only made me feel bad and upset. From then on, I would apply only for a job I thought was worth the effort.

With the government's attitude towards boat refugees becoming more insane by the day, a few outraged groups raised their voices. I attended a big meeting where a few of these groups had gathered.

There were some great women at that meeting (predictably enough, very few men were present and no one of public importance). One of these women was Carmen Lawrence. At the time, she was an Independent Member of Parliament. She used to be in the Labor Party and had quit the Party specifically because of its refugee policies, but later on she became the president of the Party.

At the end, they asked the audience to take home a petition and gather twenty signatures. It was going to be sent to the parliament asking to review the current policy on asylum seekers and their treatment. I hesitated but took one.

I didn't know what I was getting myself into. I realized later how difficult it was, how hard it was for me to go to strangers in the street and start talking. They look at you with suspicion. So, I tried the neighbors, some of them didn't even open the door, even though they knew me. The neighbor next door said he didn't want any asylum seekers in his country and wouldn't sign. I asked why, but he just kept repeating, he didn't want them here. When I first saw him, I had this feeling I had seen him before. Looking at him from close that day and listening him talk, made me remember where I had seen him. He looked exactly like the mushroom farmer.

Knocking on doors wasn't for me, either. I decided to do it differently. I was going to sit on a bench on the footpath and just pick a passer-by at random.

"Maybe a good idea to get a pen and a clipboard".

From my petition adventure, I calculated that the views of my neighbor are shared by maybe about a ¼ of the population. So, is it the minority that rules the country?

Anyway, when I finally managed to fill in the petition, it gave me a pretty good feeling. Once I got it right, it wasn't that hard at all. I just had to be on the right place, at the right time, when people are relaxed and less defensive, when they are having a drink, eating or chatting in front of a café or at some public entertainment event.

Then I realized that if every one of the 800 people that were at that refugee meeting had taken a petition letter, we would have gathered 16,000 signatures. Wouldn't that be amazing?

My renewed interest in natural food made me stumble upon the food cooperative of Friends of the Earth (FoE), which in turn brought up in me the idea of doing some volunteer work. Since the job seeking was going nowhere I thought maybe, volunteering would lead somewhere. I didn't see myself fitting really well in there, but it was a way of staying up to date with what was happening at grassroots level and hopefully getting some work experience.

The fresh food department wasn't much and working in the kitchen didn't really excite me. So I tried working in the office. I liked the very democratic and open way they ran the whole thing, with decision making on all levels open to anyone, but I did have difficulty with the mess in the office and everything seem to me to flow in a rather chaotic way. I've got already enough chaos in my head. I need my working place to be orderly and my difficulty understanding people on the phone made me quickly move on to editorial work at their magazine, but lack of experience with their software, finally landed me on an aboriginal advocacy group.

Meanwhile with the oldies in Wallangarra things weren't going too well. Mumboy had her knee operated on and Dadboy's tests results didn't look good at all. They had found cancer in his blood and brain and he was having too many side effects and reactions. They would stop treatment. It didn't look good, but doctors didn't know exactly how things would go from there. I found Greg often with tears in his eyes and I was so glad I could be there for him.

We were getting to the end of March and most of the previous two months were spent trying to mediate the problems between Tayna and his father. Information I got from both was always contradictory. At one time Tayna was all right: working hard, with a reasonable idea of where he was going, not understanding why his father was giving him such a hard time. At other times, he was completely lost and confused, not knowing what to do.

One day, he would be in tears and completely out of control and a few days later, it was as if nothing had happened.

In 2001, I had to let him go, fearing so much that he would get into trouble, but watching him suffer and struggle with the consequences of that decision, was even harder. He was drowning and there was precious little I could do.

The situation made me feel more and more restless.

I started an on-line self-help program; I worked a lot on it, especially on the goal setting part. It helped me focus a bit, but then after two months the website crashed. I started to make a bigger effort with the meditation and I started to pray more and in a more regular way. I spent hours planning my days and trying to get some organization in my head. It often felt so messy, so busy... Days in which I got very little done, became more often. I tried to re-think my routine, set my priorities, but I only felt as though I was going round in circles.

I intensified my cyber activism. I started to help some of the NGO's I subscribed to, with translations and often I found myself overwhelmed by the amount of letters that I felt I needed to write, especially for Amnesty International. I spent hours on the weekends writing letters for all those people being tortured, kept hidden in some dirty, dark cell somewhere in the world: China, Papua New Guinea, Colombia, Palestine, Uzbekistan, Mexico, Tibet, Zimbabwe, South Africa, Myanmar, you name it. There's so much suffering in this world...

I worried so much about everything. What would happen to Tayna's visa if he didn't come? I worried about my stuff in Brazil, the humidity. My slides and equipment that were so precious to me. I called the oldies. I asked my mother to open all the boxes to check if things were still all right, put them somewhere safe, if needs be, but she had got a problem with her arm and she couldn't go carrying boxes around.

I asked Tayna if he would see my stuff at the oldies during the Easter holiday, which was approaching. Two days at the oldies would do, I said and they would love to see him.

Would he bring some of my stuff that was at the oldies, if he came? He misunderstood me again and thought I was asking him to send everything over, so he just ignored my questions and never answered.

His father kept telling me that I was protecting Tayna, that every time things got a bit difficult he would run to me. He basically told me to stop talking to him, to tell him that I don't want him here before he finishes Uni and to let him handle it. According to him all Tayna needed was a good kick in the ass. I shouldn't comfort him, but tell him to bugger off instead. How can someone in his right mind ask a mother to do that, after the phone calls and e-mails I was getting from him?

In one e-mail his father told me Tayna didn't have it in him to study and that he should stop studying for once and for all, be a laborer if needs be. I strongly disagreed. I told him, Tayna had got some issues in him that needed to be sorted out and once that happened, I was sure we would be very proud of him. I told him we had to believe in our son. We needed to understand him. I couldn't let him become a laborer for the rest of his life, just because he wasn't able, at the moment, to see the future and understand the true consequences of his actions, even though he was supposed to know better. We all want our children to be independent and follow their own path, but I just didn't believe that that would happen the way his father thought it ought to happen. I believed Tayna's place was close to me.

My way to bring a bit of order in the chaos was to set out what the options for Tayna were, in Brazil and in Australia. I had put a lot of thought into it. I told Tayna he needed to analyze, study the options, and make a decision.

I thought that to be able to help Tayna, we needed to sit down and discuss all the options calmly, without pressure, without threats and ask him the right questions. I told his father that whatever decision Tayna made, we had to be united to support his decision. There was no point supporting him or even getting tough with him if he didn't make a conscious, thoughtful decision on his own first. I truly believed this was the way to handle Tayna then, but again, I didn't manage to get my voice through. Everybody told me that pressure was the solution, but I thought that the pressure we had to make together was not to force a decision upon him, but to confront him with his immature view of life and let him find a solution and make a decision himself. Then and there was the time, no matter how difficult, to find a way to connect with him. We had to find a way to reach him, to make him realize we loved and cared about him.

But, how do you talk sense into someone when he doesn't want to listen?

I was trying so hard to do what was right, but when years later, I read all those e-mails I sent, it became all too clear how confusing they were, how useless, how each of my e-mails probably, just added to his confusion.

Today I understand that the issues involved, the false beliefs, the emotional luggage build up over so many years, would never have been set straight with a few talks. A solution or a definitive decision would never have come quickly, but I still think that was what we should have done.

Instead, everybody seemed to have their minds made up.

Everybody had their own solution and no one would give in.

Nobody paid attention to anything I said. Nobody sat to discuss the issues and the options.

It was depressing to watch the news and realize that it wasn't my life alone that was in turmoil. The whole world seemed to be in disarray. The way Americans where rushing the UN process of negotiations and the search for weapons in Iraq resembled the way Tayna's father was trying to solve the problems with him.

When I look back today, it seems that, like the Americans, we were all forcing our own solutions through, screaming and shouting good, altruistic intentions on the way, when in fact we were all just desperate to solve our own problems, at any costs.

And so, the deadlock with Tayna went on. Go to Uba? Don't go? Continue Uni? Quit Uni? Go to Australia? Stay in Brazil? Work? Don't work?

I felt overwhelmed by the unbridgeable gap between his father's and my views on how to deal with the boys, the charging, the constant feeling that all the efforts I made, all my good intentions are always thrown away like rubbish, misunderstood or ignored. How much anxiety and frustration can a parent bear? I wrote in my journal one day:

"What a misery. What a mess. What a complete failure of parenting. What an agony it is to see your own child muddle through life like that. When is this going to end? How do I stop this vicious circle? How to transform this battlefield? This battle wherein everybody seems to be losing? Will I ever see the day I can hold my sons' hands and feel a true connection, feel that we deeply understand each other? Will I ever look at my sons, with peace of mind, in the certainty that they are going in the right direction? All I can do is wait and hope. Wait... Hope... knowing there is more frustration and more hurt to come. Parenthood is nothing else but a path to holiness."

As days passed by and Tayna didn't make up his mind, his father decided to set a date for him to move to Ubatuba. All arrangements made, on the set day, as they were putting his stuff in the car Tayna tells him he didn't want to go. His father went berserk. They argued. Tayna walked away and got ready to go to Uni by bus. His father then, enraged, took all his things to the house in Ubatuba anyway, without Tayna's knowing and he went afterwards to Uni to tell him he didn't have to go home any more because from then on he lived in Ubatuba. He wasn't welcome in Paraty anymore. He called me to inform about the whole episode and that I had to pay the rent immediately. Basically, he had thrown Tayna out of the house. I was so angry that things had been sorted out that way and then him telling me I had to pay the woman and support his decision. I was still waiting for Tayna to make a decision himself. I didn't want to force him to make any decisions. I felt manipulated.

And then the war in Iraq started.

What a terrible confirmation of the stupidity of human greed. What a mess. What an unbelievable suffering cast upon the Iraqi people who had already endured so much. The destruction of their entire meager infrastructure, the history of humanity looted away from the museums, the children and innocent people being blown up in the crossfire. Everything basic to life was plundered, looted and destroyed while Bush and his accomplices appeared on TV, with smiles in their faces: "It's all good, folks. It's all in the name of democracy and freedom!"

Did they really managed to fool masses of people or is it that masses of people just didn't give a damn?

One thing I know for sure, it's neither Freedom nor Democracy they are protecting here, it's Capitalism and in its most outrageous and immoral form.

There are no honest or moral reasons to start a war. We have something called a Defense force, to defend us from attackers. We don't have an Attack force! All wars were, are and will be started with an eye on profit. It has been like this since the beginning of human history and it will never change. People are the last things any warmonger is worried about.

What about democracy and freedom in China? North Korea? Zimbabwe? Myanmar? Is it just a coincidence that these countries haven't got the natural resources America needs?

Of all the things necessary for the people to survive in Iraq, water, hospitals, schools, you name it, what have Bush's warmongers chosen to protect? The Ministry of the oil building!

It's not against Democracy that radical Muslims are fighting; it's against this cannibalistic form of Capitalism and the corruption it brings with it. And before anyone thinks I'm sympathetic to what terrorists do, I categorically say that I oppose it with every cell of my body. I don't see how the killing of civilians will bring about the changes they want to see happen, therefore I think it's stupid and any terrorist act must be seen as a terrible crime and treated accordingly within our Justice systems.

But, don't give me this nonsense about just and democratic reasons for war. Not everybody is as foolish as those who started and supported this illegal war.

In spite of the problems with Tayna, my worries, anxieties and war, I tried to live my life the best I could.
The thought that I would have to get an Australian driver's license at some stage in my life, came back to my mind, now and then. I didn't dare to drive in Melbourne, especially after failing three practical driving tests in much smaller towns. All the trams, pedestrians, bicycles, buses, cars and cheeky drivers all over the place, all sharing the same lanes, the strange rule in some places downtown, where on certain crossings, one needs to go left first when one wants to turn right... I didn't know the streets either, so I had to go slow, looking for names of streets, trying to find out where I was and put up with impatient and neurotic drivers behind me, at the same time. Thank goodness for public transport!
I decided that the only way I was going to get a license, was to start from scratch and have driving lessons.
When my first lesson finished, I told the instructor, who was as relieved as I was, that I have a Dutch driver's license. To my delight, he said I could transfer it to here, without having to do the tests again. I told him to check that out because transport officials in Queensland and NSW had told me that was not possible. He got his book, had a look in it, confirmed it and made my day. Those were 45 bucks well spent!
I got a copy of my driver's license from Holland, translated it, filled out some forms and voilà, I finally had an Australian driver's license. One can't always lose!
To pay for that license in Holland, I sent Ilona and my cousin Georgy an e-mail asking if they could make the payment for me.
My mother was going to be in Holland in a few months and she could pay them when she got there. Raoni could then pay grandma when he got in Brazil.
Both Ilona and my cousin made the payment straight away. I had put both names on the "to" header in the e-mail, so they could see that I had sent the e-mail to both of them at the same time. I really didn't expect them to make the payment straight away. As my cousin was the first one to say she had made the payment, I immediately wrote Ilona to tell her not to make it, but it was too late. She was furious and resented me deeply. Many e-mails had to go back and forth before she could forgive me. It seems it was quite a hassle for her to get her money back.
I really believed they would get back to me first before making

the payment. I would! The ironic thing is that both said in the e-mails they sent me after having made the payment, to make sure no one else would pay it also. How could I have done that if they paid first and then told me they've done it! Why do I always assume everyone thinks like I do?

Nonetheless, I appreciated it that they were so quick to help me. I do have friends, after all...

In time, I got used to driving in Melbourne, but I had to get five parking tickets to learn to use parking machines and understand parking signs.

I started dancing in a new belly dance group and again I had to ask myself if I was supposed to be there.

It was good to dance again. It was a big school, with different teachers giving different styles of belly dance. It didn't feel as if it was doing my back any good, so I saw two different physiotherapists, but again it was absolutely in vain.

When I went to a presentation of the school, I had to remember the e-mail argument I had with Greg about freedom. I went to that presentation alone. He was too tired to go. When I wrote that e-mail back in 2000, I had Holland on my mind. Back then, I didn't mind going out on my own, but I must have changed. Today I reckon going out alone sucks.

With the exercises at home, I started to understand how the state of my back was the result of years and years of bad postural habits, in which some muscles and the related tissues are overused and become tense and painful, while important muscles that are responsible for sustaining the spine get underused, weakening the support of the spine. I realized I had to engage in a long process of re-educating my body, by exercising those underused muscles and making sure that I don't use the ones that are not supposed to be used. It forced me to be a lot more mindful of how I move and do things.

I also started to go to the regular meetings of the aboriginal advocacy group, at FoE. Soon I realized how big that whole issue was and how I could easily end up overwhelmed by it and that was not what I was looking for. The proposal was to transform a huge area of red gum forest across state borders between north Victoria and south NSW, an area with deep rooted and different economic interests, into a National Park, to be managed by the Yorta-Yorta people, the (ab)original inhabitants of the area who in turn hadn't had control over the land for a very long time!

I have always been interested in understanding aboriginal issues. I was hoping to gain a better insight into those issues through that group and although I was having trouble understanding how to fit in, I decided it would be good to spend some time with them and understand what they were up to.

One day, on my way back home from one of those meetings. I decided to stroll through Sydney Road to have a look at the shops. I had bought a pillow and was walking with it under my arm and then I went into another shop. I only saw they also sold pillows when I was already inside. I had a look around and then left. The owner or manager of that shop followed me on the street for quite a while from a close range. I started to feel uncomfortable, so, I stopped and looked at her. She asked where I had got that pillow from. Only then, I understood that she must have thought I had taken it from her shop without paying. Man, people are strange! How far would she have followed me if I hadn't stopped? If she was so keen to observe who left her shop, she should also look at who entered it. She would then have seen me going in with the bloody pillow! Does this kind of thing happen to other people or only to me?

Another day, I found out about a writing fellowship of the Victoria State Library and I applied for it. I proposed to do a study on suicide and it's relation to cultural values.

But, as one would expect, it didn't lead to anything. The fellowship was given to a successful and established writer... Why do I keep having these illusions that anybody would help someone without being absolutely sure that there's a profit to be made? Tell me about not having to prove yourself to anyone...

My marriage annulment at the Catholic Tribunal would also come back to my mind, now and then. I had lodged all my papers at the Tribunal in Queensland, from Stanthorpe, but they had told me I had to send it to Brazil, because I got married there.

So, I translated my twelve page story and send it up. The response from the Tribunal in Brazil was that I had to pay about US$ 800. That was more than what I had paid for a lawyer in my civil divorce, a lot more if I take into account that the boy's father and I split the legal costs 50/50.

I reckoned that at the end, it's all about money. I told the priest in Brazil that I didn't have the money and he never replied. Because of the prospect of us going to Melbourne, I threw the whole thing in a drawer.

But, now that we had settled more or less, I decided to have another look into it and contacted the Tribunal in Melbourne. Had I known this was going to be the frustrating enterprise that it has been for so many years, I would never had started it.

Negotiating the price of the whole process was a very tiring and frustrating process. I ended up paying A$ 400 in eight installments, through the mediation of my brother Ji. Half way through the process, almost a year later, after he had paid everything, they sent him and me a letter saying we hadn't paid and that therefore they would stop the process immediately unless we paid the full amount of US$ 800 at once. With much insistence of my brother, they told him that computer problems had destroyed their records, but still they continued the process only after my brother sent them the copies of the process price agreement and all the receipts of the bank transfers he had already made.

I managed to see one good thing in this entire process; it forced me to thoroughly re-think that whole period of my life. A lot of the insights I have today about what went wrong in my first marriage started through that exercise. It helped ease the strong feelings and they have since faded a lot more. I was able to see that I had hurt as much as I had been hurt, that I was the one who decided to go and that he was not the only reason for my unhappiness. It made me remember the happy moments too and it reassured me that Tayna and Raoni have always meant to be here and are the result of the love that once existed between us. It often brought tears to my eyes when I thought of all the pain and sorrow and how it all could have been either avoided or greatly minimized.

My leg was also slowly but steadily getting worse. Between joining the gym and buying some Pilates books I opted for the latter. I realized that if I had used the A$ 2,000 on a good Pilates training program instead of wasting it on useless chiropractors, physiotherapists and acupuncturists, I would have been much better off.

As I expected, the Ubatuba solution didn't last long. After a couple of weeks at his new home in Ubatuba, Tayna decided he was not going to stay. His e-mail read:

"Mum, I feel so lost, I'm so sorry for all this mess, but I really can't help myself. I don't want to stay here. I won't."

I told him I loved him but I also told him of my agony and that he was like a wooden board floating at sea, at the mercy of the winds and waves.

He still wasn't sure about coming to Australia and the agony of the situation made me do the same as his father was doing. I charged him with a decision. If he didn't come up with a decision on what to do with his life once and for all, I would not send him any money and he would have to sort it out himself. I couldn't live with that situation any longer. So, I told him again, to think about the possibility of coming back and staying with us.

His father was furious when he heard that there was talk of going back to Australia. Yet the situation had to deteriorate a lot further before Tayna finally decided to come back. I realized then that he was making that decision for the wrong reasons and that his priorities weren't in the right place, but I had been dragged into the Ubatuba solution, forced to put money into a situation I didn't believe in and I was convinced that the situation between him and his father wasn't going to improve. Everybody told me that I shouldn't support him coming over, that I should have left him face the consequences of his decision to go back, the tough reality of life in Brazil, but I couldn't.

One day, after a particularly distressed e-mail from Tayna, I tried in vain to reach him. I fell asleep that night worrying if he was all right. I had a nightmare and I woke up screaming, but I couldn't remember what it was. I often cried myself to sleep thinking of him.

At times, on the phone, he would be sobbing, completely confused. It was to me he came when he felt like that and didn't know what to do, no one else.

I wanted to put a stop on his father telling us what to do and manipulating us. My mind would be more at peace with Tayna here, but most of all, I truly believed that here he would have a better life.

I spent hours and days on the net looking for tickets. I had sent him a list of travel agencies with phone numbers in Brazil, so he could ask around and find a better ticket deal, but he ignored my e-mails completely.

The e-mails that I did get continued to show his confusion. Even though we were making arrangements for his coming, he still seemed lost, not knowing what he really wanted to do. He thought about other study and other career possibilities, so I did extensive research and sent him several links for courses here, only for him to tell me a few e-mails later, that it was better to stick to what he had already started.

With Tayna giving me so much trouble, I thought I had to give my younger son some encouragement. I was really feeling proud of him. Life had been so hard for him and still he never gave up. He replied:

"I'm proud of you too mum. You have helped me be what many rich people spend fortunes trying to make their kids be.

Life's not about success, it's about feeling happy and making life simple. I don't think anything of myself, I'm just humble and that's how I get the respect and trust of people. And that, amongst other things, is what makes me happy.

There are so many things money can't buy. It requires a lot of psychological strength to get through our own barriers, to be a better person for ourselves first and then for the community around us.

I will never waste all the dedication, tenderness you gave us and the effort you made for us,

I love you, Raoni."

After a lot of phone calls, e-mails and research on the net, I found a travel agency in Brazil with great ticket prices. I could pay the ticket in five installments if it was paid with a Brazilian credit card. So, I had the brilliant idea of calling my brothers and ask them if they would pay the installments in advance for me. I thought that paying in installments would ease the impact to Greg's pocket.

Phone calls and e-mails went back and forth. Confusing information for a while but eventually both ended up saying they couldn't help. Oh well, so be it.

Greg said afterwards, that at the end, the hassle wouldn't have been worth it.

Everything would have ended there for me, had it not been for the e-mail Tayna sent me days later, saying that my sister-in-law had called his father, outraged, urging him to tell me that Ji was not going to help me. They were in a very difficult financial situation, she said, which she was keeping hidden from the rest of the family. (A few weeks later, they went to Cancun with the whole family) It was the second time she had had a reaction like when I asked my brother something. Like the first time, I was totally flabbergasted. I really couldn't see what the problem was.

She never really put it to me in black and white, but the sense that I made out of the e-mails that we exchanged afterwards, was that she thought neither the boys' father nor Greg, knew anything about Tayna's coming, that I was dragging my brothers into some sort of plot behind their backs. That explained one e-mail I got from her, in which I read dumbfounded, "Take care! You are putting your marriage at stake".

That hurt me a lot. Don't get me wrong, I really haven't got anything against any relatives. I just find it incredibly frustrating that I cannot understand nor be understood by them. Is there something wrong with me? With them?

Thinking about this whole episode years later, I came to the conclusion that it all came down to my inability to make myself clear: I wasn't clear about what I needed, I didn't really have it all sorted out in my head, I didn't know how to send the money nor how their credit cards worked exactly. Seeing that they were already on their limits, any delay in payments would have meant fees, interest and penalties for them. That explains my sister-in-law's reaction: it would jeopardize her trip to Cancun! But why couldn't she explain that to me, instead of coming up with an entire conspiracy theory? It seems I'm not the only one with communication problems!

Why do people immediately think the worst of me when I can't express myself clearly? It hurts so much more when it comes from the people close to us!

Short after that, one night the phone rang at 11:50. I ran out of the shower, as I knew it could only be one of the boys. It was their father. Dripping on the carpet, I listened as he told me he had agreed to Tayna's coming and wanted to make sure I wasn't going to spoil him!

By mid May, I finally managed to make the payment for the ticket in Brazil with Greg's credit card. It didn't go without complications but at least it was done. That same day, Greg got home from work, bringing in the mail with bills and more bills.

Raoni's mobile phone bill was four times higher than ours. I had promised him I'd pay for his mobile when he went to Sydney, until he had sorted himself out.

"I was just experimenting, Mum. I wanted to find out if it would really be more expensive if I made all my calls from the mobile instead of the land line!"

He started paying his own bill when he came up with another "experiment" a few months later.

It was also by mid May that I finally got a referral for a specialist to look into my back. My leg was very bad, by then. I really wanted to hear some expert advice.

I found consolation in my new life in Melbourne. There are lots of interesting things to do and places to visit. I love the parks; I loved our new home, the big glass door in the dining room opening to a little private garden. I loved to look at the wind going through the leaves of the old gum trees over the fence, on the banks of the Moonee Ponds creek, or at the surreal metallic effects the sunshine made on them. The sky behind them was sometimes completely blue, sometimes dark and heavy as lead and other times yet, I was blessed with the sight of an amazing sunset. I would sit there for hours, if I could.

I spent long hours in the garden. On one of those days, while I was weeding, my mind went back to my last year at Uni in Holland. I had just handed in my major research assignment.

"So, what now? Are you going to go home and play housewife?" My supervisor asked, with a smile in his face.

"Do you think I've been through all this to become a housewife?" and he laughed. But, today that's exactly what I love being.

I am astonished by the things that make me happy these days: being home enjoying the freshness of the house after a big clean up, looking in wonder at the little mushrooms growing amongst the carpet of tiny little white flowers in the garden in autumn, watching the butterflies in spring and summer, the birds having a ball with the chopped stale bread, the clothes on the line, flapping in the wind in a sunny day, the big oak tree in front of the house announcing the changing of the seasons...

Days started to pass by quickly... There was Raoni's trip to Brazil and Tayna's trip back here. There's always something that needs to be done.

I put a lot of thought into what I wanted the boys to do for me in Brazil. I wanted them to check out my stuff at the oldies, take my computer that was with Tayna in Paraty to my mother and set it up for her and get her connected on the net again. I even researched for the best internet connection in Brazil. So, she could exchange e-mails with the rest of the family instead of those bloody snail mail letters. It took two to three weeks for a letter to get here and the same time to go back. When she got an answer for her letter, the situation had already changed. She once told me she would love to talk to us more often. Come to think about it though, I reckon she enjoyed writing all those snail letters. There's nothing she loves more than feeling busy!

I sent Raoni in Sydney a box with presents for people in Brazil and another long list with recommendations and things to do plus the print out of the e-mails from the embassy in which they told me Tayna wouldn't have problems at the airport with a one-way ticket. Brazilians can only go to Australia, on a tourist visa, when they show a return ticket at check-in. There was also a list of things I wanted them to bring for me from Brazil and I made sure Raoni had all the lists with him when he left.

Since Tayna's decision to come back, I had been trying to make a new deal with his father to help us a bit financially. We had agreed before that he was going to pay Uni fees and a private teacher for Tayna, so it seemed fair to me that he sent that money every month: about 250 bucks a month, which would cover about ¼ of our expenses with the boys over here. Several e-mails went, but no reply. Until one day, I got a very long one:
He was tired of spending his money on Tayna. He was going to spend his money on more interesting things. Tayna didn't need it, he said, otherwise, he would be making a bigger effort to study and work. It was all my fault, of course. Everything about Tayna was my fault. I protected and spoiled him. I was always making Tayna change his mind; I had made him give up Uni.
I had made them come over to Australia, so it was up to me to sort it out. He wasn't going to be a sucker, not Tayna, not anyone would live on his expenses!
Again, I was left wondering: A father sending some money for his sons to study abroad, a sucker?
That e-mail upset me so much. I got so angry, but I held my horses and I didn't say a word.
He expected me to help him with Tayna in Brazil but I shouldn't expect him to help them here. You go figure. I couldn't.
I struggled with my frustration for days, but I finally realized I needed to stop expecting a change of heart. I had been beating on a dead horse far too long. The way I thought about anything never mattered to him and it never would. I needed to stop expecting support from him. The thought that with Tayna's coming I wouldn't have to deal with him ever again gave me some relief.
I hoped all the frustration would finally come to an end.

The FoE group started to stress me out as well.
I had put aside time to work on a database for the group but I needed their input and there seemed to be no interest. I started to doubt the usefulness of my commitment.
I had my first encounter with the Yorta-Yorta at a reforestation day on a sacred site.

I noticed the reciprocal trust and respect between them and the FoE group members. They got on really well and I thought to myself that that was a great achievement in itself, even though I couldn't really see how it would contribute to solve these people's problems.

With every meeting, I felt more and more out of place within the group. There was one girl in the group I found particularly difficult to handle. Ironically, she lived near my place and always asked me for a lift home. I didn't really have anything against her, apart from the fact that I felt incredibly uncomfortable next to her. She complained a lot about my driving. I wanted to tell her to take the tram, but instead I explained that I had just started to drive in Melbourne and everything still felt a bit strange to me. Maybe I needed to get to know her better, know what her story was. Sometime later, she arrived at the meeting with a heavy flu. She coughed and sneezed a lot in the car all the way home and I got a really bad case of the flu, with a high fever that threw me in bed for days. I had to take antibiotics and cough medicine for weeks. Why don't these people just stay home when they are so sick, instead of infecting others around?

Often, I thought, I would definitely be better off just staying at home doing the things I like, working on my own projects, but somehow I felt I had to help them.

Since Tayna's decision to come back and for a great part of June, my head was a mess, very busy. I felt anxious, irritable and harassed. I felt relieved only when I thought that I would have a bit more control over him and make sure he got decent education and a life for himself. I had it all sorted out, I wanted him in Melbourne, but he had it all sorted out too. He wanted to go to Sydney.

I got anxious when I thought about the extra expenses, worried about all the things that had to be sorted out. Schools, courses, enrolments, tickets, etc...

I often thought that if I had a job I would be able to do a lot more for Tayna. The fact that I didn't, made me feel guilty. If I had a decent job, none of those problems would be happening. I would go almost crazy trying to understand why I didn't have one. Why could alcoholics and inexperienced kids get a job and I couldn't? Why was I expected to do the worst and lowest kind of work available when I had two degrees and spoke three languages? How was I to know that I wouldn't get a job in this country? How come I could get a reasonable job in no time in Holland or Brazil, but not here?

Maybe employers could read in my face that there was nothing out there I really wanted to do or believed in enough to be happy doing every day, but does everybody love the job they do? Doesn't the majority of people work, just because they have to? Just to pay the bills? Is it because I'm not subservient enough?

We had enough money at the time, but what was going to happen with us in four months when Greg's contract expired?

I felt anxious and overwhelmed by my publishing and writing plans, the house needed so many things, I felt terribly bad about not having absolutely anything of my own.

There was my back, the tensions at FoE, my difficulties dealing with people in general, the cultural shock that never seemed to go away. I kept telling myself that culture's just like the color of our hair, that what really matters is to find the right people, but I didn't seem to manage to find the right people.

I wrote in my journal then, "Why am I so complicated? For some people life seems so simple... saying what they want to say, such an easy thing, so black and white... why do I feel so overwhelmed, so breathless, as if the air doesn't fill my lungs. Tears fall so easily... Why are there always so many things to be done? Why all these problems? Why can I not just do what I want to? "

My mind raged for days on end. It's hard to explain exactly what went on in my head. It was like being trapped in a small cage where I could hardly move and someone / something kept threatening me and I couldn't fight back nor run away, I felt paralyzed, stuck. The feelings of inadequacy about my parenting and about my dependence on Greg became stronger than ever.

Not knowing what to do with my life and my sons was an agony that's hard to describe. I felt so confused, I felt responsible for the whole situation, I felt I was supposed to know the solution for everything, but I didn't.

I could hardly write and it was hard keeping to my routine.

I would get cranky for no apparent reason or start some stupid argument with Greg about nothing, only to calm down a few hours later and want to hug him non-stop.

I couldn't fit him into all this. I started to doubt our relationship again. I felt bad that he was supporting me and two grown up kids who weren't his. No matter how much he said it was okay, it has never felt to me as if it was. When it came to help the boys financially, it always felt as if I was begging, I felt misunderstood.

I didn't really feel supported in my difficulties with the boys. The way he reacted to anything that had to do with the boys was never what I expected it to be. I often felt that the boys were making a bigger effort to reach out to him than the other way around. There were times I even doubted he really cared about them. With Tayna's coming, everything would just get worse!

Every attempt to address the issue with Greg only gave me half of the reassurance I needed. I always ended up feeling as stuck as before.

Adding insult to injury, the things that priest told me about my situation with Greg also kept coming back to my mind, making me feel even more confused about us, about my whole life. Questions turned around in my head: Why do I care so much about what the Church says, anyway?

Am I supposed to be with Greg? Is he really the guy for me? Do I really get from Greg what I need? Is this love? Am I in denial? And what is it that I really need? What is it that I really want? What am I doing here? What have I achieved? What was all the effort for? Was I in that situation because I had run away from my situation in Brazil? Am I not following someone else, again, instead of leading my own life? Why is all this happening? Why does happiness keep evading me?

When I decided to come here, Australia seemed such a great country in which to start a new life. I wasn't sure about that any more. I had been here for so long and nothing really good had happened.

Around my birthday, things only got worse. I used to see my birthdays as a time to look at where I was in that point in time. I always got depressed when I saw that I still wasn't where I wanted to be.

For the third time since I arrived here, I came very close to leaving. Again, I thought of Holland and the possibility of leading an independent life; I believed my self-esteem would probably rise and I would feel able to raise my own kids and not have to be dependent on anyone. I felt terribly unhappy!

It was in that state of mind that I received a phone call from Raoni one Saturday night. He was with Chica at the oldies farm and was asking what I wanted him to take from my stuff. I got pissed off. Didn't he have the list I sent him several times, by e-mail and snail mail?

"I lost it" he said. I had tried to call Paraty two days before, didn't get him on the phone, only Tayna and I reminded him not to forget the list and the presents. Obviously, he didn't get the message.

He said he was in a hurry and would only stay with the oldies overnight. He would probably not bring half of what I had asked him to.

I had also made several phone calls to the oldies and convinced them to make the 5 hours trip to Paraty to pick the boys up and the computer, so that the boys didn't have to take the computer in the bus.

When they got there, Tayna couldn't get bothered going to the farm and he told the oldies the computer couldn't go either because Ney was using it!!

I couldn't believe it. I went berserk. I wanted to kill them all. Greg ran into my office and looked at me with a dropped jaw: I was screaming on the phone...

I did hours of meditation and I cried myself dry all weekend, but my entire body felt tense and the rage took over every time I thought about it.

In the middle of my rage I sent e-mails and called Tayna, only to regret half of what I had said later on and then, regret that I regretted it. I was so mad at them, feeling so sad.

Their father, who has never given me a cent to help with the expenses here, had taken my computer!? The grannies had done so much for us, they loved it so much to have the grand children around for a few days but Tayna couldn't bother... I couldn't figure out why it always ended up like that. It was so frustrating. Why couldn't I communicate with my sons?

Tayna resented my big mouth. He was thinking of not coming anymore. I was too heavy. But as usual, in time he forgave his crazy mother. Raoni, as usually, didn't even realized how pissed off and upset I was and hadn't even read my e-mails. As to my mother the last thing she wanted in the world was to see another argument between the boys' father and me because of the computer, so she quickly said she didn't need it and for me not to worry about it.

I kept telling myself that I had to be patient, that things don't happen overnight, and, like Greg, I should just take life one day at a time, taking it easy while I wait for better days, stop worrying about tomorrow and learn to live with uncertainties and some degree of discomfort.

I still had my hope to keep me going, the hope of one day finding happiness here and a great future for myself and the boys.

I would re-focus on the book and hope things would get easier.
But, hope alone didn't really help. The anxiety got unbearable
and a deep depression took over. I'm no good. Life is no good.
Everything is wrong and I cried for days.

I told Greg one of those nights that I thought our relationship
was all wrong. That I wasn't happy without a job, he wasn't
happy bearing all the costs alone. He said we had been through
worse times and we would get through this one, too. The next
evening he came home with a bouquet of red roses (not without
whining about how expensive they were and that his intention at
first was to buy only one).

I thought all that confusion in my head wasn't normal, so I
decided to see a counselor. The Council offered a free service.
Counseling sessions, plus new self-help programs, meditation
and prayers have helped me gain some relief to my state of mind.
It helped me clarify what I was willing to sacrifice and what not
and that it was up to Greg to accept that or not and he had
accepted it. I did want to build a life with him, but I was not
going to kill myself to stay in this country. I had come here for
him, but I had two sons that still depended on me. . I didn't lie to
him about the boys. I had told him the boys would be my priority
for a few years and that I couldn't be happy if they weren't happy.
I decided I was making sacrifices enough. It wasn't my fault.
I never again felt bad about the fact that I wasn't working or
guilty towards Greg because of it, at least, not to a point where I
would feel anxious about it.

I still don't really know what happened to my head in that period,
but all the ideas I have very clear in my mind today about what I
want to do with the rest of my life started to take shape then.
I quit the counseling sessions after about two months. I came to
the conclusion that it wasn't really helping me any more. The
counselor had more problems than I had!

I have been wondering about my head for a long time. What are
these periodic emotional upheavals that I have had all my life
and that made me feel absolutely miserable, all these emotions
that seem to erupt now and then, are they the result of stupid
periodical hormonal changes? Imbalances in the chemistry in my
brain? Do I have an anxiety disorder? Am I bipolar?
I have spoken to about half a dozen of shrinks in my life and

none of them saw anything wrong with me. Am I just looking for an excuse?

Not long after that, a well-dressed, cool looking dude knocked at my door. Presenting himself as someone from an educational institution he invited us for some info night about a property investment course. Greg, as usual, was not interested and gave him that black look of his. I understood it was some kind of high level, specialized course and I accepted the invitation. On the day, I kind of had to drag Greg to it.

First, we had a shock because of the number of people there, probably over a thousand. As the invitation said it started at 6.45 p.m. and it was already 7.15, Greg started to look black again. When it ended, over two hours later, I was all excited. I thought Greg was too, but he was just relieved it was over. We made an appointment for another interview in which I enrolled in this property investment course. The promises where great. They would teach us how to buy property and make a (very good) living out of it. I was a bit shocked with the price of the course, the same as a year's university fee, but I believed it was a comparable course.

Something deep inside me didn't feel completely comfortable, it all sounded a bit fantastic at times, but I always believed property is the safest long-term investment one can make. Greg didn't see anything wrong with it either so I reckoned the whole thing was okay. I would finally have a decent job! I believed that in a year's time, I would be able to make some money out of property and I started to dream about our little piece of land in Byron Bay.

I didn't give up looking for jobs, though. I kept looking now and then. I got another interview with an organization that gives refuge to victims of Domestic Violence. I had been short listed with some other people. I was quite excited about it.

The interview was on the same day I had an appointment with the counselor. I had to kill three hours between the appointments. After walking and looking for about half an hour for a decent place to have a coffee on Sydney Road and spending about another half an hour drinking it, I got into a huge co-op shop; it's easy for me to lose myself in a place like that. When I remembered to look at the time, it was already 5 p.m., the interview was 5:20 and I was nowhere near it. There was no time for the bus, so I almost ran for 30 minutes down Brunswick Street, with two huge bags full of things, my makeup getting messed up in the drizzle and cursing half the world. I got very close to throwing away the bags. I got so upset with myself that I had forgotten time. When I got to the place, I was dripping with sweat, in spite of the cold weather. The woman who opened the door, the team leader, I came to know a few minutes later, just said: "I'll give you a few minutes to get yourself together". She must be used to seeing messed up women. The interview lasted less than 10 minutes. I had a good feeling about the place. I hoped they had a good feeling about me too. It was not far from where I lived. On a bike, it would take me about ten minutes to get there.

Back at the FoE group a few days later, there was excitement about some funding they had received. They would open a paid position for a coordinator. I thought it would be great if I could get that job, so I asked if they already had someone in mind and of course, they did.

I thought it was fair enough that the coordinator be someone who had been in the group the longest and I didn't think again about it. But, I kept thinking that it would be great to get paid to work in that group, I reckoned that there was work enough there for more than one person.

I sent an e-mail to the group with a proposition to get some funding for myself to do the things I thought needed to be done to complement the work of the coordinator.

I expected some surprise in the group with my proposition but I got a lot more than I bargained for. I had kicked a holy cow. The issue was put into the agenda of a meeting. I didn't have great expectations of success due to the big reaction the e-mails had caused, especially from the would-be coordinator.

In the meeting I said I would use my own time and resources, no one would have to move one finger for it, yet the whole process of writing the proposal would be a very transparent thing with input from everyone in the group. I said we needed to liaise more often with the local groups in the Park area, especially the objection groups. We needed to sit at the table with all the parties in the region, understand their economic interests, be more present in the area, participating in events and meetings, understanding their needs and worries, finding out alternatives together. To have stronger arguments to lobby, we needed to do more research and liaise with the scientific community to come up with strong evidence of the ability of the Yorta-Yorta to manage the natural resources properly. I wanted to do all that but I needed to get something in exchange for my time and effort.

I reckoned that even if I didn't get my proposition through I would at least understand better the way they think and do things. But I got neither. I talked and talked and no one said anything for quite a while. Then a girl said, "I don't know, I cannot explain, but I don't like it". The other explanations that followed were even more confusing. I could not really make any sense out of them.

They didn't see the importance in any of what I had said. They didn't see any need to look for more funding.

Someone said that priorities and the need for funding have to come from the group as a whole, not from particular persons, especially not if they have an interest in it. When the whole bureaucratic process of finding and getting funding is finished, then, the paid position that may come with it is opened, for everyone to apply. There was a paid person at FoE in charge of looking for funding. It was not something anyone just came up with.

I was told that this idea of individuals looking for funding for themselves was a big taboo inside FoE. Someone had tried to get this idea through for a while, but it had always created a lot of controversy every time it was brought up.

Then, I don't know if it was because they thought there was something wrong in the way they did things or if FoE's direction told them to do it, but they started a very pedantic process of writing down the position requirements to publicize it, so anyone could apply. For as far as I'm concerned I was the only one interested in it and being aware of their preference, I would not question it. It was a finished business and I couldn't understand who outside the group would have the hide to apply for it. I found the meetings that followed totally useless, unbearable would be a more appropriate word.

I kept no bad feelings and no resentment. Very much the contrary. I actually like the coordinator and other people there, but I had an enormous feeling of frustration. They looked at me as if I had done something bad or wrong and I couldn't see what the problem was. No one really showed me what was wrong with the idea. Again, I felt in the wrong place, at the wrong time, with the wrong people.

After that, it became more and more difficult for me to take part in the activities of the group. I had never understood their way of thinking, but now even the willingness to understand them was gone. I started losing my patience and feeling really annoyed with the never-ending meetings and time spent on things that for me were totally irrelevant. And I wasn't the only one. FoE's president told me he was pissed of with them as well, with the way they had handled things. But, I had promised to work on that database and I felt I had to. I felt a bit stuck with them. I felt I couldn't just walk away and they eventually handed me enough material I could work with.

I had to rethink that whole volunteering thing. I had to ask myself what I had to offer to whom. Maybe I shouldn't volunteer at all, if what I really wanted was a job.

It all reinforced my belief that I'm a loner. I have always been and will always be.

The date to finally see a specialist for my back had come. I didn't believe it would really be of any real help. I had to go through yet another bunch of tests and x-rays and I was put on a waiting list for intensive rehabilitation at the Public hospital. If things didn't get better after that, we were going to look into more radical stuff: cortisone shots and surgery. This all meant that I had to put up with my leg for another month and I could forget about the belly dancing for a while.

At some stage, I remembered our Immigration process. We were supposed to have received something from them in February or March. When I called then they told me they were running late with the processes and that there would be a few months delay. I also informed them that we had moved to Melbourne and they asked me if I wanted my papers sent to the office in Melbourne. Knowing these people and foreseeing complications and more delays, I told them to continue processing my papers in Brisbane. Two and a half months had passed. I called DIAC in Brisbane again. I got to hear they had sent all the files to Melbourne. So, I went to the Immigration office in Melbourne:

"Irene Elizabeth who? No, I'm sorry; I don't have you in our files."

"What? Are you sure? What do you mean, "I'm not in your files?"

"What do you think I mean? I mean you are not registered with us. I mean we don't have anything of you with us. How long have you been in Australia? Are you sure you have applied for the right visa?"

"Look there must be a mistake. I applied in Brisbane. I've been waiting for this visa for over two years" I showed her the papers I had from DIAC in Brisbane.

"Hmmm..." And she types the file number in. "No, I'm sorry, nothing."

"Can't you ask the people in Brisbane about it?"

"No, I can only handle files that are in the system"

"But..."

"I'm sorry. Next one, please".

Okay, I had to find out what happened to my file; I needed to find out who had handled it in Brisbane, who had sent it down and who had received it here. Cursing and swearing loud and clear all the way through my investigation, I discovered that some clerk here in Melbourne had misplaced the file and it was just gathering dust on some shelf.

I kept calling and asking what they were up to, until one day, I was told a letter had been sent.

Finally! Something was going to happen.

About two weeks later the letter arrived with a request for another truckload of documents and forms. All I hoped for at the time was that when that visa soap opera was over, the boys could get a little bit of support with their study and things would be easier for us. Maybe then, I could manage to do a few of the things I wanted to.

I spent days filling out forms. Among other things, DIAC wanted Police clearances from Australia and Brazil. I sent the Australian Police the forms requiring the Clearances. They ask people not to call all the time, because they are too busy and to allow a month for any reply and so I did. After more than a month, I still hadn't received any reply. When I called, they said they never received the forms. I had forgotten to write some code on the envelope, without which, a letter is not forwarded to the respective department. They just throw it out, I guess. So I had lost another month and I could start from scratch again.

Raoni and his father tried to get the Police Clearances from Brazil. More missed phone calls, unanswered e-mails and running to and fro, but eventually the papers arrived. Everything was translated and posted, only to hear a few weeks later that they were not the clearances they wanted. I needed to sign another form and they themselves would get the clearances they needed directly from Brazil.

Meanwhile, problems with the repayment of my study loan in Holland got ugly. I had forgotten to send up the forms I have to send them every year. I also forgot to send them my new address in Australia. As a result, they started to charge me monthly for the maximum repayment amount. I never received their letters and I never replied, so they sent me to the debt collector.

I still don't understand how they think. When you earn below a certain amount you don't have to pay anything that year.

I had been sending them the low-income forms for years. Then, one year they don't get the form (two years, actually) and automatically they assume I could pay the maximum installment. I could have just ignored the whole thing. Greg himself suggested I do so! The only address of mine they had was my parents' house in São Paulo and they had moved on. They didn't know I was in Australia. Would they have bothered spending a lot of money to find out my whereabouts? I find it hard to believe. But I decided to sort the mess out with the collector. I had to negotiate a way to pay a large amount of euros.

As I dug into the mess in the following months I had to admit, surprise, surprise, that I had no one to blame but myself.

My debt had increased a lot due to some stupid things I didn't even remember I had done, much less, why I had done them. I had cancelled my Uni enrolment in May 1992, when I went to Brazil, without finishing my course. I think I did that because I didn't know how long I was going to be in Brazil for or maybe I just decided to give up Uni. That caused a chain reaction that, with the addition of interest, made the debt grow out of control. I felt so overwhelmed and depressed when the whole picture became clear. How did I manage to make such a mess?

After a difficult negotiation process over snail, e-mail and phone, the debt collector finally agreed to let me pay it out in small installments.

From then on, I had to periodically send money to Holland. I tried several possibilities, involved friends and family in Holland to no avail. Finally, I decided to send my cousin my card, from a free online savings account, which she could withdraw from to make the payments. It took me three years to finally find a great, cheap way to make payments abroad. Why does it take so long to learn something?

One morning, not long before the boys' arrival, I had woken up in a great mood, something rare in those days; I was full of beans and had big plans for the day. But then I got an e-mail from Tayna. He said he didn't want to stay with Raoni, that it wasn't going to work; he said Raoni doesn't like him and doesn't want him in the flat. I didn't know what was going on. They must have had an argument, I thought. He wanted to stay somewhere else in Sydney. My plans for a nice, calm day evaporated like drops of water on a hot pan.

I had done a lot of research already looking for schools and courses for him in Sydney. I had pre-enrolled him in three English courses, pending his passing the entrance tests. We had agreed that he was going to stay in Sydney with Raoni and come to us just for a short visit of two weeks to talk things over before classes started.

I had a long conversation with Greg. In my heart, I wanted Tayna to be here with me. We decided that the best thing to do was for him to stay with us. It was hard for me to explain to him that we couldn't afford to pay two different apartments in Sydney and that he has to come and live with us. He wasn't really happy about it, but resigned. I thought it was the best thing to do, though I somehow, worried about how it would be.

Now I had to find courses for him in Melbourne and applications had closed already. I tried desperately to find a course he could still get into. The only thing they could do was to put him on waiting lists. Without any certainties about him getting a place in Melbourne, he had to do those tests in Sydney. If we didn't get him a place in Melbourne he would have to stay in Sydney and sort it out with his brother. On top of that, the dates for tests and start of courses here and in Sydney were clashing. It wouldn't be possible to do the tests here and in Sydney and then make a decision depending on where he got a place.

I was really stressed out with the situation for many days, frantically searching for courses and spending hours on the phone.

Hating every single second of it, cursing and swearing, I asked myself why everything always had to be so chaotic, why I ended up doing everything in a hurry, always in damage control. Why did things always go wrong? Why couldn't I make the right decisions? Why did I always plan so much if the effort was invariably wasted, why did we always end up with the worst alternative and usually the most expensive? Worst of all is to realize, always too late, the far-reaching consequences of all the wrong decisions made.

By mid June, I got a phone from the domestic violence mob, yet another "no". At least, for the first time ever, I got some feedback. They didn't think I had made a big enough effort "to sell" myself. Meaning, I didn't brag about myself enough. Well, if that is the criteria, I'm not sad I'm out. Since when is bragging a measure of how one is going to perform a job? They also didn't think my activism came through strong enough in our conversation. All my letters for Amnesty international, Greenpeace, WWF, my involvement with FoE, my petitions for refugees, apparently I had to brag about all that as well. I had already talked about all that in my application letter. I think it's one of those things we don't talk about to people all the time unless someone asks and they didn't. I reckon that if someone cannot see enough qualities in me, that's not the place I'm meant to be. I did think it was a bummer, though. I had been thinking of all the things I wanted to do with the money and I really believed I could be happy doing that work. But I didn't linger on it for too long. I didn't get upset at all. Actually, a few days later I felt relieved. I reckoned that in the end that job was going to be much more than I had bargained for. The chaos on the day of the interview was already a sign that it was not going to happen. I was glad I could continue doing the things I was doing at home, but with that last disillusion, I did decide my job searching was finished once and for all for the rest of my life. It became clear I had to give up for once and for all my struggle to fit somewhere and be part of something I didn't really believe in. I will never manage to do anything under strict rules and procedures that make no sense to me. Maybe I have a problem with authority. Maybe it's just one of my problems. But, I don't know how to fix myself. I don't know how to accept and adapt to the world around me. I cannot change the core of who I am. How long does one try? How many times do I have to hear a 'no'? How many times get it rubbed in my face that I don't belong? I finally accepted that my place under the Australian sun did not exist. I would have to create that place myself. I decided to believe what I have thought all my life, that I was meant for something bigger. I could get back to my book, which I had neglected for some time and spend time on my property investment course I had just started.

It often gives me consolation to think that Jesus never had a boss either!

After only a few meetings of the "course", I realized what I had got myself into. It wasn't what I had expected at all. I thought it would be a sort of sophisticated long distance course, I expected to see a classroom environment but it was just guys talking. Seminars they call it. I had never heard of these things. I tried to know more about it and started to read and hear things about how seedy these kinds of seminars can be and I didn't really like the kind of people I found there. People who think money's the essence of life itself. They had told us we only had to spend a few hours a day, but these guys talking there were real, full time businessmen. That's their life. The whole thing was contrary to my beliefs. I got to know that the whole thing was put in place by Henry Kaye, a so-called property guru. I started to have doubts. It felt a bit like I had been sucked into it. I wasn't sure we had done the right thing anymore. I thought I had been impulsive again. I got confused. What now?

Did I have to shift the perspectives I was looking from? Should I become like these guys, get serious about earning the big bucks, was that what I was supposed to do after all? I could do many good things with the money, give the boys a good future for example, or was that exactly the illusion they were selling us? Would I enjoy doing it? Would it make me feel proud about myself, would it give me satisfaction in life? Is that it? Make money?

And what about my writing plans? How can I write a book saying that we must have faith, persevere in what we most love doing, to do what we have been called for, because when we do so we will eventually get everything we need? How can I say that and stop doing what I love doing to do something just for money? Or is this whole writing thing with me just an ego-trip? Will I ever make any money with books? Am I doubting myself again?

I felt stuck; I had no other alternatives, really. We had made the commitment and we had already paid for it. I had to continue with it and hope that at the end I would achieve my goals anyway. The property thing would have to be the priority from then on. So writing was put aside once more and bit-by-bit I got into the property "course" in a very intensive way.

On the 26th of June, Tayna was in the plane, on his way to Sydney. Even though I didn't manage to talk to him before he left, I felt so much more in peace with the thought he was coming back. I really believed everything was going to be all right with him from then on.

I was disappointed that he didn't call me immediately when he got into Sydney. His flight from Brazil was delayed by eight hours. I must have called Raoni's flat about ten times that day. When he finally arrived, instead of calling me, he went to town first.

I called him two nights in a row and then I thought I shouldn't call the third night. I thought I was being too intrusive. He said he missed my call the day after. Will I ever get it right?

After a week in Sydney, getting more acquainted with the people, he didn't really want to come down to Melbourne, but I told him he couldn't keep changing his mind like that.

I continued to look for courses in Melbourne and I finally got confirmation from one. It wasn't as good as the ones I had managed to guarantee for him in Sydney, but that was what we got.

I told him not to enroll at the schools in Sydney, although, by then he had actually passed the tests and got a place in two good courses.

With his coming, I needed to re-arrange the house. I moved the dining room into the living room. The dining room became my office. My office became our bedroom and Tayna got our bedroom. Greg had to make new network connections for the computers, most of the furniture had to be completely taken apart and then put back together again, because we couldn't get it up or down the staircase.

I bought Tayna a desk, but I thought he wouldn't like the color, so I hired some tools and sand it and repaint it. It took me a whole weekend to do it, outside in the freezing winter wind. My arms got sore, but it looked great afterwards. At the end, I would probably have spent less money if I had bought a new one. Did Tayna give a damn? Of course not. Moving all the furniture almost killed me. I couldn't move for a few days and my back was very painful for more than a week.

In July, I started my back rehabilitation program: hydrotherapy and physiotherapy. I didn't believe it would really help me. Many of the exercises were similar to the ones I had already started doing on my own. I showed the books I was following to one of the therapists and she thought they were all right. I took their program very seriously. I really wanted to get my problems fixed. I bought a Swiss exercise ball and practiced at home every day for an hour, apart from the four hours a week at the hospital. The result didn't take long to show up.

Tayna arrived in Melbourne on the eighth of July. I was nervous waiting for him at the airport, maybe a hint, a gut feeling of what was to come. He had made a friend in the plane, Otto, a Brazilian boy, about the same age and they started to go out together. He was enthusiastic; he had a positive attitude and started looking for work very intensively, straight away. He left résumés everywhere and he was positive about his career choice.

As days passed by, things didn't work out very well between us. We argued a great deal. I became so annoyed with the way he did things. He got annoyed with the way I did things. He hadn't been here for two weeks when we had a big argument and he decided to leave, no matter what, or he would kill himself, he said. I didn't know what to do any more, so I got Greg and the three of us had a talk, which was rather disappointing, as usual. All Greg said was to wait a few days. I really thought the situation warranted a whole lot more than a "let's wait and see" response, but Greg didn't see the urgency in the situation. Was it again a cultural difference?

Tayna called his father. He promised to send him some money and support him until he settled in Sydney, or so Tayna said. Tayna asked if we would advance him the money so that he could go and he would send his father's money as soon as it arrived. How bearable would the situation have become if I had said no to Tayna? Greg was silent again; he later said he felt we had overturned his decision.

His father never sent the money. Years later, he told me he never told Tayna he would send any money. Either Tayna made that whole story up or his father made him a promise he didn't keep. I guess I will never know what really happened as nobody remembers that episode in detail anymore, or so they say. For my side, I could have checked with his father, but, as usual, I only discover too late, what I should have done in a certain situation.

My mind went off, spinning again, worrying about all the things that had to be sorted out for Tayna to go back to Sydney. He had done the tests in Sydney but missed the enrolment dates. Trying to get him back in the schools I had previously contacted, was another huge and stressful task. Then there were the tickets, organize his stay in Sydney, etc...

I had a terrible night the day he left. After a few restless hours of sleep, I got out of bed before 4:30 a.m. It was cold, the temperature must have been close to zero, I almost regretted getting out, but I needed to get things out of my mind. I needed to write:

"I don't think I will ever manage to express the pain I'm feeling at the moment, the tears are pouring down; I can't see the letters on the keyboard."

Tears for me are a blessing. When I cry I know that it won't take long for me to feel better again. But, when I can't cry, the turmoil in my mind just gets greater and I feel I'm going to explode. It's hard to explain. It's a mixture of rage, frustration, and confusion that's unbearable. I can hardly breathe.

Why has parenthood always been such a torture for me? The constant unbearable discrepancy between what I know is the best and right thing to do and what I always end up doing...

Writing helps me put my mind in order. After writing for a few minutes, I managed to start seeing life from a brighter side.

The feeling of frustration and sadness with the whole situation with Tayna, lingered on for days. I was trying hard to accept the situation when Otto came along...

He had gone to New Zealand to check out some work possibilities over there. But the whole thing turned out to be a bit seedy and having nowhere else to go, he called us. He asked if he could stay a couple of weeks, until he found out what to do next with his life. The two weeks turned into over four months. But, all in all, although it did mess up my routine, it was good having him with us.

I thought that a lot of what he was feeling then was the same I felt in my first year in Holland in 1986. I was his age then. So many expectations, the feeling of having the entire world at my feet, a whole world to conquer. Feeling a bit lost, excited at the possibilities on one hand and the fears and insecurities on the other.

We had so many interests in common: real estate, natural food, yoga, meditation, Christianity. He listened to me. We spent hours dreaming about a property empire, we spent weekends looking for houses, we talked for hours on end. We visited parks, beaches, went to the movies. It made the days and weeks pass easily. He became my surrogate son. He filled the gap my own sons had left.

I put a lot of energy and time in helping him get a job in a mill. Milling had been his family business for generations. We actually succeeded, which was for me kind of a miracle, because I knew all too well, how difficult it is to get decent work in this country; he didn't even have a working visa nor spoke the language fluently.

Raoni in Brazil came up with ideas of bringing Chica back with him, ideas about marriage, I freaked out and so did his father.

I sent him a very serious e-mail urging him not to do anything if he feels pressured somehow. I worried this thing with Chica wasn't real. I urged him to know very well what he was doing and why; to be completely honest with himself and his feelings towards her; to think about his future and hers and to be aware of the enormous responsibility a marriage entails. I told him to think especially about the possibilities of things not working out well. He had to have backup plans.

By mid July, Raoni returned from Brazil and it didn't take long, as I had expected, for the problems between him and Tayna to start. They had a flat-mate, in one room, so they had to share the other bedroom. Raoni thought it was all right to take a girl to bed with him while his brother was sleeping three feet away from him. He thought Tayna had to sleep somewhere else if he was bothered. Tayna on the other hand felt embarrassed to go in the room when there was someone else in there, so he couldn't get any of his stuff when he needed it. As usual, I got different versions of the story, so it was hard to sort out things or say anything useful under these circumstances and all I could do was to try to calm things down. They would have to learn how to live together and share one way or another.

Raoni continued working on his plans with Chica for a few months but, thank God, slowly they turned their minds to other things and the whole issue cooled down. They were too young and irresponsible. That was no time to be thinking about marriage, unless they could prove they really knew what they were doing, which was definitely not the case. Before the end of the year, the relationship was all over. One good thing was that with Chica's coming in mind, Raoni put a bigger effort into finding a better job. That got him out of the café and into a Marina, more in tune with his career choice.

Besides their normal expenses, the boys' needs for extra money never ended. One day they needed to clean the carpets, the other the bond needed to be paid back to a flat mate that was going, overcharged phone bills, mobile phones and broken computers...

When tax time came, Raoni had a hard time trying to get his work papers sorted out by his boss from the café and it took him another year to get him to pay his superannuation.

Tayna had to organize many papers to apply for the course he wanted to start in 2004. He needed references from Brazil and school papers. More translations. Now he could have a taste of how hard it was to get any paper coming from Brazil. He started to miss Brazil and his friends again, but knew there was no other choice for him but to stay. He started to feel bored with the

English courses. He wanted to work and make money. I told him to talk to the counselor at school for some advice, but it was in vain. He started dragging the courses, skipping classes; he practically abandoned one of the courses altogether.

By the beginning of August, I made a big discovery: phone cards. Raoni had told me about them before, but I didn't pay attention. There is room for technical improvement, but the amount of money that we have saved since has been well worth it. Telstra charges over a dollar per minute for a call to Brazil, the card charges two to four cents. There are different cards with different prices and each has their plusses and minuses.

It was in August too, that I made another, less fortunate discovery. Less than two months into the Property "course", I stumbled upon something on the internet about the course I was doing and Henry Kaye. He was up to his neck in legal problems. I saw alerts, advising to stay away from anything to do with him. I wrote what I found in an e-mail list of people doing that course and someone in the list replied by saying that I was a chicken, that I didn't believe in myself. Another guy said people like me, who worried so much about everything made him sick.

I desperately tried to get out of that course, cancel it, but it took the bastards weeks to reply to my calls and e-mails. When they finally did, all they said was not to worry and that everything was under control. It was too late to get out, anyway, I had made already the first payments, I had to resign and hope they were telling the truth. I continued trying to learn as much as I could, I bought books and I started to go to every property related event in town.

In The Garra, the news that Dadboy would not make it for more than a couple of months hit the family pretty hard. He was losing weight at a very fast rate. Everyone's consolation was that he wasn't in pain, so our worries turned to Mumboy.

Russ and Kay moved down to Stanthorpe from Airlie beach, something they were planning to do for years.

This way they could be closer to Mumboy.

At the end of August, Greg and I went up there to see Dadboy. It was a very emotional and difficult reunion and Greg kept going to Wallangarra on a regular basis after that.

I didn't see the need for me to go every time. Dadboy would hardly speak to me when I was there. I think being with his sons was all he needed. I spoke to him often on the phone and would always send him a small letter through Greg. With those trips and all the new expenses with the boys, all the money we had managed to save was quickly disappearing and with it, the deposit for the house I dreamt about.

In the beginning of September, I finally managed to sort out something that had been worrying me all the time I'd been here. The boys' father had promised to keep an eye on the farm and the block of land I had in Paraty, but he never did. There were rates that had to be paid and because the farm was so far away from everything, there was a real danger of invasion. I managed to get someone to keep an eye on it for me, at last. That gave me great relief. At about the same time I finally decided to put an official end to my commitment with the FoE group. I hadn't gone to any meetings for quite a while, anyway.

By mid October, we finally received our definitive resident visas. I had expected I would be so happy when that day arrived! I would jump with joy, but strangely enough, it didn't make any difference. It did absolutely nothing to me. The hassle and the effort to get it had just been too much. Three years of anxieties and hardships. I had given up too much, I had gone through too much to get it, we waited for too long. I had seen more of Australia than I should. My vision had changed so much from the one I had in mind when I decided to come here. Both boys were working, by then. We didn't need any help any more. I could not even smile about it.

By the end of the month, Raoni bought himself a car. I was so glad he got something back for his hard work: scrubbing boats on his knees, in the rain, in chilly winds, putting up with rude managers and being underpaid. He didn't feel really happy. He said he had become grumpy and life wasn't as much fun as it used to. I tried to tell him that when we are really enjoying ourselves, we are not really improving ourselves. This seems to be God's design. There are no roses without thorns. That's what maturity's all about. Doing the things you know are right, even if it's not much fun doing them! Not surprisingly, it didn't make him feel any better.
Greg meanwhile, stopped being a contracted worker and became a regular employee and that meant a considerable salary cut.

At the end of November the organization that was giving the

Property Course collapsed, i.e., went into administration. Hell broke loose. Unbelievable, with all the money they were making! Of the one-year course I was supposed to get, I only got five months. I got myself into the creditors committee of the administrator to try, as much as I could, to minimize the damage and make sense out of the mess.

An incredibly stressing month followed, but worse was the feeling that with all the effort and stress I didn't really managed to change anything. I think that if I hadn't done a thing, everything would have turned out exactly the same. For the rest of the year my life was reduced to reading corporate law papers, trying to understand procedures, going to meetings, talking to lawyers, finding out what would be the best thing to do and getting in contact with some of the 3,500 people from all over Australia, who were also caught in the mess.

What a mess, what a nuisance, what a waste of time. I was so angry, so upset.

As the end of the year approached, a general meeting was arranged in which Henry Kaye would present his company deed, explaining how he was going to pay for the damages done. From what was coming out of the Administration meetings, I knew that no one could in sane consciousness, trust Henry Kaye. I decided to vote for liquidation and would try and convince as many people as I could to do the same. Some experts had also said that was the best option.

From then on, very few things would cheer me up, but an e-mail from Raoni was one of them:

"Well, for no reason I was thinking...
I might send you an e-mail, although we have just been speaking on the phone for two hours...
Maybe I forgot to mention...
We Love you mum!!!"

Tayna on the other hand, had abandoned one of the English courses and left a second one several times, always coming back. One of the teachers got fed up with him and sacked him. Out of the three courses he enrolled for, he got a certificate for only one. I thought I needed to go see them, so I spent Christmas in Sydney. Raoni got embarrassed when I showed up at the marina where he was working in army pants and my new very short hair-do. I was a bit surprised to know he felt like that about me.

We were going on a sailing trip with the boss. The trip was good, even though the weather was dreadful, but being there with my sons, watching them take turns steering the boat made me really happy.

There was the usual friction and a few arguments with Tayna, he too, thought my army pants were 'out'.

After Christmas Raoni was allowed to get another boat and we went for another trip, just the three of us and a few of their friends. The weather was wonderful and we had an unforgettable day.

2003 came to an end with Greg and I in Wallangarra for the New Year.

It was a shock to see how much weight Dadboy had lost; he was about 49 kg. But he was still lucid most of the time. We stayed with him in Hospital most of the time. Because he was a terminal patient, the hospital staff was kind enough to allow the dogs in and they slept on his bed all day. How comforting that was for him and Mumboy.

We spent most of our last day there at the hospital, going to Kay and Russ late in the afternoon. On our way back to The Garra I told Greg to stop at the Hospital once more. I had a feeling I wouldn't see Dadboy again. I needed to give him a last hug. Greg gave in, very reluctantly. Having to say good-bye to Dadboy was terribly hard for him.

He was half-unconscious. He looked a bit confused at us. We gave him a big, long hug. It was the last time we saw him. He passed away a few days later.

More Skeletons

We arrived in Melbourne one day and the next I was straight back into the Property course fiasco, with all the stress that came with it as a bonus. Apart from related companies and creditors, other parties got involved, a few so called "consumer defender organizations". It became obvious to me quick enough that the only interest they were defending was their own, using the disgrace of all these people to push forward hidden agendas, while pretending to care.

It's hard to describe the frustration and how upsetting it was to deal with all those people. The rudeness of those from whom one would expect the most understanding: consumer defenders, lawyers and even the people who were caught up in the mess. It was pretty shocking. I'd expect people to get strength from unity to try to control the damage. What an illusion!

It turned out people had been trapped into this mess by different means and had different amounts of money at stake; there were several different "courses" being given at different prices and with different payment arrangements. There wasn't a one-fits-all-solution. People became divided and turned against each other. We were all in the same boat, sinking together and yet some tried to throw others overboard and some just refused to help in the hope that they would lose less. What a despicable situation. I had another great opportunity to see the worst in people, all the greed and selfishness.

I could write fifty pages if I was to get into the nitty gritty of this mess. Suffice to say that the whole episode cost me six very stressful months of my life: anxious and restless nights and days dragged into legal courts and meetings, only to minimize the damage. No amount of prayer or meditation would ease my worries. I did so much more than was healthy for me to do.

It kept me so busy that I wasn't able to give Mumboy the necessary support when Dadboy passed away. I couldn't even go to the funeral, because we would be away for a week and I had important meetings in that week that had taken me a great deal to pin down. I felt bad about it, but the family was very understanding.

At one point, I arranged a meeting with Henry Kaye himself, in the innocent hope that I could propose a better way out of it all, because the company deed he had proposed did nothing but to outrage everyone.

Instead, all I found was an exhausted and expressionless face and icy cold eyes. He seemed to me utterly indifferent to what people were going through. All he cared about was his own skin. Of course, I didn't even manage to say half of what I had planned to say, nor did I achieve any of what I wanted to, but at least I tried and just because of that, I think the experience was worthwhile.

No matter how much time I spent reading and trying to understand the legal and technical aspects, no matter how much I learned, I was never completely sure of what was the best thing to do. My gut feelings were playing the major role in my decision-making. So, I decided to get a small group of people willing to put together some money for a second legal opinion. They charged us A\$ 4,000 to read the DOCA (deed of company) and give us their impression of it in plain English. In theory, because lawyers never talk in plain English! They always say things in such a way that, may they be wrong, they won't get into trouble. Never ever will one get a black and white answer from a lawyer!

Nonetheless, it did make me more confident that liquidating Henry Kaye was indeed the best thing to do.

On the other side of the story were the credit providers. The major ones were associated with Kaye in one way or another. Even though the "Training Institute" had collapsed and people didn't get the complete course they had paid for, these credit providers wouldn't let people go; they wouldn't review nor ease the loan payments people had taken. Like starved vultures, they wouldn't let the rotting carcass go. In time, one of these consumer defender organizations managed to get a law firm involved that is, to this day, trying to organize a class action against the major credit provider for that "course", but the class action has so many ifs and buts that it will be completely useless to a large number of people, including us.

After a relentless effort, I managed to settle the case with one of our lenders through the Victorian Civil and Administrative Tribunal and with the other, I managed to arrange a stay of the payments until after the class action, when the validity of the credit contracts will be analyzed. Out of the A\$ 18,000 (interest included) that we would have paid for the entire "course", we paid A\$ 5,000 for half of it and we were lucky! Many people lost a lot more than that. Relationships broke up and many were in danger of losing their houses. It could have ended a lot worse for us. But, this whole issue is not finished yet. It will drag for years.

There is still a shadow hanging over our heads. If the Courts decide that the credit contracts are valid and God only knows when that will be, we will still have to pay the rest of the money. It is unlikely that it will happen, but we can't be sure.

The Government and the media spared no efforts to blame, accuse and brand us: bunch of stupid, greedy dipsticks.

In response to the alarming number of people being caught up in seedy financial schemes in the country, the then treasurer, had the brilliant idea to set up a taskforce, to try to do something about all these "financially illiterate" wooden ducks. He believed that before disaster stroke, there was nothing the government could do about scammers. They are too damn quick, too clever, always ahead of the law, they say. But, if we have a look at the mechanisms they have in place to catch tax evaders, it's obvious they don't think *they* are fast enough for them.

The taskforce recommended that another mammoth organization be set up, a coordinating body that would put together all the information regarding consumer behavior, for organizations to tap into and "help" consumers on how to better deal with their money. These organizations, mind you, are the same organizations that will provide them with the financial services!

Judging by what they do to protect people, I can only conclude that the thousands, maybe millions of vulnerable people that fall prey to these scams every year are, for the government, nothing but faceless and inevitable casualties. There can be no winners without losers, who cares if the winners are few and the losers many?

The whole experience just made me feel overwhelmed with the complexity and confusion that is this world. Every little step forward in this mad society we live in is an all or nothing decision, a lifetime enterprise, an enormous amount of time and effort. It's not by reading a few papers and going to a few meetings that we are going to change anything. In fact, I think that in all the meetings I've been to, specially the ones set up by the government, the so called public consultation meetings, everybody's agendas are fixed already, they know exactly what they want. It is not as if people go there with an open mind, with a willingness to listen and find alternatives. I had the strong impression that they are set up only to check out how hard or easy it will be to set forth plans that have already been decided upon.

Huge financial scams happen all the time in this country. Adverts with the most outrageous promises ran freely on TV, internet and newspapers. They can call us stupid, but the way these people presented the course to me, really made me believe I was dealing with a genuine, traditional kind of training institute, they went a long way to present that image to us. It never crossed my mind I was getting into property investment seminars.

I noticed that the majority of the people that fell prey to these cons were simple, ordinary people and a great proportion were immigrants like me, without much knowledge of the country, who believed that it wouldn't be possible for anyone in a country like this, to present themselves as something they were not. We believed that the government would have regulating mechanisms in place to avoid these things from happening.

Have I learned something from all this? You bet!

We live in a capitalistic jungle were everybody's trying to eat everybody else and in this wilderness it's every man for himself.

There are regulations, of course, maybe too many of them, but there's always a way around them, always a loophole to be explored.

I did have some soul searching of my own to do, though. Why didn't I react to my gut feelings? Before we signed the contract, I spoke to a few guys that had something about them that didn't really click with me. Why didn't I pick up the clues?

As if my stress and frustration in Melbourne, during the whole administration process weren't enough, in Sydney, Tayna missed the enrolment day for his new course and he had to settle for a lower level diploma course. The one he was supposed to have enrolled for filled up very quickly.

By mid February, after Henry Kaye was liquidated by a small margin, I sent a farewell e-mail to the fellow "students" I was in contact with during the whole process, explaining that I had decided to get out of the committee to get my life back. I got this reply from one of them.

"Irene,

Words cannot express the feeling of overwhelming relief from achieving the task we set out to do, mingled with a twisted feeling of sadness and sympathy as you get on with your life after sacrificing so much of what you obviously didn't really need in your life. The fact that you have completed a task that's nationwide and have brought a finality in the lives of so many people who were hanging on the end of an unfinished story... a bit like wanting to know where your life is and wanting something to close the chapter and you have certainly provided that for me and no doubt hundreds of other people. Who knows, this could in fact impact on many more thousands of people in the future and in my eyes, you have helped write history and I'm glad that I got to meet you and have you represent me. I thank you ever so much. Please keep smiling and know that you challenged the odds and won. Good overcame evil, as cruel as this sounds, but the people who were taken advantage of finally took control.

...Maybe our paths will cross again and I can give you that big hug. Be proud of what you did, no matter what people may say. You did the right thing because you believed in it and it was not out of greed or to take advantage of anyone.

God bless, C R"

It almost brought tears to my eyes and it made me feel proud too.

Being out of the committee, didn't mean the whole thing was over for me. I still kept talking to different organizations and lawyers and closely following the events, but not having to deal with so many people all the time, made it possible for me to get back to things I really found important: writing for Amnesty and my pen pall on death row in San Quentin, get in touch with the boys, work in the garden and get back to the book.

When a few days passed without the boys calling me with some sort of problem to sort out, I would call them. I e-mailed them one day to ask if coming to Australia had been worth and to tell them that I loved them. To my surprise, Tayna replied saying that he thought it had been very worthwhile.

I asked them the questions I was asked in my self-help programs: What are the three things they love doing the most? What in the world would they like to change?

Both guaranteed to me they were doing the things they loved and felt they were going in the right direction.

But, not long after that, Raoni called. He was a bit depressed. He missed Brazil and Chica. He often thought of going back. Tayna wasn't really happy either and had to drag himself to school and work, but at least he was doing both. He also started a relationship with the flat-mate that was living there. She was a good girl and she would prove to be a great support for him.

It was great being back to my normal life, enjoying the house and spending time in the garden. We never know how much we have until we lose it.

I love to work in the garden. It's so therapeutic. I get so many insights when I dig my hands into the dirt!

It was in the garden one day, that I saw clearly how focused I am on the results of what I do, when in fact it's the process to get there that's the most important. It's what we learn on the way that matters, not what we get at the end. It's not about what, it's about how!

And Pink Floyd comes to mind:

"Everybody's searching for something, they say.
I'll get my kicks on the way" ("The Gold It's In The..." Obscured by clouds, 1972)

One day, I decided to make a big revolution in the garden. Many plants were overgrown, others needed to be transplanted and others yet, to be cut back. It was still quite hot and as I watched, afterwards, how the once strong and beautiful plants died or struggled to recover in the heat, I realized how reckless I had been with them. I realized how reckless I had been with the boys and myself. People, like plants, have roots. Once they grow to a certain point, we can't put them somewhere else without causing a lot of trauma. How unaware I was of the depth and strength of our roots, our uncertainties.

I remembered a story told in the family many times about my grandfather, whom I never really got to know. He never recovered from having to leave Indonesia for Holland after the Independence war. He had a stroke en route on the ship and lived in bed for the rest of his life. I thought of the boys, their loneliness, our feelings of alienation, of how different the life I always led in Brazil was, compared to my life in Australia.

Why did I have to uproot myself so much? Why have I been avoiding letting my roots grow somewhere for so long?

I thought of all the years spent here and how difficult it had been at times.

How long would it still take for things to start happening for me? When I looked at the garden many months from there, the differences seemed so small! Had it all been worthwhile? Yet, I knew that those questions were useless. It didn't really matter. As the garden had been changed, I was here. There was no going back. I had to make the best of what I had. Life wasn't too bad, all things considered. No doubt, my life had improved. I just had to let the roots grow strong enough, so that my life could flourish again. I had come a long way, but I still had more miles to go.

An e-mail I once received would often come back to my mind. It was a story about a bamboo.

"After the seed of this incredible shrub is planted, one won't see anything happen for a long time. Apart from a tiny bud that slowly shows up, absolutely nothing else happens for four long years. For four years, the bamboo is growing underground, a massive network of roots that spreads vertically and horizontally in the ground. On the fifth year, that tiny bud starts to grow and it grows and grows until it reaches 24 meters in a very short time!"

It was also in the garden that I often thought about the past. Many times, I wished I could turn back time, to when the boys were little, do it all over again. Back to that magic time that passes us by as quickly as a breeze, never to come back; the time when every little thing in their lives is a new wonder to be discovered and be amazed by, those bright little eyes full of life, the screams of excitement, the happiness shining off their faces. So many of those precious moments missed, because I was too busy looking for myself, looking for I don't know what, running around for nothing.

All the things I found important then, now look so ridiculous, in comparison to the memories of the blessed moments I did spend with them, when their innocent eyes were still wide open looking up at me, when they still believed that whatever I had to say was important.

All I can do now is accept the fact that I will have to painfully watch my sons muck around in life until they do find some balance of their own and that will probably take a long, long time.

After working in the garden so hard, a stupid male cat decided it was good enough to use it as his toilet on an almost daily basis. He kept coming back for months, until the creeping plants covered the whole ground again. Every time I picked up his poo, every time that foul smell got into my nose, my feelings towards that cat became nastier.

I always loved cats, I still do, but it was the first time I found myself hating one and the first time I experienced what it is not to have a cat and be the neighbor of people who do.

I tried to hit him with a shoe a few times, but he was always too quick for me, I thought of putting glass shards on the fence or an electric wire or spreading mouse traps around; I thought of catching the cat himself...

As I thought about what I would do if I did catch him, I became aware that I harbor a fair bit of anger inside me and then I realized that a lot of the tension and pain in my back and neck could be related to that anger.

In spite of all the mess I got myself into because of it, my interest in the property business never went away. I still believe that it can play an important supportive role in all my other projects. I kept going to other property related events and reading about it.

In March, an opportunity showed up for me to get a reasonable job in property management through a person I had met during the Administration process.

But, going through that whole fiasco had made me re-focus and reset my priorities. I had given up my responsibilities as a member of the committee to work on my book. It had been a while since I gave up hope of a decent job. I had finally set my mind on a purpose and then I got that. Someone who believed in me, a job where I would have some responsibility, a position of trust, something I could even enjoy doing in exchange for a decent salary. I got all confused again and I had to think hard about it and drag myself out of the confusion to finally decide that I was going to do what my heart most wanted.

One day in April I was coming back from yet another property event. I had got the tram in the wrong direction and ended up somewhere in Preston and it really annoyed me. Is a sense of direction genetically determined? Because if it is I must be a mutation. I really haven't got any! I got home after 11 p.m., after spending two hours on a trip that was supposed to last 20 minutes. I wasn't very happy.

In the long trip home, I thought of all the things I had heard on that property event. It was full of wealthy people, who had worked twenty, thirty years of their lives and now had money to invest in property. I didn't have a cent. What had these people gone through to have the money they now have? What had they given up? What do I want to sacrifice?

I decided that more important than to think about what to do with the money we've got is to earn it in the best possible way. I concluded that money cannot make anyone happy, that happiness comes from what we do and from our relations with others, not from what we have.

At some stage, Greg needed to have four sunspots removed. It cost us almost A$ 800 and afterwards, some of them got infected. I gave the doctor an earful. For over ten years, Greg had had sunspots removed in Tenterfield, in a bulk-billed consultation, without them ever becoming infected.

I get so annoyed when politicians on campaign go saying on TV, that the Medicare system here is the best in the world. Have they ever been abroad? I cannot understand why people have to wait for years to get a free dentist consultation. I went to one in Stanthorpe one day that told me to point at the tooth that was aching. I said I wasn't sure. I got home with a filling in the wrong tooth! I don't understand why physiotherapy is not bulk billed. Why are there so many neglected old people? Why do people with mental disorders end up in the streets? It's such a rich country, with such a budget surplus. How much to they spend on political advertising and on armament? It's so sad and so wrong.

When I saw a private dentist and paid A$ 750 to treat one tooth, I remembered how much I earned at the mushroom farm, A$ 200 – A$ 300, before tax, for a whole week of hard work.

He was a great dentist, no doubt about it, but how can people charge so much for an hour and a half of work?

It was only in 2007 that a new Medicare program was introduced that allowed a patient to be referred to a mental health practitioner by his doctor, and have A$ 75 of the consultation reimbursed. Still, with an average of A$ 120 per consultation; many people still can't afford counseling when they need it.

And then you only get twelve consultations a year. Or five for physiotherapy. Everybody knows that for most cases, one needs a lot more than that.

With Easter the boys dropped by to stay overnight with five friends on their way to the Bell's Beach surf championship. I didn't get to talk to them, not even for a moment. The house looked like a backpacker's hostel in high season. I hoped they would stop by on their way back, even if it was only for a cuppa and a little chat. I even had chocolate eggs in the fridge for them; but they didn't stop, not even to bring back the blankets they had taken. I wanted so much to help Raoni reframe his dissatisfaction with his job and to know how Tayna was doing in his search for jobs.

Trying to reach Tayna in Sydney was so frustrating. When I called him, he always had some excuse for why he couldn't talk to me at that moment. E-mails were never answered.

Tayna kept jumping from one menial job to another and I worried. He had been in Australia for almost a year and didn't stay in any job for more than a month. He seemed to be struggling so much and he still had another two years to go with his study. Often he would get terribly depressed. I suggested many times that he see a counselor or the career counselor at school, but the answer was always the same, "They don't know anything".

Again, I had to ask myself if I had done the right thing by bringing them over. Their slaving in stinking cafés or scrubbing decks and floors, I really wondered. Greg said it would do him no harm. I wasn't sure.

Just hope that some good would come out of it all, was not very helpful, but it was all I could do.

I needed to see Tayna moving in some direction. I felt that I had to say something, bring him to his senses, telling him that time was passing by, that he shouldn't be depending on us so much anymore. More than being independent, he needed to find a direction in his life, to know where he wanted to go, but I never knew what to say, how to say it or even if I should say anything at all. I often told him what to do, while so many times, I myself wasn't sure about what to do with my own life.

I pushed him, but at the same time I asked myself if I wasn't being too hard and no matter what I said, he always got upset and threatened to go back to Brazil. The situation between us was always tense.

Now and then I would lose it; I would threaten him, only to tell myself afterwards that I was trying to change him, saying the things I promised myself I wouldn't say. Then I would get depressed and at a loss, not knowing how to help them. In one of those days, I wrote in my journal:

"When is this agony going to end? Is all this pain and frustration necessary? I try so hard to teach them something, but they are the ones teaching me. Will I ever be able to communicate and connect with my sons? Every time I try, I feel there's a wall there and every time I try to break it, I hurt myself or I hurt them, time and again. Come to think about it, I feel that wall with a lot of other people as well. Maybe the wall's around me."

I felt selfish and guilty when I thought of better ways to use the money we were spending on Tayna. Greg would often tell me

Tayna needed to get real, but it didn't really make me feel better. At some stage, Tayna decided to try construction work. I found that so unsound; he had to wake up at 5 a.m. Why didn't he look for something in his study area?

Raoni was easier! I sent him an e-mail telling him how proud I was about the way he was dealing with all the seemingly useless little jobs and holding tight. I told him this would all be to his benefit. One day he would understand.
"I love you very much too mum!!!
The way I was brought up allowed me to do whatever I wanted (most times) and I always had your support and comprehension. Some times more support and other times more comprehension but you are always by my side, caring and wishing me all the best this world can offer. That helps me a lot and makes all the difference through difficult experiences. Knowing that I have a loving mum makes me feel very special. I miss being closer to you, mum. Being closer to our family, granny, grandpa, the cousins, uncles, aunties... our family may have many problems (like any other family) but I still thank God for the family He gave me.
Love you Mum!!!
Raoni."

As soon as my leg and back got a bit better, my exercise sessions at home became further apart. I was still going to hydrotherapy, once a week, but I knew that wasn't enough. So, in May, I finally got myself together to become a member of the pool and to my surprise, I really enjoyed it. The water was nice and warm. It's amazing how we just put beliefs in our minds and then live according to them and limit ourselves. I have always believed I didn't like swimming. I had never seen myself swimming on a regular basis.
Seizing the moment, I bought more Pilates equipment. With new books and videos, I designed myself a new exercise program and I have kept to that for over a year. Now and then, I would understand a little something more about how the muscles worked, about centralizing and balance.
Swimming at night also helped me establish a better eating routine. I stopped having dinner (cannot swim with a full stomach) and that solved my long lasting problem of taste incompatibility with Greg. I could eat what I liked at lunch time and cook Greg's favorite food in the night. Perfect!

June arrived and with it, my birthday. It was a dark, windy and rainy day, the sky was grey and that was how I felt, immersed in the somber thought of another year gone by without achieving any of the things I wanted. The thought that I had wasted so much of my life trying to get out of the mess I repeatedly got myself into: my previous marriages, my businesses attempts and even education in Holland and here, had transformed into a huge problem. I remembered all those I've hurt in the process. I compared myself with others and decided that my life had been senseless, mediocre and insignificant; I cried most of the day.

I was getting more and more worried about Tayna. He was always stressed out and unhappy. I looked for a psychologist in his neighborhood, around where he lived. Although the money was short, I started to think Tayna really needed some help to cope with reality and to learn to take his life in his own hands. He wasn't interested, but he did followed his girlfriend's advice and saw the school counselor. Apparently, the counselor thought there was nothing wrong with him. "Good gracious, what does it take for a counselor in this country to realize someone needs some help? How messed up does one have to be?"

Now and then, he would come up with the sweetest of things, out of the blue. Like the call he made one day, just to say hello, saying he had to call me because he had remembered my taking care of him as a baby and what a good mum I was. But, that was the exception.

One day, he called to tell me that life was too hard, he was working so much and the work was so stupid, so unrewarding. He was so tired. There was never time for some fun and yet, in spite of all the effort, he never had a cent. I asked him what he was willing to do to change the situation. I asked about looking for other jobs, writing letters, networking.

"I don't know how to do that", he said.

"I'll help you. Just write a letter introducing yourself, saying what you are looking for, so you can send it around, see if someone's got work for you that you could do; send it to me, we'll go through it together".

"Yeah, okay, I'll try", but he never did.

Ten minutes after I put the phone down, Raoni called, also quite depressed.

A change from wine to water after the call he gave me a few days before, all excited about a new job possibility in Wollongong.

He and his flat-mates had woken up at 5 a.m. on a weekend to go to a National park to surf, but the trip had been a flop. It rained, the sea was flat, they got lost and he was pissed off that he had spent a fortune on petrol driving around for nothing. Even the new job possibilities weren't looking that good any more. What was he going to do all alone in a dead, small town, two hours from Sydney? He couldn't see meaning in anything he was doing. The weather was too cold. He was being exploited and underpaid. He couldn't see anything in Aussie girls; he said they are only after material things. He felt lonely. He didn't feel he belonged anywhere. Everywhere he went he felt rejected. Life was no fun. Why did everything have to be so freaking hard? He wanted to go back to Brazil, where people are friendlier and life's much more fun. Where he had a sense of belonging and a sweetheart that loved him for what he was.

Somehow, I knew that part of what he missed was living without responsibility, the moments with friends where he could lark about and be silly and everybody would just laugh. Here he was only frowned upon. I asked him if he wanted to play the silly clown forever. He answered with silence.

The way they felt ripped my heart to pieces. These were the hardest moments to be apart from them. I wished so much I could be there with them and hug them.

I knew exactly what he was feeling.

I had gone through that as well. The difference was that I had a loving man who was always by my side; I had many more years of life experience. It was so much harder for them.

Without managing to stop my own tears from falling and my voice from getting chocked all the time, I told him one day he would see the worth of it all. I remembered how desperate I was for some kind of acceptance, a smile, a sign of friendship, at FoE, the mushroom farm, everywhere. Everything felt awkward; every word they said made me feel that I didn't belong there. I told him, I didn't feel like that anymore. I felt stronger. I didn't need to feel accepted anymore. I didn't need anyone to reassure me of my worth. I didn't feel less than anyone else. I didn't have to put up with people I didn't like.

I told him that happiness was not outside ourselves and that the only thing that can make us really happy was not people, but God. I think this was all a bit too philosophical for him and I don't think I really managed to put it in a way that could be more useful to him. What I was trying to say wasn't as clear to me then as it is today. I didn't really feel I helped him that much and I worried so much that he would give up everything and end up getting stuck in Paraty, when he could have the world.

I called a few times, afterwards to make sure they were okay. They had calmed down a little bit, but I knew it wasn't over. I knew it was just a little battle in a war that was far from over. Again, I fell back into a deep conscience search. Did I give them false hopes about Australia (false hopes I myself had?) Did I force things? Should I have given them more time? Was their father right all along? Is Brazil indeed the best place in the world to be?

I got another proof that out of tragedy, something great and good always comes forth. The Property course collapse brought about friendships that are dear to me to this today. One of these friends was Justine, a catholic Vietnamese-Chinese immigrant, who arrived in Australia as a little child with her family on a boat, about thirty years ago. In those days, boat people weren't treated like criminals.

She gave me the book "The purpose driven life". I was a bit disappointed that the author is connected to the Evangelical movement in the US, which I am very suspicious about and I don't know exactly how connected he is, but the truth is that this book helped me clarify many issues in my life. One of them was in regards to writing my book. So often, I got stuck with it. How many times didn't I doubt the whole thing? How many times didn't I think of forgetting about it all? How many times did I asked myself who could possibly interested in what I had to say?

Inspiration to continue came from little writings I stumbled upon, here and there. A poem, a little something about a philosopher, a saint, a writer that would give me renewed motivation. However, I never knew exactly why I was writing it. After reading that book, everything became clear. I'm writing this book because there are people out there going through the same struggles I am. Maybe by reading this, they don't feel so alone, maybe they will gain a new hope. It had become clear to me that I *had* to write it.

That's not to say that I never had doubts about it afterwards or that I never got stuck again, but it never crossed my mind not to write it anymore.

That book also convinced me of the importance of reading the Bible and I decided to wake up earlier to read the Bible every morning. From all the good habits I tried to introduce in my life, this was one of the best, with the furthest reaching consequences.

One day, while I read the Book of Daniel, the memory of my parents and specially my mother came to me, in a very strong way. It was the first time in my life that I had managed to see her beyond her ways, which I have always find so difficult to deal with. All I could think of that morning was how much love she and my father had given me. It was as if Love itself had embraced me for a moment and I felt so much peace, a contentment that made me feel completely satisfied and not wanting anything. I wished that could last forever. I realized how much I have been given when compared to the abuse and neglect that so many children have to endure in this world; I realized how much my parents and especially my mother had done for us. My entire life I hadn't been able to be grateful, nor see beyond the things I didn't like in them. That experience rekindled in me a long forgotten certainty that all we need is already in our hearts.

The insights I gained in all aspects of my life, due to this pursuit of understanding the Bible and the teachings of Jesus, were so many that I would need to write another book to explain them all. It helped me so much to understand my purpose, my destination and myself. This was the very beginning of my acceptance of my life as it was. I never again thought that my life could be better somewhere else.

Apart from that, I didn't make much sense of Daniel at all. I found it quite difficult to digest. So much so, that it took me a few years to gather the courage to open the Old Testament again. I did read the New Testament four times, since and I keep going back there and I also started reading biblical scholars. Since then, many questions I always had about the Bible have become a lot clearer to me.

Yet, nothing drastically changed in my life. It went on with its usual ups and downs. There were peaceful days. Days in which the simple sight of a cute pigeon picking dried, frizzy little stems in the garden for a nest made me happy. Days in which life seemed to run its natural course and I would even enjoy the cooler days and the chill in the air!

And there were days when everything would annoy me, days in which life looked messy, when the smallest of things, a simple phone call could upset me, days in which I felt choked and overwhelmed by all the little problems of life, the difficulties with the boys, my contradictions, my doubts about myself, my messy eating habits, which I finally concluded, would never really go away unless I made some drastic changes to my lifestyle,.

I got angry when I looked into the past and thought that I had got into trouble despite asking for advice and even paid for it in some occasions. Like the accountant I paid when I had the shop in Brazil and ended in debt with the Tax office, because he didn't explain to me the right procedures to follow. There were days I felt heavy, drowsy, not in the mood for anything but to be a couch potato, only to feel guilty afterwards and tell myself I couldn't waste my life away in front of the TV.

Since the crisis I had in the middle of 2003, I had been putting to paper many of my projects. What had been many loose ideas for years, started to take shape in a coherent way. Brainstorming and detailing them became an ongoing process ever since.

From that time I learned that if we have a problem and we haven't found a solution for it in one week, we won't find it a month or in a year, either. We need help. And is it any surprise that exactly those who need the most help are exactly the ones that can't afford it? Since then I had been thinking of creating a counseling group that could offer that help.

I started to dream of little communities spread all over the world, everywhere were there's despair and hopelessness, everywhere where people are struggling in their lives. So many people are falling through the cracks. So many living a lesser life... I so often think about all the people out there, having difficulty fitting and adapting to this system we live in. People with a lot to offer, with an enormous potential to do good for the world, but who, somehow end up just messing everything up and suffering needlessly.

I watch the news and documentaries and think so much about all the mess that is this world: the refugee problem, war, poverty and criminality, pollution, human trafficking, degradation, human rights abuses, corporate corruption and what have you; I feel such a strong need to do something concrete to change the situation and make a difference.

To be a positive force in the world, we need to get together, support each other, and join forces.

In these communities of likeminded people, we could live a life of self-reflection, mindfulness and prayer, dedicated to the causes of peace, reconciliation, fraternity and to the building of meaningful lives.

I have always felt the need to be part of a supporting group, to help me keep focused, a group where people could be really true to one another. Since adolescence I've been struggling with ordinary everyday life, the unbearable small talk, the insignificant things that seem to make up most of people's lives; difficulty ignoring the disguise in people's faces, their reluctance to talk about themselves, about what's in their hearts, their avoidance to look at themselves and their irritation with those who do.

To grow, we need feedback from people we can trust, people who understand what we are trying to do. But, this mad world is tearing people apart from each other. More and more people are becoming alienated in the business of the rat race and when they do have some time for themselves, they don't use it to reconnect with themselves and each other and face their issues, but rather to forget them.

In the swimming pool one day, I started to imagine living in a caravan and travelling around Australia, visiting all the beautiful places and stopping at poor communities, using our creative minds to improve lives. When I got home and told Greg about it the first thing he asked was, "Who's going to finance the project?" I didn't know, but we ended up laughing out loud, as we imagined ourselves in a revisited version of the movie "Easy Rider".

Jokes aside, I still think it's a great thing to do. It seems so senseless to me to live stuck to a place somewhere for a lifetime, going to and from work everyday to pay the bills, when there are so many people out there needing help and so many beautiful places to be visited before they all disappear. I told Greg it wasn't a revisited "Easy Rider" but a revisitation of the life of Paul, the Apostle.

July arrived and with it election time. Although I wasn't allowed to vote, I did pay close attention to the whole process. The Labor party was under severe attack from the US for wanting to withdraw troops from Iraq, but it seemed to me that the opposition's attitude was just to be against for the sake of it, without really giving answers or offering any alternatives.

How long must the madness go on? How long must innocent people suffer because economic considerations are always put before moral and ethical ones?

Politics is such a dirty game, always compromising what should never be compromised, all in the name of power. Good ideas are only used to get one into power. Once they are there, nothing really changes.

I wish politicians stopped fighting so much amongst themselves, the role of an opposition is to come up with real alternatives that don't look pathetic to anyone with an IQ above 70, not to be ambiguous or viciously attack the Government for not doing enough or ask for someone's neck every time the smallest of mistakes is made. How despicable is the way they talk to each other in Parliament, on TV, for the whole world to see. Have they never heard about communication skills?

At least we know where the minor parties stand! Or can they afford to be coherent only because they are small? There are good politicians out there, Carmen Lawrence (Labor), Natasha Stott Despoja (Democrats), Bob Brown (Greens), there are even some decent people in the Liberal and National Party, but they are a minority amongst a sea of indifference and short-sightedness.

Beyond Australia, the situation was even sadder.

Following the US ignorant use of force in Afghanistan and Iraq, violence has increased all over the world, as has the abuse of human rights. Everyone now thinks, "If the US can do it, we can too!"

Now even brutal governments have got a good excuse for torture and abuse: everyone opposing the government these days is a terrorist! How can these men be so blind and tell the world that it has become a safer place? Bush's war has brought violence even to places where it wasn't originally a big problem. His war has made everybody a target today. The world's more dangerous than ever.

If the apocalypse is right, this world is going to end up really badly one day. Deep inside I think I always knew that, but I have always had the feeling that we were heading there in second gear, now it feels we are on fourth gear and in a much more powerful car!

To top everything off, Mumboy, who hadn't completely recovered from Dadboy's loss, had to see her oldest brother, who lives here in Victoria, deteriorate to a critical condition from his prostate cancer. She stayed with us for a week. Her sister also came from Queensland. I drove her around (She even complimented me on my driving). We visited the Botanic Gardens and she loved it. Albert died shortly after she left. The good part of it was that the four brothers and sisters came together for the first time in more than forty years.

Up in Sydney, Raoni finally accepted the job offer in Wollongong. In the interview, he was told he would work as a naval architect, but quite often, he was sent off to work on the production line and do the lowest kind of work in the factory. He was bullied and called wog (which is a derogatory slang for immigrants from the Mediterranean). The manager was a very rude Dutchman who often humiliated him in front of all the other workers. All that for an increase of A$ 2 per hour in his salary. In spite of it all, he believed he could learn something there. His bravery made my heart fill with tenderness and pride. Tayna had been brave too, in his menial jobs, washing and scrubbing pots until the early hours every day and studying full time. He had been hanging in the restaurant for a while and I hadn't sent him any money in months.

A week after Mumboy left, I went to Sydney. Since that phone call in which both the boys were so depressed, I had been worried about them, so I thought showing up with some support would help somehow.

In the morning I was to come back, Tayna was in a terrible mood. The night before, the restaurant where he works was unusually busy. He worked very hard until later than usual. He was upset, that no one let him sleep in. He expected complete silence in a student flat full of people. His back and legs ached. He said he was going to quit work, which upset me a lot. We argued and he locked himself in his bedroom. I could hear him cry and my heart was ripped to pieces. I started to cry as well, yet he wouldn't let me in. We did talk briefly at some stage, but I don't think he listened to one word I said.

I spent a week with them and another one to recover from it. I felt so drained. My whole body felt minced, but worst of all was not knowing if there was any use in all the effort. It didn't help me, it only hurt and I didn't think it helped them. They appreciated the clean clothes, the nice food but, in the end, they want to do their things their own way.

In Melbourne, Greg was already waiting for me at the airport with his sweet hugs.

I had left for Sydney, complaining that I hadn't have the time to tidy up the house, but looking at it after a week in a student flat, I thought it was the most beautiful palace on Earth.

In the world outside, the coalition in power won the elections again. They won the majority of the House of Representatives and the Senate as well. That was dreadful.

This government lied about boat people and threw sick, pregnant women and children in detention camps. They lied about the war with Iraq in exchange for economic gain. These are people for whom there's only one thing in the world that matters: money and there's only one priority: benefit those who make it. Do I have to conclude, from the results of the election, that this is the main concern of the majority of the population as well? Couldn't people see that giving them so much power couldn't do the country any good?

The labor party looked more like a circus than serious opposition, it seemed that there was no alternative, but there was. People could have voted for the Greens or the Democrats. Imagine what the country could have looked like! Imagine what a world without fear could have looked like!

I hadn't yet recovered from Howard's re-election here, when the news of Bush's re-election in the US broke through. It was so depressing. Lies had prevailed over honesty. The belief that a man's morality can be measured by what he says and not by what he does. It was a victory of delusion and denial, of the belief that money is the centre of human's existence. Selfishness and the consumerism that only creates more emptiness in life have won again. It seemed to me that materialism and brutal force were taking over the world. Common sense was defeated by fear and obscure religious misconceptions. Backward ideologies and policies that will turn back the clock of civil rights in the western world by decades, maybe centuries, will be put in place, because no one showed up with alternatives that were believable enough, because people were lost.

Okay, some good people were re-elected or got in and the majority is only a very close majority, but still, I couldn't get rid of a certain sadness that lingered in my mind for days. What is becoming of this world? More war? More injustice? More disrespect for human rights and the environment? More benefits for the rich? Further squeezing of the poor? More prejudice? More madness? Where are we going? And I prayed. More than ever, we needed to commit ourselves to our love for humanity, truth, peace and reconciliation. May God help us all.

By mid October, an e-mail from Tayna said he had been kicked out of the apartment for lack of payment. As usual I panicked, got stressed out and annoyed with it all. Even though Raoni had moved out, he was still the official tenant and had to make the payments. Tayna and the other boys deposited the money into his account every month. That month Raoni forgot to pay. He could have been more considerate, but on the other hand, the others should have made sure the payment was indeed made and remind him if needs be. After all, it was in their interest.

Too late, I realized that instead of getting annoyed with it I should have seen that Tayna had just panicked. Several phone calls clarified the whole issue. Two days later, everything was back to normal.

A month later, he called saying he couldn't pay the bills. As usual, I gave him what he asked. I have always thought he really didn't have the money, but one day, he let escape that he was saving money for a trip to Brazil. I didn't say a word straight away. I didn't want to get upset with him. I really thought about how to manage the situation, about how to say things. I promised myself I wouldn't lose my temper. I called him to talk about it one calm day, but he said so many absurdities that I lost it again. I ended up very upset and said things I should never have said: "You've got no character: your father has got no character; you lie to your own mother and I don't want to be your mother anymore".

A few days later, I was still feeling bad about it. Why does it always end up in an argument between Tayna and me? Why do I always say things I shouldn't?

After our argument, he called his father in tears. The impact of what I said was much harder than I wanted it to be. Oh, man I hate myself so much for being like this. Raoni sent me an e-mail asking me how I could have said that to Tayna. I felt miserable and cried bitterly about it. Praying, in tears, I asked God why I never changed. Why do religious books say that faith changes you? Why didn't it change me? Why did I keep making the same mistakes, over and over? Why, in spite of all the exercises, prayer and meditation couldn't I be the calm, meek, accepting, understanding and smiling person I wanted to be? Why did this angry, impatient and hard person I hate to be, keep showing her ugly head, especially with Tayna? Why do I understand that deep inside us there is wisdom and peace, freely available to tap from, but in reality all I do is get lost in the turbulence of the world around me?

I wrote Tayna a letter of apology for my big mouth, but he didn't want to talk. My son decided to believe I hated him and I didn't have a clue about how I could fix the problem. He blocked all my attempts to talk to him and we didn't speak for a long time.

I decided to go to Wollongong for Christmas, hoping to make things up with Tayna, but it didn't help. We argued again. He looked right through me, as if I wasn't there. Everything I did, everything I said was wrong. I just felt I was another of the numerous problems in Tayna's life. Even though I said I would get him and bring him back to Sydney so we could have a Christmas dinner together in Wollongong, he still thought it was too much of a hassle.

If I needed so much to be together for Christmas, I and Raoni should go to Sydney, instead of him coming down to Wollongong. Okay, he was working, it was a bit tight for him with his work schedule, but I couldn't stay in a messy, smoky student's flat. The kitchen was too small, there was nothing I could decently cook with and to make matters worse, there were cockroaches everywhere. Raoni was living in a big comfortable flat, were I could at least cook us a decent meal. Raoni drove me around to see Wollongong and its surroundings, but on the second day, the car broke down. It was quite expensive to fix it too and we spent the rest of the holiday without a car.

The news of the Tsunami near Indonesia only sank in a few days later when I was in Wallangarra for the New Year. What a terrible tragedy that was! Why did so many innocent people have to die?

Away from my own personal tsunami in Sydney, the peace of Wallangarra with its sunsets and lorikeets, was lovely as always Greg had just bought a very expensive SLR digital camera with several lenses. I still had my old one and we could interchange the lenses. We never stopped making pictures ever since.

I decided to take Buster back with us. Mumboy was having a bit of trouble, alone with the three dogs and I reckoned Greg would be happy with Buster in Melbourne. Trying to convince the real estate agent that we should be allowed to keep a dog had been a difficult process, but I was proud of myself for having managed to convince him without losing my temper.

A House

2005 was a fairly peaceful year, compared to the previous ones. I managed to keep myself out of major trouble.

One day, in March, Greg and I were watching TV on a lazy, warm weekend afternoon when we saw an ad about a builder, selling houses for a price we thought we could afford without much stress. The same day I started to look more into it and soon it became my newest obsession. I didn't do anything else for two months. Everything else became second plan. I wrote very little during this time.

I researched about twenty different builders and about the same number of lenders, I looked for dozens of established houses and blocks of land. I finally found a block of land for a very good price in a new development in Wyndham Vale. It was about 40 km from Greg's work, but we reckoned it was better to live far but in a new house, than to live closer but in a run down house that we wouldn't be able to fix soon. I studied dozens of house plans and we decided to build a small, standard three-bedroom house. A new house closer to downtown would cost us twice as much. Needless to say, dealing with mortgage brokers, lawyers, sales men and builders was a very upsetting and frustrating exercise at times and I worried about that big step as well.

At the end of July, Tol and his girlfriend stayed over for a few days. She had graduated and was moving down to Melbourne for a job she had got at a University. Her parents had moved down a few months earlier when her mum got a job here. Tayna gave her a hand with the moving. We went to the planetarium and the Botanic gardens. I was really surprised when Tayna held my hand there and gave me a smile. But again, my heart was ripped to pieces when we had to leave him at the airport, his eyes filled with tears. I thought it would be so much better for him to come down too, but I didn't insist. He would think I was trying to control his life again. After he left, I thanked his girlfriend and told her I didn't know what I would do without her. She didn't say a word. Our relationship has always been a bit awkward. I never knew what sort of picture Tayna painted of me.

It didn't take Tayna long to realize that it was indeed better for him to stay in Melbourne. He wasn't coping alone in Sydney. Once again, I moved everything around in the house, took furniture to pieces to get it up and down the staircase and then put everything back together again.

Greg installed a wireless system for the computer this time, so we wouldn't have wires all over the house, such an effort, such a chore. My back once again, was absolutely buggered.

At the end of August, he arrived. He had to do his last assignments for school, so he took over my computer. I could only use it when he wasn't there.

He seemed to wait for me to get home from the pool at night before going into the shower, so I often had to wait. He always left the bathroom or the kitchen in a mess. I showed him how simple it was to quickly tidy things up after he was done. He said he would do it, but never did. He left doors and windows wide open while it was freezing outside and the heating was going. He pushed me to the limit every single day, always complaining about the way I organize the house and the food I cook.

"In my girlfriend's house they make great food every day, people don't care so much about keeping everything tidy, they know how to live. You are a couple of old sour people."

Every time I tried to start a conversation, he would tell me he was not interested. "You are too serious. I hate serious people. Why don't you just keep your views to yourself and shut your mouth?" If I said one word, he didn't like, he would slam the door behind him and take off to his girlfriend for a few days. This all upset me so much; it hurt me so much. I needed so much to reach him somehow, make a connection, but it never happened. Wiping the tears off my face, I would tell myself he didn't know any better. I didn't know any better either.

I was absolutely convinced that he was going to finish his course, find out what it was that he really wanted to do with his life and get a better job. He started to talk about being a fire fighter, something that has been a dream of his, since childhood. I promptly encouraged the idea. He got a job at the cafeteria of the Uni where his girlfriend was working. The hours were normal, just as he wanted, no more working until the early hours. He could now, in his own time look for something better. He had saved enough money to buy a car, another one of his dreams. I was still hopeful he would finally, find his way.

But then, suddenly, one day in September, he announced he was going back to Brazil. He wouldn't even wait for the results of the school exams; he wouldn't buy a return ticket. His mind was made and I realized he had made it up before he arrived in Melbourne. Again, I had to see him throw away all the possibilities he had in his hands, knowing he was going to get into trouble in Brazil.

What was he looking for? What did he expect to find there? He never answered me.

Even though he didn't want to hear, I made it clear to him that from the day he left he would be on his own. I would not help him back and I would not help him in Brazil.

I knew it would be too late when he realized what he had left behind here, what he had lost.

"Are you leaving your girlfriend behind?" I asked. "She's done so much for you!"

I understood there was a vague agreement that she would go to Brazil in a few months.

When we finally left him at the airport, she looked so sad... I wished, from the bottom of my heart, that she too, one day, would find her place under the sun with someone who could truly love her and give her what she needs.

I was so sad. I couldn't stop crying.

"Don't waste your tears, my dear", Greg said.

"I have a fountain of tears inside me, that can't be stopped", I replied.

For days, that melancholy lingered in my heart, that longing for the times long gone, the feeling of loss, the longing for a time when we would all be together and happy again.

I feared I wouldn't know what to do nor what to say if he called me again in a crisis or completely lost and in panic. I knew it was just a matter of time.

I had to accept it and hope God, in his wisdom, would, one day, bring everything to a happy ending and I thanked Him for Raoni. At least he was more sensible; he seemed to be settling down.

Eventually, I took a deep breath and thought to myself, "Life must go on", I had a book to finish.

Tayna called me out of bed very early two days after his arrival in Brazil. He needed to tell me that his girlfriend was pregnant and that very day she would be terminating it. He was feeling bad about it.

"How can you people be so irresponsible? How could you leave your pregnant girlfriend behind?"

"She only told me at the airport..." he said.

I don't think I'll ever know the whole story. I called her that day, asking if she wouldn't consider giving the baby for adoption.

"No. It has impacted on my body too much already", she said

Her Mum was with her, giving her all the support she needed. She told me not to get so upset, "These things happen." There was nothing else for me to do but to wish her all the best and cry myself to sleep again that night.

I called a few days later; she seemed okay. That was the last time I heard of her.

Two weeks later Tayna called again, sad and confused; going back to Brazil had been a bad idea, he said.

When the dust and my emotions settled down a little, in this new chapter in my elder son's soap opera, I decided to concentrate 100% on the book but, as soon as I started working on it, I stumbled upon a request on a website I like very much, on communication skills. They were looking for a volunteer Portuguese translator for their workbook. It seemed like a good idea at the time. I never imagined it would keep me busy until almost the end of the year. It was a lot of hard work and, at times, I felt my work wasn't really being recognized. It was a big exercise in humility.

I don't think I would have done it, had I known what it would cost, but when I finally finished it, I thought I had done a good job. I can now only hope that all that effort will be useful to other people, somehow.

Raoni came to spend Christmas with me and Greg went to Wallangarra to spend it with Momboy. I reckoned this way we both could have our sons to ourselves!

I had a few lovely days. It helped me step into 2006 with a smile on my face.

Acceptance

2006 didn't start very well. In the first days of January Tayna's papers from school arrived. He had failed two subjects. When he told me he was going to Brazil, he swore to me he had finished everything and passed all subjects. I was supposedly just waiting for his conclusion certificate. I don't know if he really didn't know he still had to do those subjects or if he was barefacedly lying to me. It upset me so much and more tears rolled.

In my despair, I sent his girlfriend an e-mail in the hope she would help him find out what had gone wrong. She never replied, but I was woken up by a phone call early in the morning two days later. Tayna didn't say hello nor asked how things were going. He was just screaming like an enraged madman. "How dare you contact her? She hates you. She doesn't want to know anything about you. If you contact her again, you'll regret it for the rest of your life!"

Shaking from the shock, I put the phone down without saying a word, while Tayna was still screaming. When I told Greg about it, he said I should have apologized! I said "Never".

I still don't think I have done anything wrong.

I called him a few days later to try and convince him to look into the issue with the school, maybe it was an administration error, maybe he could sort something out with them and still get his diploma. He wasn't interested, not in the least and he never did anything about it.

A few weeks later, I got an e-mail from him. Could I send some money for the ticket for him to come back? His girlfriend would help him out too, he wasn't asking for the whole ticket.

I wanted to scream. Instead, I sent him an e-mail, a few days later.

"Tayna,

Greg and I spoke long and seriously about you.

You don't listen. Not to me, not to your father. What did I tell you before you left?

Twice we paid for your ticket to come here. We paid for your English courses. You abandoned them. We paid half your Advanced Diploma course. You didn't get your diploma and you couldn't care less. We have helped you so much already, Tayna.

Today, I'm convinced I should have left you in Brazil in 2003.

I'm so tired of this, Tayna. You are twenty-six. Take care of your life yourself. You can do it. You've got many talents. Use them.

I'm doing this for your own good. I don't think it's going to do you any good if we give you this money now. I'm doing this because I want to see you become a man and not this immature and irresponsible person you are now.

You made your decision, now assume the consequences.

I love you and I wish you well. If you can't understand this today, one day you will.

Love you

Mam"

He didn't get upset. He didn't answer. He would have to sort his life out and we had our life to take care of.

The last few weeks of the house building were incredibly stressful. I was called to inspect the house for the last time, before hand over. There was a problem with the way they had layered the brick on the side and rear of the house. I told them I wanted the bricks replaced. They didn't expect me to complain about it. I had to get quite upset and call in an independent building inspector for them to agree to replace them. When they finally agreed to do it and gave me a date to finish it, I gave notice to the real estate agent that we would be leaving the house.

After ten days I got a call from the building supervisor telling me the problem was fixed and when I went there to see it, it was worse than before and this time he wouldn't accept any complaints. To fix the problem on the side of the house, they used a very similar brick, but not the same one as the rest of the house. I had to take it or leave it. I went berserk. I told him I would go to the head office and wouldn't leave until everything was as I wanted it. He called in the general manager who was almost 2 meters tall and probably about a 150 kg. A real bully, who did his best to intimidate me, but I was so furious that it didn't work.

With a week left for us to get out of the house, they finally brought it to the standard specified by regulation, or so we thought. It took us months to find out that they had actually, rendered and painted the bricks individually to make them look like the rest of the house, instead of changing them. They did a good job, because we didn't notice it, but still they cheated, the bastards! Then they got some young, inexperienced workers to put in the dishwasher and they wrecked the cabinet under the sink. It would have to turn into a court case for them to fix that the way I wanted it to be fixed, so I let them fix it the way they wanted to do it, which was basically just to cover up the damage with some sticky stuff. To this day, every time I think of it I get pissed off.

I will never trust a builder, again! And that was one of the biggest builders in Australia! Some people told me it can get a lot worse than that.

We will not live in this house forever; one day we will build our definitive home and when that happens, I will take things in my own hands, even if it takes a lot of my time. I will be at the building site every single day and make sure they do their job properly.

As we prepared to move, I found out that there were still many things I needed to sort out. Electricity, gas and telephone had always been something that showed up miraculously by making a simple phone call. Getting these things to your own house was much more complicated. Many people had to come and go; many wires had to go through pipes, before we could move in, but in the end, we managed to get out of the house one day before the deadline.

I felt a bit sad, while cleaning the house for the last time. We both liked that house in Brunswick so much. We had spent many good moments there. Another phase of our lives had finished.

We moved to our new house by mid February. Again, Greg couldn't get his broadband. We had to wait for more than two months, for Telstra to upgrade the infrastructure so that it could handle the amount of data Greg wanted to work with.

We spent a month working really hard, trying to get all the basics in the house. Lay the lawn, put curtains at the windows and a fence around the front yard to keep Buster in. For some reason, he was freaking out in the new house and had run away twice, making me spend hours looking around for him in the neighborhood.

I cleaned up all the building debris from the land around the house and started to lay the top soil for the lawn myself. I had worked incredibly hard for ten days under a scorching sun, when I realized I wouldn't get out of it alive. My whole body felt minced and the mountain of top soil in front of the house didn't seem to have lowered a bit. We had to call in a guy with a bobcat to help us, but he too gave up when it came to putting the 35 m² of lawn down.

So we did it ourselves and spent a week recovering from it.

By the time it was safe to walk on the lawn, the nights had

already started to get cooler. We would have to wait for next summer to spend sometime outside at night, looking at the stars. It was only when Raoni arrived to spend Easter with us that I unpacked the last boxes that were still scattered around the house and everything finally landed in its right place. It all took so much longer than I had expected even though some said we got ourselves sorted out pretty quick. Only after all the work was done, did it sink into me that Greg and I had taken another huge step and moved to a next stage in our life together, we had settled into each other a lot further.

I thought of the enormous respect I have for him, his love for me, the tenderness and the passion that fills our relationship, our long conversations and I decided that we had done the right thing. I am reassured of that every sunny day, especially in the cooler days of the year, when we sit out in the backyard to have breakfast or a drink, lazy, talking about life, throwing time away, looking at the grass we've planted together and remembering all the hard work. In those moments, I smile and think to myself that it had all been worth it.

At the end of March Tayna called in a crisis like never before. That was the month his girlfriend was supposed to have gone to Brazil to meet him. They would come back together. She would lend him the ticket money, but instead, she just called him one day, telling him it was all over.

Tayna lost not only a girlfriend: he had lost his future. I don't know what the exact reason was: did she found out Tayna was seeing another girl in Brazil or did she just woke up to the fact that she had a boyfriend who was going to depend on her?

Anyway, whatever the truth was, Tayna was feeling real pain and holding back my own tears, my heart torn apart, I tried to say the right things to calm him down. I had to put the phone down, without really knowing if he would be all right.

Not too long after that, it was his father's turn to call, he too, in panic, at a dead-end with Tayna.

There we go again; life just seems to go round in circles...

He wanted us to sort something out for Tayna to get back here.

He would help pay for his ticket this time, he had serious worries of what would happen to Tayna if he stayed. They had had a serious argument and Tayna left the house.

He stayed with a friend for a couple of days and then moved in with the girl he had been seeing.

That girl, he explained, was a well-known troublemaker and

druggy in town. He had tried to convince Tayna to stop that relationship many times but it always ended in arguments.

Things escalated out of control when he tried again, to talk to Tayna about the girl he was seeing. That was a few days after he had called me. He wasn't aware of how depressed Tayna was or of his plans and that it had all gone down the drain.

He had also heard rumors her family was planning to build a house for them on *my* block of land. "Are you aware of that?" Thank goodness, he reassured me he would make sure it didn't happen.

I told him I would not spend another dime with Tayna, unless he could really prove to me that he knew what he was doing and he never did.

When I put the phone down he had calmed down and he would let things cool down for a while.

If I was in Paraty, I would probably try to help that girl Tayna was seeing, but at such a distance, I could only think of the worst: Tayna getting into drugs; she getting pregnant; it could all end up really badly for everybody. It was such a frustrating situation. I worried and anguished.

It was in my long conversations with Greg about Tayna, that the meaning of "suffering with our children" slowly started to make sense to me. When I read "The Road Less Travelled" quite a while ago, I learned that parents must suffer with their children, so that they can accept that pain is okay. I understood that we need to learn to accept pain and we need to teach our kids to do the same, because life's not always fun and easy.

Pain is unavoidable and we grow through pain. But it was only at that time, many years from when I first read it, that I fully understood the deeper meaning of it.

I realized that a lot of my anguish in relation to my sons in all my parenting years had to do with my own inability to accept pain. I understood that the need to control is the fear to feel pain. This is why I needed to always do everything I could to avoid their suffering, spending so much time planning everything in advance, only to get upset in the end because everything always went wrong anyway. How many times had I said that seeing my kids get hurt, hurt me a lot more than it did them? I couldn't let them get hurt, because *I* didn't want to get hurt.

Once I understood and accepted that Tayna needed to go through his pain and I with him, much of the anguish and all the guilt I felt about him slowly disappeared.

This is not to say that anguish and guilt don't come back now and then, but I finally managed to let Tayna go. I always knew I had to. Everybody always told me I had to, but I never managed to.

I had to let Tayna do whatever he has to do to learn whatever he has to learn. My role is just to be here when he falls, to calm him down, to console him or just to cry with him.

Like a miracle, after a month or so, all the things that were worrying me to death about him all disappeared.

One day I got an e-mail from him, telling me he had broken up with that girl and was living with his father again. Their relationship has steadily improved ever since.

Today I understand that without pain, growing as a human being is not possible. To accept pain is one of the most important things we need to learn in life. To accept pain is to accept our limitations, accept the challenge to change what needs to be changed, accept our responsibility in the mistakes we make.

It can be very hard to accept that we often allow things to go wrong in our lives or accept the truth about ourselves and the world around us. Finally, we need to accept that there will always be people that cannot love us nor understand us, people who can't accept us for what we are.

I know for sure that the most wonderful people in this world are the ones who have embraced pain most bravely. Only through pain, can we dive into the essence of our humanity and become who we truly are. Pain is what makes us rich as human beings and quite often, also literally.

In Easter, which is also my father's birthday, the family in Brazil was, as usually, at the farm for the long weekend: Johanna, Ji, Paulo and all the kids. One night they were surprised by three armed robbers. In balaclavas, they held a gun at my father and Ji's heads and pushed them around the house, screaming.

They took off with all they could get, including Ji's company car.

They wanted to take six years old Paula, Paulo's daughter, as a hostage, but my mother told them she would go. She was released a few kilometers from the farm unharmed and Ji's car was found the next day, thanks to the GPS tracking system in it. My father got some bruises, as he had to play the hero and risk being shot or getting someone else badly hurt by refusing to obey the robbers, who in turn punched and kicked him.

One of the robbers was found months later. They were stupid enough to take off their balaclavas at some stage.

They had been very lucky, because the burglars were clearly inexperienced, but I was not the only one who was sure that they would come back one day and probably with more experience and more violence. So everybody decided that the oldies had to move out of there and they started to build a new house in a nearby secured condominium.

The World Soccer Cup came and went again, leaving behind only disappointment. The hopes and dreams of entire nations destroyed by the short-sightedness of a few umpires. Why don't soccer officials introduce cameras and replay the dubious moves, like they have done with Rugby for quite some time and recently also with Tennis? It would avoid so much injustice!
What was supposed to be a show of technical strength and passion had been transformed into a show of deceit. Again, the usual talks of match fixing and corruption that we will never know for sure. It was so disappointing. How vain and stupid human pride is. What is the pride in winning at all costs? Who's really winning something this way? I think we all lose. What a difference from the last world cup. Different too, was the fact that Greg sat by my side watching many of the games. Australia had finally made it into the World Soccer Cup!

Raoni finally had enough of Wollongong and moved back to Sydney to work for a renowned naval architecture office there. People were very friendly, they respected him and the salary was higher. He had lost his former car on a crash and didn't have insurance or the money to fix it, so he had been using his bike to move around for over 6 months. He could now afford to buy another car. His life could really start for him, but alas, he decided he had enough.
He reckoned he had done a lot and stayed long enough.
Loneliness was still a constant presence in his life and a constant worry for me. He has never really adapted to the culture here, never really felt at home. It fills my heart with so much tenderness, love and pride for him, people may think what they want, for me he's a winner. As he said, he just wanted to prove to himself he could do it and he did.

So, by the end of August, he was back in Brazil. They are both gone and I found comfort in the thought that they are both back home, amongst everything that's familiar and comforting to them. I called him a few weeks after he arrived in Brazil and I asked him for his impressions there.
"Good..." he said.

"c'mon... say something..." I begged.

"Okay. I'm feeling quite comfortable in the mess and the chaos that is this country!"

I smiled. He's fine!

He had good prospects for work in Brazil. On his last trip to Brazil at the beginning of the year, he had met a new girl and he was glad to be back with her. I knew he was going to sort himself out, one way or another. He always did and always will.

Tayna had also settled down. He had got the job he always wanted. A tour guide in the biggest tourist agency in Paraty, driving tourists across rugged forest tracks in a Land Rover. Yet, he still complained and felt bored now and then. He had finally decided to face his demons and started going to a counselor on a regular basis, which was helpful for a while, but in Paraty, you can't get too deep into anything. I know that he too, will, one day find out how blessed, how beautiful and what a wonderful human being he is. My biggest joy was to hear from him that he was going to Church. A lot in our conversations these days is about the Bible and it's only in these conversations that I feel he's really listening.

I still don't feel a connection as strong as I would like it to be. I don't feel like they are where they are supposed to be, which is the same as saying that there are still things I need to learn and accept as a parent. I had finally, found peace in myself in the acceptance of their decisions and in the understanding that they have to do what they believe they have to do. They are big boys now. Who knows what the future holds? They may both come back one day. This story ain't finished, yet!

The relationship between their father and me has also improved. The problems with Tayna made him do some soul-searching of his own. For the first time ever, in a phone conversation at the end of August he admitted his share of responsibility in the problems with Tayna. For the first time ever, it wasn't all my fault alone and he too had gone a few times to the counselor.

As October came to an end and I prepared for my long awaited trip to Brazil, I looked at my life at that point in time. It was with a sense of relief that I saw that some long-standing issues had finally been resolved.

I had paid the last installment of my debt in Holland. If from then on I made sure I sent in the forms every year and kept them aware of my whereabouts, I should get into no more trouble.

Another issue was the Church marriage annulment. It finally

came through, after four and a half years. It cost me so much time and money that, like the immigration papers, it really didn't matter anymore and I don't think the effort was worth it.

When I decided to start the whole thing I had my reconciliation with the Church in mind, but I have more doubts about the Church today than I had before I started all this.

They have granted me the annulment on the basis that I didn't have the maturity nor the clarity of mind to make such a big decision at the time I got married; they made me do the MMPI and the Rorschach test but, I read somewhere they are not reliable methods to judge one's psychological state. They wanted to find out what I might have been when I married. During the tests, I made lots of comparisons between today and then, but still, how they were able to deduct from my state of mind today, what it might have been almost thirty years ago is beyond me. The lady who did the tests was very old, over eighty I guess, or very close to that. When I asked her if she found something wrong with me. She answered that she was not a psychologist: "If there was something wrong with you, someone would have found that out!" I got confused. Was that not the reason why I was doing those tests? To find out if there was something wrong?

They didn't even bother talking to the boys' father. They could have summoned him, but that is not the way they do things, I was told. A letter inviting him for a talk, which he completely ignored, as usually, is all they do. I really expected them to get into the nitty gritty of the marriage and make a thorough evaluation of it. This verdict kind of made me feel the marriage failure was my fault. I'm sure the fault wasn't only mine; it would have been great to hear an acknowledgement of that.

Yet, receiving the final sentence from the Church would not be the end of it. The process still had to go to an Appeals Tribunal for review. Without the review, the sentence had no value and I was expected to pay another A\$ 700 for that review. Nobody had ever told me there would be more expenses down the track. I didn't understand why a case had to go to an Appeals tribunal when none of the parties required it. The final sentence by the Appeals Tribunal had been given and the process closed, but I would only get to see the final papers after I paid.

I had to go through months of negotiations again, involve local Parishes and the Tribunal here to settle on another agreed discount and send money over. As this book comes to an end, I am still to see the papers!

I got very excited with the idea of meeting the whole family again in Brazil. Everybody would be together for the 50th anniversary of the oldies. Ursula was coming from Mexico, Georgy and her partner Jet, came from Holland and Ilona would be there too. Greg was supposed to go too, but he had to stay for his work, to the disappointment of everybody in Brazil. I expected it to be an unforgettable event in our lives.

My mother still didn't have her computer and she still mentioned now and then that she would love to get in contact with her sons and daughters more often, via e-mail, so I thought of giving her a computer. I paid excess luggage and made a superhuman effort to take a desktop computer with me to Brazil. I got her a webcam, special headphones, a microphone, the whole paraphernalia. In Brazil, I bought her a very good monitor and my brothers bought her a multi-functional printer. I spent hours with her teaching her how to use everything, I wrote manuals in Dutch and Portuguese, put little reminder notes on the wall next to the computer but it was all in vain. She just couldn't get herself to learn. She would get exasperated and even cry in frustration, notwithstanding the fact that she had have computer classes before.

When I left, I arranged for a young guy to come once a week to continue tutoring her. She did it for a few months, but when he couldn't come any more; she stopped trying the new things and just stuck to the e-mails. Yet, I get fewer e-mails from her than I used to get snail mail. My brother Paulo asked if he could have the webcam a few months after I left and I wonder how long it will take until everything else disappears.

As it often happens, it turned out I had too many expectations. I thought almost seven years apart would have made everyone in the family keen to be that much closer, to go beyond the pettiness of everyday life. I had hoped for a deeper and stronger connection, but, absolutely nothing had changed. Exactly like seven years before, everyone was still living in their own little worlds, with little interest in what goes on outside it. The same arguments, the same senseless rivalries, the same gossip, the same small talk and the same stories, told so many times before. All everybody cared about, was the new house.

I had hoped we would be able to talk about some issues I thought we needed to address as a family. I thought that would be *the* time to do it. When would the whole family be together again?

But I had forgotten that in my family, like it has always been, coming together is not meant for anything deep. Let's just be together, drink, eat and smile for the cameras!

It reminded me that, like so many other things in life, family is something we can't change.

I did manage to sort out many other pending issues, though. Issues I had left behind when I came here in 2000. I went through all my stuff, gave a lot away and brought some home. The most valuable things are safe and sound and everything else has been repacked.

I got the surprising news that the problem I thought I had with the taxman in Brazil wasn't as nearly as big as I thought it was. A few small fines paid and everything was clean and clear.

I put in order all the land papers from both the block and the farm and I finally closed some pending issues in regards to the shop I once had in Paraty. It's great to know that every little thing in my life is under control now. It feels so good not to have any unfinished business haunting me in my mind.

It was so good to see the boys and be reassured that they are all right.

Raoni has got a job with a catamaran builder and prospects for the future are good. Tayna has started and abandoned another University course, Pedagogy, this time, to teach children. I always told him that together with sports, I thought working with children was his true calling. He seems to be much more at peace with himself, but he still has a long way to go and I think he knows it.

Conversations with his father have resulted in him giving Tayna a little piece of land where he started to build a tiny house where he could finally live on his own. He's also buying a motorbike on installments.

I came back home with the certainty that the boys are, in their own ways, going in the direction they are supposed to. They will get there, they are able to cross the dire straits and survive it.

I gained a renewed appreciation for my house in Melbourne, my space, my life and my dear husband.

Moving to the new house at the beginning of the year had messed up the good balance I had achieved with the swimming and the eating; so, 2006 was again a year of struggles with my poor eating habits. To this day, short periods excepted and especially after spending two months in Brazil, which threw my normal routine out of the window for good, I still haven't found a truly satisfactory new balance between food, work and exercise. I often watched too much TV and I didn't tidy up the house as much as I'd like to, but I did manage to stop my chocolate and cookies binges. I finally understood that cravings are symptoms of a metabolism that it's out of whack. The only way to get it in balance again is by eating proper food, square meals at regular times. Giving into cravings is like having a cigarette when we are trying to treat a lung disease. But, having square meals at regular times is a complicated issue. It requires us to spend hours in the kitchen everyday and that's why, starting a slow-food, organic restaurant is one of my plans for the future.

As I finished yet another year and another chapter in my story, I saw the situation in Iraq getting totally out of control, the situation getting worse in Afghanistan by the day, more bills pass through eroding civil liberties and human rights and getting upset at the stupidity, hypocrisy and lack of creativity of our governments.

I saw North Korea testing nuclear bombs and Iran going that way and I think this is all because they are scared of the US and don't want to see happen to them what happened to Iraq.

I heard the debate on stem cell research heating up again. Some think scientists are going against God's will when they want to research the possibility of easing the suffering of millions of people with terrible degenerative diseases. Do they think God would blow a soul into a bunch of cells produced, without sexual intercourse, with the sole intention to ease the suffering of human beings? Do they really think God is that stupid? Are they not the ones, who scream out loud that there's an intelligent design behind creation? They sound so much like the Pharisees who criticized Jesus for curing people on a Saturday.

To commemorate the 5th anniversary of Guantanamo Bay, the "Getup" people (a progressive political lobby group) asked us to write an e-mail to the politicians to apply pressure to release David Hicks, an Australian caught with the Taliban in Afghanistan.

I wrote, "It has taken humanity so long to put in place basic agreements on how we should treat each other in case we think someone has done wrong.

The greatest satisfaction we can give terrorists is to go back to the barbaric times in the past and start treating our suspects like terrorists treat theirs, without any respect for law and due procedures, without any respect for life itself.

Terrorists could never have dreamt of a better result. Their enemies have become like them and they didn't even have to take the West over by force!

It's obvious that our politicians think economic benefits are more important than life itself, but we don't have to accept that. It's obvious that we alone will have to restore respect for life and law. If not for the world, at least for ourselves. It may not bother you, because David Hicks is not your son, father, brother, husband, in-law, not even an acquaintance, but when we allow people to be thrown into solitary confinement for five years without proof of guilt, if we don't fight this, we, or a loved one may be next."

But, in spite of the world, I looked forward to 2007. That would be the year I would finish and publish my book and start turning some of my dreams into reality.

Looking forward

I did finish the book before the end of 2006, but sending it out to the printers didn't happen as near as soon as I expected. There were so many details to take care of, time just kept running away from me and I am too unfit to catch up with it.

2007 just slipped away frighteningly fast and of it, I will only mention three events.

The first one is that in November the labor Party won the elections by a landslide. John Howard lost not only his job as prime minister, he also lost his seat. This was also the first time I voted in this country! I wish I could say that the Australian population said no to the inhumane treatment of refugees, no to the arrogance in relation to aboriginal issues, no to the war in Iraq, no to the denial of the world environmental crisis, but I can't. These issues were all present in the last election and not enough people cared. What they said no to, was the squeezing of the working class. After 11 years in government the conservatives became so arrogant that they thought they would get away with scrapping employment rights that workers had fought so hard and so long for.

One way or another, there's an atmosphere of hope and renewal in the air. Let's see if promises will be kept. Let's see if this country becomes the more humane place we all want…

The second one relates to Piveti, our maid for over forty years. She died shortly after I left Brazil, in the beginning of the year. No one in my family thought it was necessary to tell me. When I sent her a birthday card in April 2007, my mother sent it back saying that she didn't need it anymore. I cried all day, that day. I loved her so much; she was like a mother to me. I can't wait for the day I'll see her again, somewhere, somehow. It was shocking to hear that no one in my family went to the funeral.

The last one relates to my decision to confront my family about some issues that had been bothering me for many years.

If I had thrown a dirty bomb amongst them, the consequences would probably have been less disastrous. Even the shrink I visited a few times afterwards told me I was being a cat amongst pigeons!

The honest conversation I expected as a result never happened and the hatred I got thrown back at me, for disturbing the good order of their lives was very hard to bear.order of their lives was very hard to bear.

My father did have a talk with both my brothers, something they appreciated very much, but they couldn't get bothered talking to any of their daughters, not that my sisters gave a damn, anyway.

I like to dream of a day in which we would look into each other's eyes and hold each other's hands as people that truly care about and love each other, but deep inside I don't think it will ever happen and I will have to struggle with this for a while. The echoes of my father's cold, enraged words still keep coming back to my mind.

I don't know what I could do to feel like I'm part of this family; I guess I would have to stop being me, be someone else.

They hurt me without noticing and I have been biting back all my life, but I grew old and tired of the vicious circle and the smiles for the cameras, tired of pretending that everything is fine and denying so many issues that need to be addressed. From a very young age, I have always had the feeling I didn't belong there. This episode just gave me the certainty that I never really did and never will.

I gained a new appreciation for being so far away. Loving them and accepting them for what they are, is a lot easier when I am on the other side of the planet. I think it's best for me to let them pigeon around, if that's what they want.

From this distance, without their slapping my face all the time (and I theirs), I can, at least, remember times long gone; a time I believe there once was love and innocence. Only then can I think of all of them with love and tenderness.

It reminded me too, that there cannot be lasting peace in this life. There will always be an issue, a problem we need to dig ourselves through. I think that's what life is all about: a succession of challenges that we do best by accepting, because it's by overcoming them that we grow.

I know this will not be the last challenge I will have to face. They will keep coming until the day we die. I know there's a lot more that I have to learn about gratitude, acceptance and forgiveness. Many questions still remain unanswered.

This story, like life itself, doesn't finish here, it will continue for as long as I live. This is not...

The End

Part II

Making sense of it all

As I observed and reflected on the events as they unfolded in these seven years, I did slowly and with many ups and downs, gain some insights that helped me make sense of who I am and why I do the things I do.
In the next pages I try to, briefly, share those insights with you. They have helped me find a new direction and see things from a different, positive perspective. I hope it helps you, too.

Cracked pots

A long time ago, in China (or was it India?)
there was a water bearer.
He had two large clay pots, each hung on the ends of a bamboo
pole, which he carried across his shoulders.
One of the pots had a crack in it, while the other pot was perfect
and always delivered a full portion of water.

At the end of the long walk from the stream to the house, the
cracked pot always arrived only half full.
This went on daily, for many years.
The perfect pot was proud of its accomplishments, perfect for
which it was made.

But the cracked pot felt miserable that it was able to accomplish
only half of what it had been made to do.
After many years of what it perceived to be a bitter failure, it
spoke to the water bearer one day: "I am ashamed of myself,
because this crack in my side causes water to leak all the way
back to the house."

The bearer said to the pot, "When we go get water tomorrow I
want you to observe the track."
The next day, when he returned home, he asked the cracked pot,
"Did you notice, in the way back, that there were flowers only
on your side of the path?

Every day while we walk back, you water them.
I knew about your imperfection before I bought you. Matter of
fact, I bought you because of your imperfection. I planted
flowers on your side of the path and without you being just the
way you are, I would not have these beautiful flowers in the
house". (Author unknown

Okay, no matter how imperfect and limited we are, we will always be part of a beautiful plan, devised by someone who knows what he's doing, even if we are not aware of it. Good to know that, but before we start wondering about that plan, I want first to understand *why* we feel this way. Why can't we see that we are a part in something beautiful? How do we become cracked pots?

A cracked pot is a damaged pot.
But, even though the crack may be visible, the real problem here is not the crack itself, a visible damage or a physical defect, but how we feel about it. The way we deal with physical limitations or imperfections is also dependent on how we see ourselves from the inside. There's nothing we can do about the physical imperfections or limitations we are born with. We don't get to choose on that, in the same way we can't chose the family we are born into. More than a physical, visible "defect", what I want to talk about here is an emotional damage.
Although this kind of damage is harder to get a grasp on, because it's mysterious and often hidden, there's a very good side to it.
Unlike physical "defects", which can rarely be reverted, emotional damage can and a good start in that direction is understanding how exactly we become emotionally damaged.

I think there's little doubt these days, that the most important single influence in determining what we will become, comes from the people responsible for our upbringing.
It's in the first twelve years of our life that the foundation of our existence is laid. The foundation that cannot be changed without destroying everything that has been built on top of it.
What our children, all human beings, will eventually be, what feelings will dominate their existence, the kind of life they will lead results from the sense they make out of all they experience and observe in people around them as they grow up.
Without no one noticing, what children feel and observe as they grow will develop into their mindset, their system of beliefs and values, which will in turn, rule the rest of their lives.
Beliefs about their value and who they are, beliefs about what the world is, what Love and happiness are, their understanding of right and wrong, good and bad. What they believe in, will ultimately become the core of who they are. These are the beliefs that will guide them in all the small and big decisions and choices they will have to make in life and determine how they cope with

the smaller and bigger difficulties and challenges they will face, from dealing with fellow students in grammar school and looking for jobs to dealing with crime and major natural disasters.

It is this foundation, their beliefs and values, which will determine the stability, strength and longevity of whatever they decide to build on it.

Like a clay pot, we get damaged when somewhere in the process of our making something went wrong, when the significant people in our upbringing, parents, carers, teachers, relatives and the odd stranger, didn't do their job properly, didn't handle us with the necessary care or have been negligent or inattentive.

The damage is done either by their actively hindering the development of our potential, by abusing us in subtle or violent ways or by inaction, by not being able to offer the support and understanding needed to make that potential become a reality, by not being there when we need them.

In other words: they either cause the damage directly or they somehow, allow the damage to happen. A great deal of what we are is the result of what they have allowed us to be.

I don't think there's need to mention the obvious ways in which children are damaged: all sorts of abuse, violence, negligence and deprivation. Instead, I want to talk about smaller, subtler and more common ways in which that happens.

This is because the vast majority of parents and carers out there, no matter how inadequate they are, do care about and have good intentions regarding their children. Most parents don't consciously and deliberately hurt their children.

Come to think about it, no one hurts anybody else completely aware of what one's doing.

Parents don't intentionally damage their children. They don't explicitly tell them they don't love them. It doesn't work like that; it's so much subtler. It's unconscious.

We hurt and damage our children because we have been hurt and damaged before and are not aware of it. It's a vicious circle.

Without awareness, it won't and it can't be any other way.

Parents and carers like their parents before them don't know why they do the things they do, they often don't even notice the consequences of what they do and when they do realize they need to change they don't know how.

If we want to stop the vicious circle, if we want to be who we are meant to be and not the result of what others have allowed us to be, understanding who we are and why we do the things we do is fundamental.

Many theories about how the mind works and human behavior try to explain the fundamental question of how we become the people we are, how we feel and act and they can all be useful in helping us understand and make the changes we need to make, but I would like to call the attention to one aspect that I think is often neglected in this whole debate: the issue of our understanding of what Love is.

I use Love with a capital L to distinguish it from all the individual definitions of love. I am assuming that there ought to be a universal definition of what Love is.

We all know it: what children need is love. Sounds so simple...

Children and everybody else for that matter and the reason why so many children go wrong, don't fully develop their potential and spend the rest of their lives feeling like a cracked pot is because most parents don't know what Love is.

What determines whether the significant people in a child's life will damage or foster her, depends largely on their understanding of what Love is.

There are probably, as many definitions of love, as there are people on earth.

Some parents believe love is providing for the physical, material wellbeing and protection of their children. And they all truly believe they are good, loving parents. But, this isn't Love. In the end, what they are worrying about is their children's survival.

This is their duty. A responsibility they have accepted when they brought a child to this world.

I look at the tenderness with which some animals care for their young, especially chimps and gorillas; it really doesn't differ much from the care and love we show our kids. They too will go to great lengths to protect their young. So, either animals are able to feel love for their young or a great deal of what we call love is just survival instinct. You decide.

In our misunderstanding of what love is we worry about our children's earning a living. We want them to get good grades at school; we want them to behave properly.

How much time is spent teaching kids the skills and knowledge needed in their professional lives and how little time in helping them to become whole human beings, able to solve not only the problems in the world around them but especially the ones deep inside themselves?

What's the point in being beautiful or having a perfect body or having diplomas or being so knowledgeable or having so many skills or earning lots of money or being the best, when at the end, we still feel there's something missing and we are still not satisfied?

So many parents kill themselves to give their kids all they believe they need to be happy, but children become spoiled, indifferent or rebellious brats while parents become depressed and stressed out.

Other parents believe good parenting's got to do with hugging and kissing; that happiness has got to do with laughter, with having fun or excitement. They spoil their children, they over feed them, they become permissive; they encourage excitement and fun in their lives more than responsibility and don't support them in the tasks they struggle with or don't like.

Most parents don't know any better, so they keep beating on a dead horse, until their personal worlds eventually collapse. Giving kids material things is often a substitute for the things children really need and which they can't give them: time, patience, guidance, respect, understanding and support.

If parents teach their children that happiness is to be found in material things, children will grow up and continue to look for happiness and satisfaction outside themselves, in the things money can buy. Detached and away from their hearts, they will continue to believe that happiness comes from what we can get from life.

In the long run, if we continue on this path, the whole world will collapse. This entire planet will be destroyed in the mad pursuit of happiness through material things.

When parents have distorted ideas about what Love is, no matter how much they give their children or how much they say they love them, they will still hurt and damage them without noticing; they will end up putting their efforts in the wrong place and neglect the most important...

To truly love our children we need to reach the realm of feelings and thoughts, their hearts and minds, the core of our children's being. Children will feel truly loved when their limitations and difficulties are thoroughly addressed, when they feel they are being guided by people who truly know and understand them, when their qualities and achievements are acknowledged and appropriately rewarded.

If we don't reach their hearts and minds, they won't feel truly loved, they will feel hurt and become damaged, they won't become the persons they are meant to be, they won't develop their full potential, they won't be whole, they won't be able to truly love, no matter how much they have or how much we give them in all the other areas.

It's not education, it's not the best schools, music, dance, martial arts and sports classes, not anything that money can buy that will make them or us happy. Nothing in the world will make them happy if they don't feel connected with the significant people in their lives on a deeper level.

The major role of those responsible for the upbringing of children is not to provide for their survival and physical comfort, but to teach them about Love. And the only way to do that is by truly loving them and all those around them. If children feel truly loved, they will go a long way, even when all else is missing!

Bob Dylan said that the answer is blowing in the wind, but the answer, my friend, is in our hearts!

We cannot truly love our children if we don't feel loved ourselves, if we cannot see Love in our own hearts, we won't be able to see it in theirs. Without knowing what true Love is, we will criticize and judge without showing any alternatives, we will point a finger without giving a helping hand, we will label, we will see people as less than they really are, we will not be able to see their beauty, their qualities and their dignity, we will miss opportunities to pay a compliment, to encourage, to support, to smile, we will yield to our weaknesses, we will deny. We won't be able to listen, nor help, nor understand, nor give some of our time.

We hurt our children every time we are impatient or unkind or jealous or arrogant or rude, every time we demand our own way; every time we get irritated, resentful, unjust, untrue; every time we give up, chose the easy way or lose hope and faith.

And we hurt them when we hurt ourselves.

We hurt ourselves when we don't allow ourselves to be who we are meant to be, when we are trapped into behaviors that don't express who we really are. When we eat the wrong foods, eat too much or too little, we deny ourselves health and the true beauty of our bodies. When we drink or take substances, when we have addictions, we deny ourselves the development of our creativity and potential. When sexual expression does not involve love and respect for another human being we denigrate love, our body and ourselves. When we let fear dictate what we do and don't do, we don't allow ourselves to feel victorious and strong, when we waste time and don't do what we need to do, we deny ourselves the happiness of achievement.

One may say that these things are too small, insignificant and harmless, but I say that they are as damaging as the more obvious and more violent forms of abuse, because of the frequency and persistence with which they occur.

Like soft water that relentlessly, drops on a hard rock will eventually make a hole in it, so do all the little unkindnesses put together that our children see and have to put up with. Every time we do these things we send our children and those around us the wrong message.

Hurting others is the natural consequence of the hurting we do to ourselves. I think of all the hurting that goes on in our homes. We call each other names; tell each other to get lost. It astonishes me how rough, sarcastic, mean, judgmental, indifferent, cold, selfish, nasty or manipulative we can all be at times and many don't even notice it.

But, unlike a real rock, a child is a lot softer and easier to harm.

The hard rock is the core of a child's being, the hole, created by all these messages, an emptiness left in their hearts.

When we hurt ourselves we teach our children and those around us to do the same and in doing so, we contribute to all the mess that's going on in our own little worlds and in the world outside, because the world outside is nothing but the sum of all our little individual worlds.

What we do to each other and the Earth, we do to ourselves.

Every time we hurt our children or anyone else, even if we didn't want to, even if we didn't realize, we hurt ourselves as well, because we are all connected and everything I do to someone else comes back to me somehow; because hurting others is not in our true nature and we cannot be happy unless we are what we are meant to be: loving beings.

What we do to others and ourselves defines what we are.

Every time we hurt others or ourselves, deep inside, without us noticing, we become a little smaller, a little less human, a little further away from happiness, from what we really are, we make the crack a little bigger.

We won't stop hurting others, unless we can see Love inside our own hearts, unless our own heart stops aching.

Children are incredibly patient, they will wait for ten, twelve, even eighteen years, for us to reach their hearts, but eventually, there comes a time when they give up, when they learn the message we have given them over and over, without noticing: we can't love them, we can't understand them, we don't have a clue.

If after so many years, we still haven't been able to truly reach their hearts, understand how they think or how they feel, they will eventually, stop talking and listening to us. Why would they bother? And when they do that, the vicious circle is complete.

They have become like us: damaged, cracked pots, people who can't see Love and are unable to love.

If we don't guide our children while they develop their mindset, their beliefs and values, they will almost certainly develop beliefs and values that will not help them in any way in their lives.

If they can't see Love in us, they won't see It in themselves. They won't feel truly loved and will believe that they are not worthy of being loved. They doubt their value as human beings, they see themselves as less than they really are, they start comparing themselves to others, they become unable to see the beauty around them, inside them, unable to see the beauty that they are a part of, unable to see that they are able of doing great and beautiful things, they look at themselves and all they see is imperfection. All they see is a cracked pot.

They grow up, get into adulthood neither hot nor cold, doing only half of what they could do, disguising and repressing their true feelings and who they really are. They find their little consolations, little remedies, follow social rules, dive and disappear into the mainstream, start relationships, adapt to expectations, settle for less, but the emptiness and the feeling that there's something wrong never disappears.

Unaware that the damage is inside them, they look for defects in their bodies, the only things they and others can see.

They hate their hair or the lack of it, they curl it when it's straight, they straighten it when it's curly; they dye it black when it's blond, they want it light when it's dark. They think they are less because of the way they look, they spend a fortune on beauty products, make-up and plastic surgery, so that they can bear to look at their faces in the mirror or present themselves before others. They spend a fortune on clothes, jewelry and accessories, while the poor in the world are dying from hunger and lack of basic medical care. They hate their own smell, they need perfumes and deodorants. They worry about what people think of them all the time. They even use fake nails, fake hair, fake breasts, fake penises, fake bums, they even fake the color of their skin, they become all fake and then they think they are okay. Anything is better than looking at who they really are, because they have a problem with who they really are.

They feel bad about not having the things they want to have.

They envy those who have them.

The things that worry us the most are the things others see in us.

We are a lot less concerned about who we really are than about the way others see us!

I find it striking that simple, humble, people living outside the big cities, older (wiser) people, nuns, monks and all those living away from the mainstream, don't seem to be so obsessed with the way they look. I think they are a lot more honest and more accepting of themselves.

We go through so much trying to fit into the norms established by others about how we should look or be, but the hurting never stops, because no matter how much we have or what we do to our bodies, our hearts are still empty, they are devoid of Love.

Feeling bad about their accomplishments or the way they look are not the only symptoms of a cracked pot, they are just the tip of the iceberg.

For cracked pots, every little adversity, every little thing that goes wrong, every harsh word is a reinforcement of their unworthiness. The world becomes a hostile place, full with nasty people, ready to hurt them. They become grumpy, selfish and materialistic whiners.

In their dealings with people, they talk about partnerships, mutual advantages and compromise, but they are unable to truly understand others, because they don't understand themselves, yet they expect everybody else to understand them. They become either lazy, full with excuses or workaholics. They know their lives could be better, but they lie to themselves and tell themselves that they are okay: they got their possessions, their TV's, their (junk) food, their grog, their hobbies and distractions or whatever it is that gives them the illusion that their lives are fine and that there's nothing missing.

They feel guilty, filled with thoughts of the things that they should or shouldn't have done. Something's constantly accusing them. They feel anxious, tense, uncomfortable, restless, fearful, panicky and worried.

People who don't have Love in their hearts worry about everything all the time, about money, about things that may go wrong, things that may happen; they fear new situations, the unfamiliar, the unexpected. They become control freaks and develop anxiety disorders. They become either perfectionists or disorganized, chaotic and messy.

They are like headless chickens, that don't know where they are going. They feel pulled in different directions by the contradictory feelings inside them. On the one hand there's the universal desire of the human heart to grow, to fly, to feel free, in charge and powerful and on the other is the fear holding them back. Paralyzing them. And if they make decisions anyway, because they believe they have to, they will always end up making the wrong one. They can't make decisions. How could they? If they don't know why they do the things they do, if they don't know who they are.

If we can't see Love in our hearts, we can't see our strength, our creativity, our ability to sort out and overcome whatever problems come our way. If we knew Love, we wouldn't worry so much.

Cracked pots feel shame, because they doubt their worth as human beings. It's shame that tells us not to seek help when we've got a problem, not to talk about our difficulties with anyone. We feel ashamed of our backgrounds, ashamed of what we have or haven't got, ashamed of our past, our family, ashamed of what goes on in our hearts and minds, ashamed of our limitations. We keep secrets we don't tell anyone. In fact, we become dishonest. For as long as we are ashamed of something in us or related to us, we will be stuck, we will not go forward. The result is that we become estranged from people and eventually, we will become strangers to ourselves. Shame is fear of what others think of us.

Cracked pots are lonely people. They feel disconnected, separated from others. In fact, they are disconnected from themselves. Disconnected from whom they are supposed to be.

Because they feel unloved, they become emotionally needy people, they become emotional beggars. Beggars often accept from people things they shouldn't. Emotional beggars give in to peer-pressure and end up doing something illegal or immoral, something they don't really want to do. If they haven't experienced a true connection with the significant people in their lives, they will look for that connection somewhere else and they will do anything to get it. This is ultimately, what street gangs and destructive relationships are based on. We become needy people when in our upbringing our minds and hearts haven't been touched with Love.

Needy people are forever trying to fit in, to be nice; they feel awkward and anxious amongst people, they can't be clear and direct about what they need, about what they like and dislike. The voice get chocked when they need to speak, they speak too loudly when they need to silence. Communication is difficult.

So much conflict in this world is the result of miscommunication. To be able to communicate properly we need to be able to listen to someone's heart and our own.

"The most important thing in communication is to hear what is not being said." Peter Drucker

Cracked pots become inconvenient; show up uninvited, always in the wrong place, at the wrong time, with the wrong people. Invariably misunderstood, people see in their confusion, signs and intentions that don't exist.

They become cowards. They can't stand up for those in need, not even their own flesh and blood. They do not confront, they rather walk away feeling awkward, resented or angry. They get easily hurt and they will eventually, hurt back.

Bullies, inflexible and arrogant people are also needy people. It's just a different way of dealing with the same underlying problem. Instead of letting others walk over them, they do that first to others, imposing their crooked views and needs upon others by force and threats. Incredibly enough, in this messed up society we live in, these people even end up being politicians, bosses and (pseudo) leaders!

They mistake arrogance and authoritarianism for strength. They make great efforts to look like roaring lions and sure, they can hurt people badly, but inside they're nothing but frightened mice. They truly feel less than others, not more.

Needy people have an inferiority complex.

A humble person may look like a mouse and be despised for that reason, but truly, humble people are lions inside, because they feel no fear for anyone, they are okay with their imperfections, they can be who they really are, they do not disguise nor lie, they have no fear for the opinions of men.

Humble people have an enlightened awareness of their limitations and a clear understanding of what they can become.

Inferiority complex is feeling less in the face of men. Humility is feeling small in the face of Love.

Cracked pots are restless and busy. They can't be still for long, they are never satisfied, always craving for something, always thinking about what to acquire next, always inventing new needs, new tasks, new "haves to".

Their needs for comfort, security and status never stop growing. The more they have the more they want.

They can't stand silence, eternally looking for distractions, for pleasure, for noise and for fun, always in search of something, always looking for something better somewhere else, forever chasing dreams, forever running around and going nowhere.

Restlessness is an awful feeling and parents and carers do a terrible thing when they ignore it when they see it in their children. Restlessness is what gets so many young people in (deep) trouble. It's a clear sign that there's something missing in their lives, that there's a hole in their hearts. A heart devoid of Love is a heart devoid of peace.

People, who feel unloved, become angry people. Anger is frustration, is feeling that we have been badly ripped off. We have been ripped off of the Love our parents and carers were supposed to have taught us about and shown us. Instead, we have been threatened, our needs haven't been met, our value and dignity has been denied, we have been shamed, disrespected, misunderstood, neglected, ridiculed, screamed at, beaten and God knows what else and our anger is proportional. We have not asked to come to life to have to put up with all this!

Anger is a throbbing wound in our hearts that makes us say and do things that hurt other people, makes us hate other people and ourselves.

Anger is everywhere. Look at all the violence and gore that fills our screens nowadays, our streets, our world. They are a reflection of the widespread anger and frustration that fills the hearts and minds of millions of people.

Anger's not a bad feeling in itself and I believe it's one of the most misunderstood things about our nature. In our ignorance and hypocrisy we find anger unacceptable and we teach our children and ourselves to repress it, because we are, oh, so polite and decent! Anger's not dangerous, but repressed, bottled up anger is. It will explode, inwards or outwards.

Depression and stress, the plague of our modern, capitalistic world today are just sophisticated and subtle expressions of anger and hatred that we direct against ourselves because we can't get rid of them in any other way. Instead of repressing our anger, we need to find safe and healthy ways to release it. Arts and sports can play an important role in this regard.

When all cracked pots see in themselves are defects, that's all they will see in others. They become judgmental and easily label people.

Anything in others that's strange to them, something they know nothing about, a different skin color, religion, culture, thoughts or ideologies remind them (unconsciously) of their own defects and strangeness and they fear and deny the people who have this "defects" the same things they have been denied: understanding and compassion.

I think of all kinds of indifference, despise, prejudice, racism, slavery, torture and genocide in the world; these things can only exist because the people who do, defend and are indifferent to these things are full of hatred for themselves. They see cracks and imperfections in themselves that they find hard to live with, they will not put up with the imperfections of others!

The reason why people defend the detention of refugees is because they see them as less and only those who see themselves as less can see others that way.

"If you hate a person, you hate something in him that is part of yourself. What isn't part of ourselves doesn't disturb us".
Hermann Hesse

And all these things are unconscious. Unconsciousness has no logic, it's irrational and unreasonable.

People that defend mandatory detention of entire families in camps that resemble concentration camps, with their razor blade wires and isolation from everything, find it very logical and reasonable to allege concern for disease and criminality. If there was any coherence in their arguments, they would have to quarantine anyone who came from a trip abroad. The only logical explanation for the belief that they are more prone than anyone else to becoming criminals or spreading diseases is a hidden belief that they are less.

Would they want a loved one or a dear friend in there?

No one who knows Love, who feels loved and filled with peace and compassion can hurt anyone or desire to see someone suffer or be indifferent to the suffering of others.

The opposite of Love is not hatred or anger, it's fear.
Look deep into all the symptoms described above and at the bottom of each one of them, you will find fear.
There's so much fear in the world, the constant, desperate and useless search for a feeling of safety that cannot and will never be satisfied. We take insurances, we gather and gather, in case we may need, we kill or let our criminals rot in jail; governments spend much more money in armaments than they do in the care of the vulnerable and attack defenseless countries, all in the name of a deluded sense of safety. The entire capitalistic system strives on fear. Fear and illusion. They always walk hand in hand. Illusion is fear's daughter. The fear of what others think of us, fear of imaginary enemies, the illusion that anything material can make us feel safer and better about ourselves. A mind without Love is a mind filled with fear and illusion.

To feel unloved hurts. It's a wound that may never heal and never stops throbbing.
When children are hurt, they feel an intense pain. The pain can be as intense and traumatic as a life threatening experience for an adult. But, they are not yet able to express in words or gesture, what they are feeling.
Under intense pain or fear, a part of our true being cracks, disconnects from the rest, goes into a latent state, becomes hostage to fear. A part of our true self becomes lost to fear.
Fear is survival instinct. Pain equals to a threat to our survival. In the face of great pain, the part in us that feels threatened withdraws and fear takes over, blocking the natural flow of Love inside our hearts and bad feelings fill the void. The connection with our heart is broken.
I disagree from the mainstream belief that this disconnection from our true self happens only under extreme situations or within the context of serious mental illnesses.
I believe it's far more common than one imagines. It happens all the time in subtle and imperceptible ways: every time we are hurt or hurt someone else.
Cracked pots are people, who have lost the connection with the core of who they are, their hearts. I believe cracked pots are the norm, not the exception and most are not even aware of it!

How much of our true self is lost or damaged will depend of the scope, frequency and intensity of what we experience.

When the natural flow of Love ceases, so does our ability to think clearly and objectively. Reason is replaced by subconscious and irrational beliefs.
We develop false beliefs and irrational truths because we are rational beings, we need to understand the circumstances around us and why we aren't being loved. We do this because our minds were unable or too young to understand the limitations of the significant people in our lives or the complexities of the world.
It's easier to blame ourselves: "I'm not loved because there's something wrong with me", "I must be bad and undeserving", or to blame others: "People are bad, people aren't fair, the world isn't fair".

In time, the original (traumatic) events and experiences that hurt us, the pain, the fear and the resulting false beliefs, all go underground, but they remain active nevertheless, in the form of unconscious impulses that dictate the way we think, our actions and choices.
The natural flow of life, with its challenges and victories, partly stops and is replaced by a succession of vicious circles, wherein bad feelings and subconscious impulses, fuelled by fear, prompt us to make bad decisions and take wrong action.
The resulting negative consequences will in turn reinforce the original bad feelings we have about ourselves and others and the circle is closed.
Bad feelings (a heart not touched by Love) and distorted beliefs (a Mind not touched by Love) need to feed on each other to exist; they depend and need reinforcement from each other.
For instance, a woman who grows up with a violent father and unconsciously harbor's hatred (fear) against him, will marry a violent man, so that her hatred and her irrational belief that all men are violent and bad can go on. She lets him hurt her so that she can tell herself that she is right for hating him and that she's good compared to him. This way, fear, hatred and irrational beliefs win once more.
Or take for instance, children who have been raised by unreliable people. They may develop a distorted and unconscious belief that no one can be trusted in the world. As a consequence, they will trust those they shouldn't, so that they can get in trouble and reinforce the belief that no one can be trusted. They can tell

themselves that they are right for not trusting anyone and because of that they don't need to change.

Guilt is another terrible vicious circle that substitutes action. Think of dieting and procrastination. We keep doing the exact things that make us feel guilty and we can't stop doing them, because deep inside we fear what we may lose when we stop doing those things. We do that because deep inside we believe that we are helping ourselves by doing what we shouldn't and we think we are redeemed by punishing ourselves with guilt.

More than anything else distorted beliefs need to prove to themselves that they are right all the time. This is how they survive. By feeding on each other, distorted beliefs and bad feelings justify themselves.

The reason why we get trapped into these vicious circles is because somehow we grew to believe that the unconscious false beliefs and bad feelings have become a true part of ourselves, unconsciously, we strongly perceive them as being a true part of who we are. To face our irrational beliefs, our bad feelings and the vicious circles they create, is to destroy them, but to destroy them feels like death, feels like destroying ourselves. That's why they are so hard to fight, once established false beliefs will do everything they can to remain existing in the mind. The mind, hostage to fear, will become very creative in finding ways to avoid facing the truth.

Even when someone challenges us about our views or actions, before we face the truth about ourselves, we will find excuses, we will deny, we will blame someone else, we will try to prove that we are right, we will say that the problem is not really as big as it seems!

What fuels the vicious circle is the fear hidden deep inside ourselves, the fear that we, or a significant part of us, will die together with the madness. This is why going against our bad habits is so difficult.

The kick that we get out of our bad habits, out of giving in to the impulses created by these false beliefs and bad feelings, is the illusion that we are doing something for ourselves; because we believe that the feelings and beliefs are ourselves, even if we feel worse or our consciousness accuses us short after.

If unchallenged bad feelings and irrational beliefs will continue to make us behave in erratic ways, do stupid and unhealthy things, develop dysfunctional and self-defeating habits, overindulge ourselves, become narcissists, buy things we don't need, eat too much, drink too much and do things that harm our bodies and make us unhealthy and ugly.

All we do becomes an attempt to fill the emptiness in our hearts.

This is the madness we get trapped into when we don't know any better, when we don't know Love. We keep repeating the same mistakes; keep getting involved with the same wrong kind of people, over and over we create and fall into situations that don't help us go forward.

With no one to shed Love over bad feelings and thoughts, with nothing to keep them in check, with no one to challenge them, these vicious circles, can take off on a life of their own. They can continue to grow, unnoticed and silently turn into true madness. They become a monster that can do real damage to others and ourselves. Think of Hitler, Idi Amin, pedophiles, rapists, murderers, madness and all the people that hurt others or themselves really badly.

The root and the reason behind all addictions, self-defeating and self-destructive behaviors, including suicide, is an abysmal feeling of being unloved, of being unable to see Love.

There are those who believe they've got it all sorted out. They tell these people who don't know any better that they are responsible for their actions; that they are adults and have no excuses anymore, that they can't blame others, not their parents or carers, no one, that it's up to them to get out of the mess, pull themselves together and clean up their acts.

But, it's often so that those who criticize and judge the most are the last ones to offer a helping hand or at least show them an alternative.

If being sixteen, eighteen, or twenty one means that one is able to sort him/herself out, how come so many don't? Outright stupidity? I don't think so. Very much the contrary.

Most of those who society sees as losers are, deep inside, intelligent, creative and original people. They can't get themselves together, because they have been left to fend for themselves for too long and have given up, because someone has given up on them a long time before, because the demons have become too big for them to fight them on their own.

These people don't need prejudice, criticism and judgment; they need someone who can show them what true Love is.

I truly believe that all the cracked pots and all the "lost" people out there, trapped in the hell of their own minds, battling their demons alone, are people who have not been truly loved, have not had in their lives, someone who could truly touch their hearts and minds long enough for them to develop in the right direction.

Most of them, given that Love would transform into people anyone could feel proud of.

I am absolutely sure, that no one develops his or her full potential on their own, without the care and support of others, without any help. If there are any who did, they are rather the exception, not the rule.

There's so much that we still don't know about how exactly our brain works and develops. Some children just need more than others. Some children get hurt a lot easier than others.

Others seem to grow well and suffer less damage under very unfavorable conditions.

Some children seem to have a bigger need to see Love in their parents than others. Some children seem to find comfort more easily in the consolations the world has to offer, some children are just different. Genes and other things outside the control of parents and carers also play a role.

Children that need more attention are often seen as difficult ones and troublemakers.

It's an awful thing to go judging these children, saying that one set of characteristics are preferable or better than others.

I think that children that get hurt more easily, who are more sensitive, have brains that are quicker to perceive what's underneath and hidden. If guided properly they could become brilliant thinkers, but if neglected, misunderstood, unaccepted or forced to conform to someone's short-sighted view of what's appropriate, they can really lose it; they can easily develop negative beliefs. If these children accept the labels they are given and the roles they are allowed to play, they become the family nut, the black sheep and worse. In time, that negativity will reflect back to the people around them and everybody will lose.

These children are born like that, God made them that way for a very special and divine reason.

Difficult children are seen as a curse, but they become a blessing when people around them accept the invitation to look further and deeper, like the water bearer did, to venture further out of their comfort zones and grow; when they accept the challenge to dig deeper into their hearts to find the wisdom to know how to put to good use, what at first sight looks like a limitation in their children.

The flowers that the cracked pot watered in the tale in the beginning of this Chapter, are the beautiful things that these children bring about, when their limitations are understood.

In this mad society we live in, our authorities only move into action when things go terribly bad, when someone gets hurt badly. Precious little attention is being paid to the madness being perpetuated, invisibly and imperceptibly, generation after generation, "with so much love" behind the walls of homes and schools. The cycle of hurting and getting hurt goes on and on.

This is why it's so important that we understand what goes on in our children's minds and hearts. If we want our children to feel truly loved, we need to learn to read, accept and guide their hearts and minds.

Very few parents and carers are aware of their children's thoughts, of how they really feel. We think they are okay just because they seem to be or pretend to be. If they have food and shelter, if they look healthy or wealthy, if they're laughing, we presume they must be all right. Most take it for granted that children will sort themselves out emotionally and even when they see them struggle they think, "Oh, they'll get over it."

This is too big a task for children and adolescents to do on their own! Sending children to school isn't enough either. Schools might fill some gaps, but they are not able to give every child the attention it needs to become who it's meant to be.

Parents are always so busy trying to give kids so much of what they don't really need. What we really need to do is to stop and listen, stop and look, stop to try to understand what's happening deep inside our children's hearts and minds.

The reason why we don't do that is because we don't stop to try and understand what's going on in *our own* hearts and minds. To do that is to go against the normal (mad) routine of life, against what comes naturally, it's so much easier not to. We have an acquired aversion to express our deepest feelings and thoughts, to get into someone's heart, to understand what someone really thinks or feel; we have all learned to accept social rules, to disguise and so we just fight our inner struggles and doubts on our own, no one is allowed to get deep inside our hearts and minds and we leave our children and loved ones alone to cope with all their contradictory and sometimes destructive thoughts and emotions.

As parents, carers, teachers and governments we need to have a serious look into our hospitals, streets, jails and social security buildings; we need to look at all these people entangled in debt, in dysfunctional and self-destructive relationships and behaviors: the mad, the neurotic, the homeless, criminals, gamblers, hoarders, drunks and addicts, doomed to muddle in chaos and confusion for many years to come. We need to stop to think and find out what went wrong, because all these people were once innocent little babies and vulnerable children in need of guidance and tenderness.

We need to get a lot more serious in establishing networks for parents, children and adolescents who seem to be struggling, unable to deal and overcome the challenges they face. We need to have a serious look at the networks that are in place and understand why so many people are still falling through the cracks.

It's absurd that so often parents are left to sort it all out on their own. For all other jobs on earth there are procedures and guidelines we can follow, there's training and certificates we need to acquire, but for the most fundamental, the hardest, the most important and the most difficult of all jobs, there are no courses available, no one to look for help.

The major mistake we are making is to believe that children will be a positive force in society and have the ability to understand and deal with the negative forces in the world and themselves on their own. And even if they eventually do find some balance, it is such a shame that they should waste so much time of their lives muddling and suffering until they get there.

If we want to break the circle of unconsciousness and hurting in raising our children we need to understand that parenting is not something we do *for* our children, it's something we need to do for ourselves. Because children are not the result of what we *do for* them, but of what we *are*.

When we are the people we are meant to be, people with a joyful heart, not afraid of facing the truth about ourselves, people with the wisdom and strength to face the challenges we need to face in life, able to love and understand those around us, our children and all around us will as well, naturally.

The truth is, we are all cracked pots in one way or another, at one time or another in our lives, we all go through life with some bad feelings inside, we all hurt somehow, we all got our wounds, fears and deluded ideas of what love and happiness are or what it is that will make us worthy. Who has never made a bad decision? Who has never said a wrong word, done something regrettable? Who has never made a mistake? Who has never had illusions?

I dare to say that it's only a small minority, who can honestly say that they are truly happy.

By happy I mean that they have fulfilling relationships with their loved ones; relationships characterized by mutual respect, understanding and affection; they can rely on a supportive network of people who truly care about them; they love what they have; they are able to assume responsibility and love what they do; they make their own decisions and don't blindly follow someone else's; they are able to lead independent lives; they are calm, peaceful people, kind and gentle to others, to animals and to nature, they tread lightly and leave no tracks behind them, only good memories; they laugh easily and smile often, they love and are loved by those around them; they feel compassion for the unfortunate in the world and actively do something to ease their suffering; they lead healthy lifestyles and are not afraid of accepting the pain that is unavoidable when we are committed to truth. In short, people who have discovered Love in their hearts, people who are well awake and live in awareness of all the feelings and thoughts that block the natural flow of Love from their hearts to others and themselves. This is not the majority, the vast majority is just floating along and too many are drowning.

It is in this scenario, armed with all sorts of contradictory feelings, wounds and delusions about what love and happiness are all about, that we decide to start relationships and have children. We are never totally rational or objective in our decisions, we behave on impulse.

No matter how much knowledge or education we have, we will still make bad decisions, because the only right decisions are the ones Love makes.

Sexual relationships and children are still, largely, unconscious decisions that have a lot less to do with Love and a lot more with unconscious selfish interests. It must necessarily be so, because relationships, marriage and having children would not happen otherwise. We don't marry someone completely aware of what it will take us to keep him or her happy; we don't have children thinking of what it takes to raise happy and fulfilled human beings. We marry and we have children because we think it will make *us* happy.

We only bring children into this world, because we have delusions about what this world is, what happiness is, what we really are; because we aren't fully aware of the limitations, distorted beliefs and wounds we and our partners carry inside.

We can't really engage in long lasting relationships fully conscious of the difficulties ahead.

Attraction, birth, death and the suffering that comes with it all, have nothing to do with Love, they are just expressions of the mysterious and natural force of life that pulses deep in the unconscious of all living beings: fear.

The cycle of hurting and getting hurt will go on and on until people understand what Love really is.

This is why it's so difficult to truly love and understand others.

This is why relationships, all human relations are so complicated and parenting most of all, because it's too hard not to see ourselves in our children.

It is in relationships, in our interactions with our loved ones, friends and all other human beings on the planet, that the underlying, not so noble reasons that brought about these relationships are exposed. It's in human relationships of all kinds that the truth about ourselves, our true colors come to light. It is in these interactions that we are confronted with the distorted beliefs and values that rule our lives.

Behind every human decision lie selfish interests and misconceptions, which will, invariably, lead to conflict and suffering.

If there's nothing selfish about parenting, why don't people who cannot have children adopt a child instead of spending a lot of time, effort and a huge amount of money trying to have children of their own? Why can they not love another child? Correct me if I am wrong, but I think it is because they cannot see themselves in another child who doesn't carry their genes. What they want, like most parents, is to love themselves through their children or even worse, maybe they feel less than people who are able to produce kids on their own.

Why not consider the possibility that what they see as a terrible curse may in fact, be a special blessing?

Don't take me wrong, I do have compassion for these people, I know their suffering is real, but it is avoidable suffering. It doesn't need to be there!

I think it's a serious distorted belief, preached by some churches, that the function of sexual relationships is to have children. This has led to so much unnecessary suffering. For human beings sex has a much bigger significance than just reproduction, we are not rabbits.

Blessed are those who have the understanding that they will not be able to give their children what they need: physically, mentally or emotionally and decide not to have children.

Life is not meant to be wasted in dysfunctional relationships and in raising messed up children for a mad world. These people deserve to be applauded and not labeled as selfish.

There's nothing more difficult than to raise a human being and right they are for not feeling they could.

Many of the people out there weren't meant to be parents at all.

If we carry any grudges or resentments, especially against our parents, any wounds that still ache, any bad habits we cannot overcome; we will inevitably hurt our children and will be perpetuating the cycle of hurting.

If we are not what we are meant to be, our children won't either.

We make irrational decisions about children and we make them about marriage. We don't have a clue of what happiness is meant to be and we marry in the hope we will find it there. We think we will find love, when we don't know what Love is. We think we have found the one who will understand us, who will love us completely and satisfy all our needs when we don't have a clue of what those needs really are. In our deluded ideas about happiness and love, we expect our partners to make us happy and sort it all out for us.

There are so many wrong reasons why people get married. Some see in their partners the parents they never had or cannot emancipate from, some see their partners the same way they see their bottle of whisky, some think they will die without them. Some see in partners a trophy, an asset, the satisfaction of the vanities of their egos. Yet others don't have a clue of why they are together at all. Some seek in marriage a safe haven for an easy and comfortable life, a refuge wherein they can relax about their little, and sometimes big, vices and limitations. Marriage becomes an escape, a hiding place.

Some want a husband, a wife, children, a house in the suburbs because that is what everybody else has, because they are afraid others will think they are less if they don't.
It's not that these things are bad, what I'm trying to say is that we need to know why we want the things we want and why we do the things we do.

"Know thyself! The unexamined life is not worth living. Socrates

They believe happiness can be bought and fall into the capitalistic trap and the madness of consumerism and debt. We spend most of our lifetimes running after so many things without ever really stopping to think about our true destiny in life. We try so hard to get the things we think we need, that we end up missing the things that would really make us happy. So much effort is put into achievement, into having, when the real treasure is in being what we really are and understanding what we really need. What a wonderful place these planet of ours would be if everyone only followed his/her true calling.

"If you are what you should be, you will set the whole world on fire." St Catherine of Siena

We do what everybody else does because we fear distancing ourselves from a pack that may resent us deeply.
We chose not to believe in ourselves and in our uniqueness and we dive blindly into the mainstream and into mediocrity, instead. We tell ourselves that success comes from adapting to the rules, from being able to go with the flow, from adopting the standards and definitions of success that prevail in our societies.

"It is no measure of health to be well adjusted to a profoundly sick society." Krishnamurti

We are three-dimensional beings, but we are forced to live in a uni-dimensional society, that is concerned only with physical and material wellbeing. We have not only a body, but also a mind and a soul that need to be nurtured as well. An underdeveloped mind is able of stupid and terrible things; a neglected soul can plunge into darkness, never to come back.
We feel ashamed if we are not a part of something, if we are not responsible for anything. We need to feel that we are important to other people, that we matter, that we are doing something,

that we are making a difference. So we get ourselves into anything: work we were not really cut out for, marriage, parenthood, volunteer work and a thousand other activities and responsibilities. We convince ourselves so strongly of the goodness of it all, that all the stress, ill health, chronic pains and aches, bad moods, grumpiness and tiredness are seen as necessary evils.

How many of us out there, mothers, fathers, carers, employees, volunteers, are killing ourselves to give our loved ones everything we think they need? Completely overwhelmed and unhappy, we stubbornly fight our way up stream on a path that's not ours and was not designed for us; we drag ourselves through because we think the world won't turn without us, but guess what?
It will and it will probably turn more smoothly without us.
It looks like unselfishness, sacrificing ourselves for others, our children and families, but truly, we are doing it for ourselves.
All the business is just because we are running away from our own, often unconscious wounds throbbing deep inside; running away from the emptiness in our hearts.
When we are stressed out and unhappy, no one profits, no one who matters, anyway. Perhaps a boss or a superior, but we are certainly not and those close to us aren't either. Of course, people grew used to our "sacrifice" and they will continue to expect it from us. The vicious circle will keep turning round, but only if we let it.
Don't get me wrong, I'm not saying that we should be all looking only at our own navels, without concern for others.
I'm trying to call the attention to the fact that under the pretence of helping others, many are just running away from the issues in themselves that they need to face.
In almost everything people do there is a hope, even if it's just a faint one, that they might get something out of it, some actually demand it: recognition for the good deeds and efforts done, a good deed in return or simply to feel that they aren't useless.
The only true deeds of Love are those who come from the heart spontaneously, naturally, without us even thinking about it, without any expectation of reward or appreciation.
No matter how big, how altruistic our actions may be, if there is a sense of "I have to" behind them, they are probably not worth doing. More often than not, all their effort, will be in vain, because it won't really reach people's hearts. It was not done with true love.

"God does not look at what we do, but at the love we put in it"
St Teresa of Avila

We don't do anyone a favor if we just push ourselves through things. If we are so busy that we haven't got time to calmly sit to talk to our husbands, wives, children, relatives and friends, if we haven't got time for the things that give us joy, that help us reconnect with ourselves or better understand ourselves. We have stopped being humans and have become robots. Robots and machines have no feelings; they "just get the job done"!

When "get the job done" is our main concern, we are, in fact, neglecting the most important, the only job that matters, the only thing that really brings joy to our hearts: feeling truly connected with people.

If we just go on "getting the job done" we will one day, wake up to look around us and see that everybody else is concerned only with getting their job done and even though, still living under the same roof, we all have become aliens to each other, living in separate worlds. Like Garry Trudeau, everybody has developed a lifestyle that doesn't really require their presence.

We top off the whole tragic comedy with telling ourselves that there is no way out and that this is just how life is!

"What about the bills?" we ask. Yes, what about them? What are we spending on, buying and using that we don't really need? Will life stop with less of without them?

So many marriages go wrong because people get so lost in the "haves to" and the distractions that they completely forget what brought them together first place: the longing to be together!

One day we have a good look around and find that the marriage became dysfunctional, our children a mess and nobody's happy.

We may one day stop to look and realize that whatever it was that originally united us has turned into either pain and resentment or denial and indifference.

One day we stop to look and everything seems lost and crooked, meaningless, stupid and helpless. We lose respect for our partners. The house looks run down, the money is never enough and life is mediocre. Staying may feel like disrespect to ourselves, a serious blow to our self-esteem. We feel trapped like a bird in a cage, miserable, seeing no way out and separation comes to mind. We decide that the answers are outside and not within the relationship, outside ourselves, not within. We decide it's over, nothing can be done.

We say we can't love someone anymore, we think someone

doesn't fit our criteria of people we could love, we think that by closing the door on someone, we are opening one for ourselves, when in fact, we are closing the door of Love for ourselves alone.
What about the famous excuse, "irreconcilable differences"? Ever heard a vaguer, nothing saying excuse than this? People think they are doing themselves a favor. They think they don't need to put up with anyone's faults and limitations.
But, here's the trick, we will feel accepted and loved in the exact same measure that we love and accept others.

No one has to stay in an abusive or violent relationship; no one has to live in fear, to put up with the addiction, alcoholism, selfishness and irresponsibility of people who don't see the need to get themselves together, don't see the harm they are doing to themselves and the ones around them, but the truth is that these are rarely the reasons why couples split. Ironically enough, self-destructive relationships are the most difficult ones to break apart.
Separation is often just another mechanism of the mind to escape from facing the core issues. People separate the same way they get together, following deluded dreams, vague and confused reasons, plain physical attraction, without having a clue of what they are doing or the consequences of it.
When we separate in this way, we leave a mess behind and we take a bigger mess with us in our minds and in our hearts. No matter how bad we think our situation is, it can always get worse. No matter what the reason for it may be, separation will only lead to a better situation when partners have had a serious look at themselves, when children have had an honest opportunity to have their say, when all have seriously gone through the process of looking for alternatives and solutions.
I believe that even very young children are able to experience great anxiety, guilt and confusion when something is not right between their parents and if their feelings are not put into the equation, if these emotions are not addressed they can damage a child for a lifetime. The damage divorce does to children is only starting to become evident.
We are not aware of what is at stake.
Without a thorough exploration of all possible avenues, without spending a lot of time and making a real effort trying to save the marriage with the help of counselors and other independent parties, everybody will lose.
Happiness in a new relationship will not happen until all the

wounds have been healed and if children are involved these wounds may last a lifetime.

I look around and I see so many divorced and separated people carrying around with them deep wounds and sorrows, financial hardships and resentments. They part, hoping the pain will end but it never does. How many people are out there carrying with them all the weight of their broken dreams, living second-rate relationships, second-rate lives ruled by unfinished businesses, how many living in loneliness and depression? How many put an end to it all?

I see far too much sorrow and despair than I can handle everywhere, as a result of broken families. I see too many lost and confused children and adolescents being hurt, caught up in the crossfire, wasting their lives without a clue about tomorrow, because their parents don't have a clue about anything.

When parenting, relationships and work feel like a struggle we need to understand what distorted beliefs and illusions we are living by and of them, none is more important than our illusions about what love and happiness are.

What we believe in, determines our lives and who we are.

To fight our irrational beliefs and to brake our bad habits we need to believe that this is not who we truly are. We need to believe that we can start again and renew. Replace fear by Love.

How many bad decisions do we need to make in life, how many mistakes, how much suffering do we put up with, how many people do we have to hurt before we start looking for the reasons why we do the things we do?

We need to take responsibility over the hurting others cause to us and the hurting that we cause to others. We need to take our lives, relationships and parenting a lot more seriously than we do. It's about time we stop mistaking Love for obscure, subconscious impulses.

If we want to make sure our children, our partners and ourselves really feel loved and become the persons we are meant to be, before anything else we need to understand what Love is.

So, what the heck is Love?

Love

4 Love is patient and kind.
Love is not jealous or boastful or proud 5 or rude.
Love does not demand its own way.
Love is not irritable and
It keeps no record of when it has been wronged.
6 It is never glad about injustice but
rejoices whenever the truth wins out.
7 Love never gives up, never loses faith,
is always hopeful, and endures through every circumstance.
8 Love will last forever...
(1 Corinthians 13)

7 Dear friends, let us continue to love one another...
Anyone who loves is born of God and knows God.
8 But, anyone who does not love does not know God, for
***God is love**...*
12 No one has ever seen God, but if we love each other,
God lives in us...
(1 John 4)

Now you can understand why I used Love with a capital L.

In my search for what love is, I found many definitions, but I always felt there was something missing. The only definition I found that is universal and doesn't depend on people's infinite tastes and likes is the one St Paul gives us in the Bible.

There are so many people out there that reject the idea of God.

The reason for that is that our understanding of God is given to us, unconsciously, by the people responsible for our upbringing. If they haven't done a very good job of showing us Love, we will have a problem with God, because for children, the adults they depend upon *are* God.

We all know God deep inside and so do children, but they are not able to understand it, they don't know it. All they know, all they see, all they need is their parents.

This is the enormity of the meaning of parenthood. This is the immense responsibility parents bear on their shoulders. As parents, our voice, our hands, our face become the voice, the face and the hands of God. If we were aware of the huge responsibility we accept by bringing a child to this world, aware of God's plan for us and for them, we would tremble just at the thought of it.

People have a problem with God, because so many parents haven't been up to scratch in their role of messengers of Love, but, when we say we don't believe in God, we are actually saying that we don't believe in Love.

We all have an issue with Love, because no parent has loved us like God would and because we were too young to know any better, we reckoned that because we didn't see Love in our parents, Love does not exist.

Sure, some parents and carers make bigger and further-reaching mistakes than others, but we all make them, because like all human beings we too, have a problem with Love. We all have our wounds and we often don't even know it.

People may say they don't believe in God, because they don't know God, but if they could see the face of true Love and true compassion, the hardest of hearts would melt, even an atheist's heart. Most of those who say they don't believe in God will be quick to say they believe in Love. What they don't believe in is a distorted idea of God given to them by others and by Churches who have lost their essence.

I don't need any proof of the existence of God. I don't need to see archaeological or irrefutable scientific proof of the existence of the persons or the facts described in sacred books. I don't need to see miracles to believe that Love is the only thing that can fill my heart completely and make me feel whole. I don't need anyone to tell me that. I just know it.

I can see Love everywhere. In the pure eyes of a child, in a small wild flower, I can see Its power in the thunder, in the roaring ocean, Its gentleness in the warm breeze, in the colors of the rainbow, Its greatness in the stars, in the universe, in the cycle of life, in the pouring summer rain, Its majesty in ancient trees. I can see Love reaching out for us in the beauty of this world, in hands that hold each other, in eyes filled with compassion, I can even see It hidden underneath the horrible events in the world, but most of all, I can feel the Love in my heart.

For I do not seek to understand that I may believe, but I believe in order to understand. St. Anselm

During adolescence, I had a few rare moments in which I was overtaken by an enormous feeling of joy and peace. A perception of the immense Love that is everywhere. An awe-inspiring feeling that I am loved beyond my wildest dreams. A feeling that filled my heart with a contentment that made me feel completely in peace and not wanting anything. This was not caused by anyone or anything and I realized it was coming from God. I became convinced that all answers are to be found in Love. I even decided to follow a religious life.

Yet, there was no one to explain things to me, to support me.

Very much the contrary, there were plenty of people to tell me I was weird and confused and in my ignorance, I believed them.

The Love in my heart and my convictions slowly slipped away, but the certainty that it was Love and lives in my heart never left me, even when, in the many years that followed, the certainty was often, no more than a faint and hazy memory.

Because I didn't follow my conviction, so many years had to pass, I had to look for answers so far away, get into and out of so much trouble, make the hole so much deeper, before I could really understand the full depth of that early conviction. I had to see so much ugliness in the world, so many different cultures and people, make so many mistakes, waste so much time, hurt so many people, get hurt so much, before reconnecting with myself again and once more find rest and comfort in the arms of Love, the Love that has always been waiting for me deep inside my heart. I don't long for Love because I'm screwed up, because I'm needy, or because I don't know any better, like those who don't believe have told me, but because it's the universal desire of the human heart.

There's something in the human heart that makes us believe in something beyond ourselves.
Mankind has always believed in something, from the beginning, from when our ancestors first came down from the trees and out of the forests. That's because our essence is beyond our physical existence. We have a soul that will eventually transcend us.
Anyone who searches honestly and deeply enough will understand that there's something much bigger than ourselves out there.
That something is Love, no matter what we call it: God, Yahweh, Allah, Tao, Jah or Buddha; no matter what prophets we follow: Jesus, Krishna, Siddhartha, Muhammad or Moses.
To believe in something is inherent to being human, it's the norm, abnormal is not to believe.
That's why we develop distorted and irrational beliefs when our fundamental beliefs are not conscious, when we are not aware of what we believe in. Even atheists who say they don't believe in anything are ruled by beliefs they are not aware of. And for as far as I'm concerned, a disbelief is a belief too, because neither can be proved!

In the former Chapter, I tried to explain that when the significant people in our upbringing weren't able to show us Love, they will hurt and damage us and we won't feel loved. And when we don't feel loved, we develop all sorts of irrational beliefs that become the rulers of our lives. I said also that when our hearts are devoid of Love, fear will take Its place. Fear, instead of Love, becomes the almighty force hidden deep inside ourselves that controls everything we do.
At some stage in our upbringing, when the people who take care of us, don't do a very good job, we stop believing in Love and in that same moment we are overtaken by an overwhelming, though unconscious perception that we are alone in the universe.
What keeps us trapped in a lesser life is the fundamental belief that we are alone. The belief that there's nothing out there to

help us and that we are not meant to be more than what others have allowed us to be.

For as long as our lives are ruled by unconscious beliefs, we will be looking for happiness in things outside ourselves and in all the wrong places, we will continue to expect that someone else has to come up with all the answers and solutions for our problems and we will continue to be only a shadow of what we can be, trapped in a vicious circle of hurting and getting hurt, finding excuses, being too busy, running away from our true self, away from silence, into the noise and the hustle and bustle of the world.

When we look for happiness outside ourselves, all we will ever manage to get is a happiness that's skin deep, that doesn't get to the core of who we are. We are not making our *selves* happy, but just our senses and our bodies. It doesn't last. It doesn't satisfy.

It's like trying to retain water in a container full with holes.

Looking for happiness outside ourselves is a very foolish business indeed. Yet, it seems that the whole world spends most of its time in this exact pursuit. Many actually, die in the process from stress, from overwork, from an overdose and from diseases that are the result of this same insane effort. That's madness, there's no other word for it.

To believe that there's no God is to believe that we can or are supposed to know it all, is to believe that we can do anything good away from Love or anything better than Love. This is the reason for all suffering, pain and hurting that has taken, is taking and will take place in the world. This is what is behind every word and everything we do that hurts other people, the environment and ourselves. We make wrong decisions because, somehow we believe we are more than what we really are and that we know more than we really do, we often think, that as human beings, we are the greatest, but we are not. Love is.

Every mistake we make, every fear, everything we say, think, dream, all our choices, our likes and dislikes, our attitudes, the way we react to people and circumstances in our lives, the sense we make of the world around us and ultimately, how we feel can all be traced to the one fundamental belief we carry inside us: either there is infinite Love, Truth, Wisdom beyond ourselves that we can tap from and be a part of or there's nothing and we are alone to sort it all out by ourselves (or our shrinks, if we can afford them).

When we feel we haven't got anything to help us out, when we don't believe that there's something much better and bigger than we can possibly imagine, waiting for us, everything is of vital importance, we can't let anything go, we can't give anything up: the bad feelings, the illusions, the vain and foolish desires, the never-ending needs of the body, we cling to all these things like a starved dog to a bone, we can't make any move forward. It's this lack of belief that makes us stick to and get stuck with the wrong people, useless things and all the rubbish we don't need, making us heavy, our heads down low, searching for the scraps on the ground. Like chickens, afraid of spreading our wings to fly high with the eagles in the sky.

All we experience in life is the result of what we truly believe in, not what we say we believe in. It's what goes deep inside our hearts and minds that counts, not the words that come out of our mouths.

What we take for truth, that's what our reality will be.
Neale Walsh

We may scream into the wind and repeat to ourselves that we are worthy and deserving, we may even be a very active member of a Church or Charity but if there's still something missing in our lives, if we still feel stuck somewhere, if our relationships with others is still not as we would like, if we still keep secrets we don't tell anyone, we can be sure that what's ruling our lives, the beliefs, the things we consider to be true are not the ones we consciously chose, but the ones that have been imposed on us.
When we decide to believe that Love is deep in our hearts, that it is, in fact, our true essence, we understand that the bad feelings, thoughts and stupid beliefs that rule our lives are not a part of us, that they have been imprinted in us by others and then took a life of their own in our minds, dictating every action, thought and feeling we have.
Unless we believe that we already got all we need to become the people we are meant to be, that we already have all we need to be happy and that unless we give up the illusion that somewhere else, someone else is better, we will never find happiness and contentment.

To give up the illusions about our condition is to give up a
condition that needs illusions. Karl Marx

We brake the vicious circle of hurting and feeling hurt when we have an honest look at ourselves and around us and admit that there's room for improvement, that something needs to change, accept that someone may have been able to mess our lives up, but no one will, no one can fix it, even if one wanted to, because no one can see what's in our hearts unless we reveal it.

If unconscious, irrational beliefs make us live a lesser life, all we need to do to brake the circle is to dive into ourselves and shed light on them, become aware of them, so that we can then replace them with a conscious belief in Love.

The way we do that is by slowing down, by being mindful of our thoughts, feelings and actions, by making time free to talk to people, to try to understand ourselves and the ones around us, by reading and learning about Love.

The New Testament has helped me a lot, but many wise people out there were helpful as well: Socrates, Harville Hendrix, St Francis of Assisi, Thomas Kempis, Teresa of Avila, Therese of Lisieux, Scott Peck, Viktor Frankl, Rick Warren, Paulo Coelho, Neale Walsch, Karl Jung, William Reich, Harville Hendrix, Kenneth Wapnick, Kierkegaard, biblical scholars and even Kafka, just to name a few.

Journal writing played a major role as well, by writing down my actions, feelings and thoughts on an almost daily basis, by re-reading them often, I started to make connections, discover patterns in thoughts, organize everything in a coherent way.

Mild exercise has helped me become more aware of my body, its connection with breathing, the mind and emotions. When I do my exercises in a mindful way, I always end up with a feeling that I have done my body much good.

Meditation reconnects us with the essence of who we are. It can take us away from the chaos of everyday, from the surface where little breezes and stronger winds make ripples or play havoc with our emotions and minds and into the depths inside us, where wisdom and peace are to be found.

Prayer reconnects us with our essence too. In prayer we turn our minds away from distractions and problems and concentrate on Love, Its beauty and Its wisdom. In prayer we reaffirm who we really are and where we are meant to be. We look at all we've got and become grateful.

Everybody's different, there are no fixed rules. It's up to each and everyone to find out for themselves what it is that brings true peace and balance into their lives, what it is that help them build more loving relationships with those around them.

But, none of them is of any use if our fundamental beliefs remain in the dark, unconscious, free to launch their guerrilla attacks against us; they will always sabotage our efforts and good intentions if we don't make a conscious choice for Love. Because only through Love can we make decisions that will have long lasting and positive results in our lives and the world.

A conscious commitment with Love is a commitment that we are challenged to re-affirm many times every single day.

So often we are not in the mood. There are so many distractions out there to make us lose our track and forget our good intentions. It's so much easier to just ignore and walk away.

The commitment to always reach out to our hearts, to always do what Love instructs us to do, is a commitment that can be very difficult, often painful and filled with many ups and downs.

It's not enough to say we believe in Love, we need to prove it to the world and to ourselves. Our belief has to show in our actions and words. We need to put into practice our new understanding of what Love is, in our relationships with everyone we meet or talk to, in everything we do.

Only then, can we slowly start to give up and get rid of all that does not truly belong to us. We don't become who we are meant to be overnight, but bits by bits, as we live our truths, beliefs and convictions in everyday life. Bits by bits we become who we truly are: agents of Love in this world. Slowly and progressively Love grows in our hearts and we start feeling truly loved and experience true joy and peace in our hearts.

Have no illusions, to make this commitment is to enter the narrow path, is to accept pain, is to enter the biggest battle of the human existence and the only one worth fighting, the battle against ourselves and everything and everyone that wants to keep us from that path.

> *34 "Don't imagine that I came to bring peace to the earth!*
> *No, I came to bring a sword. 35 I have come to set a man*
> *against his father, and a daughter against her mother, and a*
> *daughter-in-law against her mother-in-law.*
> *36 Your enemies will be right in your own household! 37 If you*
> *love your father or mother more than you love me, you are not*

*worthy of being mine; or if you love your son or daughter more
than me, you are not worthy of being mine.
38 If you refuse to take up your cross and follow me, you are
not worthy of being mine. 39 If you cling to your life, you will
lose it; but if you give it up for me, you will find it. (Matthew 10)*

I'm sure Jesus didn't mean to say that we need to take up arms
against our relatives. What he's saying is that the danger is where
we least expect, that the fight will not be easy and that we must
be ready to break long lasting entanglements with the people
around us. Trying to be what we are meant to be is a difficult
path indeed and only those who fully accept the challenge, who
dare to leave the herd behind, will be the ones who will become
what they are meant to be and find true happiness.

೮೮೮೮೮೮

Now, with our new understanding of what Love is, let us revisit
our ideas about relationships.
Is there such a thing as a right way to start a relationship?
I don't think there is, but there is probably a "natural" way for
them to start. And that's when people fall in love.
That state in which the heart of the lover is filled with awe for the
beloved. Eyes on each other, they see only perfection and
absolute beauty. There's a longing to be together that's almost
painful, a mutual attraction that will irresistibly bring bodies
together and fill both with intense happiness. The stuff of poets,
beautifully depicted in film, music, books and even made sacred
in Solomon's Song of Songs.
To see a couple in love is wonderful. It's like watching birds in
their nests, flowers opening in spring, a beautiful sunset. It's the
cycle of life turning round, the cycle of nature, as God designed it
to be. Falling in love's a blessing, a precious gift and the children
that result from these unions are blessed as well, because they
are also the natural result of the cycle of life.

Some say falling in love is only a natural mechanism for
reproduction, the self-perpetuating call of nature. It might be,
but I think it's also a lot more.
Deep underneath the turmoil of emotions and hormones, what
the heart is ultimately seeking for, when it falls in love, is to
immerse, dissolve itself in Love, it's the heart seeking out to
satisfy its most fundamental desire to experience Love.

What lovers don't know is that they have transformed Love into something much smaller and much limited: the love of another human being, which is very nice as well, but not as big as we would like it to be. The bigger the lover sees the beloved the bigger the disappointment, the greater the pain that is to come.

In an ideal world, all relationships and all children would be the result of people falling in love with each other head over heels.
But alas, we don't live in an ideal world. In the real world I live in, a lot of what people say is being in love, is nothing but deluded misconceptions about love and happiness, obscure selfish motives and distorted beliefs. Some fall in love with people that don't want them; some fall in love with people they shouldn't, some will never fall in love, others will never be loved; the real world is full with people that rarely feel blessed, they feel ugly, insecure, lonely and horny. The real world I know is a world of cracked pots.
In the real world, the only relationships that have a chance to turn into something worth having are the ones ruled by common sense and reason. True Love is rational. Peace and harmony in our homes and in the world cannot exist without reason.
Being in love is great, but if reason doesn't enter the scene early in the play, there will be no happy end.

When people fall in love, they want to be together, they want to become one. The natural function of attraction is sex. Therefore, I conclude that the main function of a relationship should also be sex and I believe St. Paul agrees with me,

1... Yes, it is good to live a celibate life. 2 But because of cases of sexual immorality, each man should have his own wife and each woman her own husband... 5 Do not deprive one another of sexual relations, except perhaps by agreement for a set time, to devote yourselves to prayer, and then come together again, so that Satan may not tempt you because of your lack of self-control... 8 To the unmarried and the widows I say... if they are not practicing self-control, they should marry. For it is better to marry than to be aflame with passion...
36 If anyone thinks that he is not behaving properly... if his passions are strong... let him marry as he wishes; it is no sin. 38 So, the person who marries does well, and the person who doesn't marry does even better. (1 Cor 7)

He didn't say those who want children should marry, or those who want a house in the suburbs or those who are looking for happiness. He said that anyone who feels a strong need for sexual gratification should marry.

This would include many church people that preach the exact opposite.

Paul saw in marriage, for those who can't go without sex, a way to better serve the cause of Love.

I do worry that someone may see in Paul's words a justification to treat their spouses as sexual objects who should be always ready for them when they need them. Therefore, I quote Paul again:

25 And you husbands must love your wives with the same love Christ showed the church. He gave up his life for her... (Eph 5)

Anyone looking for anything more than sexual fulfillment in a relationship is asking for trouble. All else, children, material comfort, security, wealth, etc, come forth naturally from a happy and fulfilling union. These things are the result, not the cause of a relationship and should not be put above it or be objectives in themselves.

There are many things couples can do for each other to express their love for one another and reinforce their union and they are all valuable, but only through sex, can man and woman feel completely and totally as one.

Sex is the most complete expression of love between man and woman.

It satisfies a basic human need, as natural and legitimate as our need for food or shelter, the need to be accepted and loved by another human being. Sex is the only thing that can truly unite them; nothing else they do together can give them the sense of acceptance and closeness that sex does. In a healthy relationship, it should remain the most important way spouses express their love for each other.

I have heard many times that people shouldn't need one another, but I think that's a myth and a hypocrisy. There are very few people out there, who don't feel the need to be loved by another, the need for sexual gratification and they alone can legitimately say they don't need anyone. These are the highly spiritualized people and the people whose mission in this life is to follow a career that takes all of their time, people who get their happiness and gratification from the service they do to the world or God, but for most mortals, sex in a loving relationship is the major contributing factor for the quality of their lives.

The quality of a relationship can actually, be measured by the quality of their sex life: the more fulfilling their sexual experience together, the more fulfilling the relationship as a whole will be, the happier they will be and the happier their children will be.

Some couples allege sex doesn't play a central role in their lives and that they are happy without it. People can even spend a lifetime together without it and that's fine, but then, we cannot call it a relationship. It's just a friendship, maybe a partnership. A relationship without sex is like a lake without water. It stops being a lake! A relationship without sex is dysfunctional.

On the other side of the equation, there are those who want to get their gratification without the need to engage in a lasting relationship, sex just for the sake of it.

The problem I see with this kind of behavior is that almost always someone ends up getting hurt, even when they think they know what they're doing, but, more often than not, they don't.

To engage in sex without the other party being aware that one's just looking for fun and has no interest in a relationship is one of the ultimate forms of disrespect for another human being there is. Even prostitutes are given the right to chose what they want to do. In exchange for money, they give permission to someone to use their bodies.

Some say, it's everyone for themselves in the jungle out there. Everyone should know what they are getting themselves into when they jump into bed with someone, but I say that for as long as people think and behave like that, they will not know what happiness or true love is, they will be trapped in the karma of hurting and being hurt, denigrating both themselves and the ones they use and becoming less human in the process.

People, who can't commit to one person alone, are people who cannot love. They can do great damage to young and immature souls who easily believe they are being deeply loved, when in fact, there is no true connection taking place at all.

These people's understanding of love doesn't go beyond the here and now, beyond their momentary needs. They get bored quickly and need to be constantly on the move.

They can be great lovers or good friends, even half decent parents, but they are not able to truly love, they cannot make anyone truly happy.

In no other area of human experience is the distorted understanding of what love is more visible than in sex. When sex stops being an expression of love for someone that's special to us and becomes a tool for self-satisfaction, it will assume many perverted forms: prostitution and pornography, sexual problems within couples, infidelity, promiscuity, etc... The reason why the world is so sick, so full of immorality is because people seek the pleasure without the love and these two things are inseparable. They seek their own pleasure and not that of their partners. The less love there is, the harder it will be to get the gratification they're looking for and the more dysfunctional and sicker sex becomes.

Eating is another of the body's natural functions that is easily perverted. What is meant to be a celebration of life, the nurturing of our bodies becomes a morbid exercise in self-satisfaction and self-destruction.

Deep underneath every attraction and relationship is a desire to find Love, but if we don't understand what Love is, we mix Love with our beloved, we are convinced that our partners, like God, are supposed to know it all, understand us completely and sort it all out for us. Our happiness becomes dependent on what they do to and for us. To "get" the love we want we give up so much, we make so many sacrifices in the expectation that our efforts will be rewarded with happiness, but they don't and we feel cheated, frustrated and angry and we let our partners know it.

We all get into relationships and marriages with the assumption that we will be happy because we will be loved. We believe that being loved is what happiness is all about, but happiness is not something anyone can make happen for us, even if they wanted to. That is something every one of us has to do for ourselves, that's our own mission in life. The happiness we will get out of our relationships is directly proportional to the effort we put into our own growth independently from each other.

We think happiness comes from what we get. In fact, happiness comes from what we are able to give. Happiness, strength, wisdom and peace will fill our hearts when we are able to freely give these gifts to our partners, children, family members, pets and the world.

Everybody talks about marriage as being a commitment to love each other, for better and worse, but a mature, conscious and loving relationship is based on the commitment to ourselves to assume responsibility over what goes on in our hearts and minds, a commitment not to our partners or anybody else, but to ourselves, to be the happiest human beings we possibly can.

We cannot love anyone if we don't know what Love is, if we are not interested in finding it in our hearts, if we continue to lose ourselves in the millions of distractions and unimportant things of life.

Our search for love in relationships is the search for Love and happiness within our own hearts. When we have decided to have a serious look at the beliefs we live by, when we have accepted who we are and accepted the challenge to become who we are meant to be, relationships, parenting, life itself stop being a struggle.

Relationships fail when people give up on growing. I don't mean only those relationships that end in separation; there are bankrupt relationships that last a lifetime. How can partners lose interest in each other if they are both committed to be the best they can?

Commitment to some sounds like a bond, feels like giving up freedom. People that think so don't know what freedom is. In relationships were people make a commitment with Love, the relationship grows wings and soars.

Free from our delusions and everything that keeps us trapped into a lesser life, we can fly.

Loving is not just looking at each other, it's looking in the same direction. Antoine de Saint-Exupery

When we make the commitment to live according to Love, we will understand that everything that happens to us happens for a reason, we have all heard it before.

Every difficulty we are faced with in life, every challenge, every time we feel annoyed, irritated, angry or sad, everything that pushes our buttons, brings up negative emotions and sad memories, everyone of these things is an invitation and an opportunity to grow.

Behind it all is a hidden mystery, a hidden truth that we need to discover and learn. The wise men of old have written it down thousands of years ago:

29 Not even a sparrow, worth only half a penny, can fall to the ground without your Father knowing it. 30 And the very hairs on your head are all numbered. 31 So don't be afraid; you are more valuable to him than a whole flock of sparrows.
(Matthew 10)

Underneath the everyday events of life, underneath the countless apparently unimportant and random events of everyday, lies an incredible and wonderful plan of Love, a divine plan for all creation.

People around us and the world outside are but mirrors that reflect ourselves. People and the outside world are giving us feedback and clues as to what we are doing right or wrong, all the time.

Every difficulty is an opportunity to become more aware and more conscious of ourselves, an opportunity to better understand who we are, who those around us are and what Love is, an opportunity to take our interactions with the people and the world around us to another, higher level.

People curse their problems and misfortunes and they curse God for them. We rebel against them, we get angry, we get upset about them, we deny, we run away and we get sad, but what we really need to do is remember that they are opportunities to grow. Opportunities to look inside ourselves, inside those around us, opportunities to dive into our hearts and find our true self, a greater, brighter, happier self. By doing so, we help our loved ones, all those around us do the same.

When we stop running away and finding excuses and face our problems with an honest desire to resolve them, Love will show us the way. Love presents problems and challenges only to those It knows will be able to solve and overcome them. Love knows what we are made of better than we do. Unlike people, when Love points to a problem It also gives the tools and shows the way. All we need to do is to accept the invitation.

We need to stop, for as long or as often as it takes, to discover deep inside our hearts the wisdom and the creativity to find alternatives and a new direction. We can all do that. We can all ask for help when we don't know what to do.

Every difficulty, challenge and problem is a chance to let Love grow in our hearts and in the world, a chance to love ourselves and those around us more. Because only Love can truly solve problems, accept misfortunes and overcome challenges. Only Love can end conflicts and bring about lasting peace.

It helps to remember that people who hurt us are people who have been hurt, too. Our challenge is to *forgive them, because they don't know what they are doing!* They are not aware of their hurting.

This is the Divine plan. This is our mission: to transform the world using compassion, open mindedness and awareness.

When we are committed to Love, the millions of big or small challenges and difficulties of a life together: diminishing chemistry or hormones, lack of money, sleepless nights with screaming babies, little things about each other that annoy us: the bad habits, the lesser personality traits, all become opportunities to grow together, as a couple, as a family, as a community.

Instead of letting relationships become a burden, or wishing things were different, or dreaming about other people, other relationships, or thinking of getting rid of what we've got with all the problems that come with it, or feeling the dream is over, or seeing in our partners only flaws and limitations, or letting love slip away, we need to make time for ourselves, sit down and try to understand what's hidden behind the events and the feelings.

Keeping the love and passion alive in a relationship, or re-igniting it if it went off, doesn't just happen. It's something we have to work on.

It's easy not to make that bit of effort to find out what goes on in the hearts and minds of our loved ones, it's easy to let the passion of a relationship fade away. In both cases, the result is the breakdown of human connection, the very thing that makes us happy.

In mature, functional, conscious relationships, where the realities and difficulties of everyday life have long replaced the illusions that come with infatuation, sex is a rational decision, not an unconscious impulse, but a conscious decision to make the effort to give our partners the gratification they need and the reassurance that they are loved. In this kind of relationship, pleasure, love and respect for our spouses are so intertwined that they cannot be separated. Chemistry, physical attraction and infatuation can only diminish; real, rational love is the only thing that can grow.

For many couples, sex quickly becomes a weapon when problems arise in the relationship, a bargaining tool in their power struggle.

With any little disagreement, sex is the first thing to go. By doing so, couples actually throw away their lifejackets, just when the boat is starting to shake.

Couples must make that little effort to engage in sex even if they are tired or don't feel a 100%. Of course, there are days we just can't, but I'm talking about the famous headache excuse, the little everyday worries and chores that slowly and imperceptibly, make the passion fade away. While couples get distracted in the business of everyday, their relationships slowly plunge into dysfunction.

People often complain that there's no climate for sex, that other things must happen before sex can happen, such as getting a present, going out, finishing a task or whatever they think is important. I think it's the other way around. The love they get in sex (if they do it properly) will flow from their bed naturally into all other areas of their lives, whereas waiting to have sex only when conditions are perfect only weakens the relationship.

What we think we need to be happy, is often, the exact same things that keep happiness away.

Like good and expensive wine, to get the most out of a relationship we need to let it mature. That's why relationships are meant to last a lifetime. But, unlike a bottle of wine, we can't just sit in a dark, cold basement (or in front of the TV), while the dust of indifference, worries and misplacement of priorities covers the relationship and love fades away.

We show our belief in Love is true in the effort we put into our relationships, a little every day. That's why we can't have more than one partner at a time, that's why we can't jump from one relationship into another like bees looking for pollen in spring.

Learning to deal with the challenges that show up in our relationships with others is to learn to know and deal with ourselves. In the end, all problems and all people are put in our lives to teach us something about ourselves.

Difficulties and problems show up when something needs to change and that something is usually none other than ourselves, because more often than not, we can't change circumstances and we can certainly not change someone else's heart.

Most of the time all we can really change is ourselves and the way we look at others, at our problems and our life.

Problems are nothing but opportunities for us to rethink ourselves and to grow. When we dive into ourselves to find our wisdom and creativity to manage and accommodate differences, everybody concerned will grow in the process.

Relationships work not because of the things people have in common, but because of the willingness to work on the differences.

People see in marriage an end, but it is just a beginning, the beginning of a *healing and discovery journey* two people take together.

The sooner we understand that this is what relationships are all about, the sooner we and our relationships will become what they are meant to be. The sooner life will start working for us.

Like children, one day need to stop believing in Santa Klaus, we need to stop believing in relationships that exist only in the imaginations of film directors, poets and writers.

There's no such thing as a perfect relationship. To believe in perfect relationships is to believe that there are perfect people walking on Earth. Perfect people become angels and live in Heaven, not on this messed up planet. In this messed up world, only messed up people live. Some more, some less.

All relationships are based on some sort of illusion. All relationships have to go through a process of purification, transforming illusions and selfish desires into true love. All relationships and all families on this planet have problems and issues they need to work on. We all have an issue with Love. We are all cracked pots.

Let's stop the useless search for that perfect someone. We are all limited and flawed. We all have qualities and defects. If we don't accept the limitations we cannot enjoy the qualities. We look for a particular quality in someone and we get all the flaws we didn't ask for. The exact same things that attract us to someone become, after a while, the reasons why we want to run away from that person.

If we can only love someone when everything's roses and we stop loving as soon as the smallest thorn shows up, soon the roses disappear and only thorns remain.

It's not money, beauty, age, lifestyle, hormones, chemistry, culture or education that makes a happy relationship. In fact, these things have nothing to do with Love, they are culturally determined and have more to do with egos and selfish interests. Examples of beautiful, rich, talented people that have lost it completely are plenty and there are even more examples of people who have it all and are still unhappy.

So, let's not look for the things in common or the qualities, but let's find out how much one's willing to work on the differences.

It would be fantastic if both partners engaged in this journey of healing and self-discovery together, but that often isn't the case.

We don't have to give up *our* journey towards happiness because our partners or those close to us are not interested (yet). When we are serious in our journey towards being a better person, all around us will follow, in time.

Every relationship is valuable. No encounter in life happens for no reason. We can learn from everything. Every relationship in our lives can bring us a step closer to what we are supposed to be. This is why I believe that no matter how a relationship started or how messed up and dysfunctional it may be, if people honestly want to get it right, they will eventually find happiness, even if all odds are against it, even if it seems impossible, even if people have hurt each other seemingly beyond repair, even if couples have been indifferent to each other for longer than they can remember, living like strangers under the same roof, even when they can no longer remember when they last had an honest talk or did something nice for each other.

Even when relationships have started for completely wrong reasons, they can transform into something beautiful, if the partners can somehow regain their common sense, get their priorities right and put Love above all else.

If the willingness is there, if we honestly want to change, all the rest is a matter of skills and skills can be learned.

Communication skills to help us reach our evasive partners and children can be learned, we can learn to tackle health and financial problems, we can learn to get over addictions and other dysfunctional behaviors and we can even learn how to improve our sex lives. There are thousands of counselors and other professional people out there who can help us; there are programs, books and courses.

But, no one can make us believe that we are meant for something bigger, that our lives can be so much better and that we already have everything we need to get there.

Love will guide us always, if only we let It.

The only thing we need to do is to believe it.

Life's quest isn't about what or who or why. It's about how. It's not about what we want. It's about how we handle what we've been given, especially our own qualities and limitations. Life is not about dreams, desires and aspirations. It's about accepting what we have and learning to make the most out of it.

To discover what Love is and learn to love, that's what life is all about.

It doesn't matter how we get there: by helping people through our work, through marriage, by raising a family, by serving the community or through a spiritual life. They are all different roads that will lead us to the same place, to peace, harmony, wisdom and joy, in other words, to happiness, if only we understand where we are going and continue walking until we get there.

Learning to love is also, what maturity is all about. The more immature we are as human beings, the more we want to be loved, the less able we are to love. The less we know about Love, the more immature, childish and selfish our relationships with others will be; the more we know what Love is, the deeper and more fulfilling our relationships will be.

> *1 If I could speak in any language in heaven or on earth but didn't love others, I would only be making meaningless noise like a loud gong or a clanging cymbal. 2 If I had the gift of prophecy, and if I knew all the mysteries of the future and knew everything about everything, but didn't love others, what good would I be? And if I had the gift of faith so that I could speak to a mountain and make it move, without love I would be no good to anybody. 3 If I gave everything I have to the poor and even sacrificed my body, I could boast about it; but if I didn't love others, I would be of no value whatsoever.*
> *8 Love will last forever, but prophecy and speaking in unknown languages and special knowledge will all disappear.*
>
> *11...When I was a child, I spoke and thought and reasoned as a child does. But when I grew up, I put away childish things. 12 Now, we see things imperfectly as in a poor mirror, but then we will see everything with perfect clarity. All that I know now is partial and incomplete, but then I will know everything completely, just as God knows me now.*
> *13 There are three things that will endure—faith, hope, and love—and the greatest of these is love.*
> *(1 Corinthians 13)*

I think the world will continue to exist until every one of us has had a chance to understand and experience what Love is.

Every one of us will be given an opportunity, be it by grace or disgrace, something that happens in our lives that will force us to face the truth about ourselves; a crucial moment in which we will have to make a definitive choice about our fundamental belief, about Love.

What characterizes the greatness of each individual human being and the evolution of humanity as a whole is not our knowledge, wealth our technological and scientific development, not the size of our houses and cities. It's the respect and compassion we are able to show towards our fellow humans.

We have come a long way. Today we have the Declaration of the Human rights and the Geneva Convention. The slave trade has been made illegal a long time ago and more and more people are starting to believe that the death penalty is unacceptable, but we still have a long way to go.

The human race is formed by billions of individuals and each one gives his or her contribution to what the world is today, good or bad; and that contribution is given in every moment of everyday, in all our little and apparently insignificant interactions with other people, other living beings and our environment.

It's the small things that matter; we all know it.

Every time we make an effort for someone else or for ourselves, when we try to become a better person, we give those few minutes when we are already so busy, when we stay when we'd rather go, when we listen when we rather talk, that's when we become the persons we are supposed to be, that's when we fulfill our universal human destiny: to share with others the Love that's in our hearts.

I think the kingdom come is a new world where every single soul wants nothing else but to love, a world ruled by Love and therefore a world with no more pain and no more suffering.

Holiness is the experience on Earth of what Heaven must be. A strong connection with God, infinite joy and immense peace.

Saints are those who, having known Love, desire no other thing but to be always close to It, every minute of the day. Away from everything that diminishes the Love in their hearts. Nothing else matters, nothing else is more important. More than anything else to be holy is to feel immensely loved by God.

They trust God in everything, they are never alone. All they want is to love without end, understand, accept others without judging, to give without expecting anything back, heal and bring people together, comfort and be in peace with each other.
This is what Heaven must be, what the Kingdom come will be.
This state of intense love among people, forever!

This is why the saints, burning with the Love that consumes them, pray:

Lord, make me an instrument of your peace
Grant that I may not so much seek to be consoled,
but to console;
not so much to be understood, but to understand,
not to be loved, but to love;
for it is in giving that we receive,
it is in forgiving that we are forgiven,
and it is in dying to ourselves that we are born to eternal life.
(St Francis of Assisi)

There's only one thing our hearts truly need: Love.
There's only one thing that can make us truly happy: experience the wonderful things that happen when we are able to truly love.
Because, every little thing we do out of Love will come back to us tenfold.
Happiness and peace is what fills our hearts when we look at the work of our hands, minds and hearts and see that we have truly contributed to make our homes and the world a better place, when we look around us and see that we have consoled, encouraged, comforted or put a smile on someone's face.
And we will only be able to do this, when we understand what true Love is.

I don't think there's anything that can fill a heart with more happiness than to fly high with the eagles in the sky, free from everything that keeps us on the ground and see our loved ones and all those dear to us, following their own journeys and flying with their own wings in the altitudes of Love.

This is freedom; this is happiness, nothing else.

Conclusion

I need to conclude this book with some final words on cyber-relationships. Let's go back to the question that originally prompted me to write this book: is cyberdating a thing of weirdoes, freaks and losers?

Of course, there must be freaks and losers roaming the net, messing up their lives even further, preying on naïve or innocent people. Why would the internet be different from the rest of the world? The internet is the world!
There are losers, perverts and freaks in all walks of life, but to assume that everybody that chat or date on the net is a freak, a pervert or a loser is pure prejudice. Prejudice is what fills the minds of those who are not spending enough time making sure they are any better than the people they judge and criticize.
Those who are truly committed about being the best they can, are not at all inclined to look for limitations in others.
Sure there will be people that will see in this book a confirmation that cyberdating is for losers, but more important than to accept the judgment of others is to know who we are.
I see ourselves as ordinary, though unique people, doing the best we can with our lives. Greg and I have our flaws and limitations and many qualities too, like everybody else. I certainly don't see ourselves as losers, weirdoes or freaks.
How different are we from any other couple?
To label and judge a person one doesn't know tells me more about a person's inability to understand and accept differences than about another person's peculiarity or limitation.
People who can call someone they don't know a pervert, a freak, a loser or whatever, can call anyone anything, really.

There's so much we can do online these days: order groceries, shop, do banking and pay bills. What's so strange about meeting other people on the net?
It seems only natural to me that the internet would become, in this day and age, yet another way to start a relationship.
I think people who dare to check out on people they have met in a virtual world, far away from their own are not freaks, but very courageous people. They are open-minded people who still believe in others, they are not ruled by a prejudice that tells them that all people on the internet must be freaks and maniacs.
They are often seen as people who are running away from their

problems, when in fact, they are trying to do something concrete to turn the table, to find a better life for themselves.

As I said before there are as many reasons and ways to start relationships as there are people on earth and every relationship is the result of what two people believe in and are looking for.
Cyber relationships can end up really well or really badly, as can any relationship on earth and this will have nothing to do with how or why it started, but with what people did with the relationship *after* it started.

People can philosophy about it, wonder whether it ought or ought not to be, but I don't think it matters.
What matters, is what we do with our relationships. If one's truly willing to make it work, if the right attitude is there, cyberdating too, can lead to fulfilling relationships and Greg and I are a proof of it. I think cyber-relationships are here to stay.

Said that, I need to look back one last time at this whole adventure of mine and ask myself, from the silence and tranquility that is my life today, if I could have done anything differently?
I go back to the beginning of it all, when Greg and I were still writing to each other and I conclude that much of my confusion and anxiety during that time had to do with seeing my going to Australia as the solution for all my problems. It would have made things so much easier between us and especially for me if I could see things for what they really were.

It all seems so simple, today. And it really was: I was going to Australia to meet a guy who seemed very nice and to visit a country that seemed really good. I was going to have a look around, see how the cookies crumbled, as Greg put it and decide if I wanted to stay or go to Holland from there.
He just wanted to see me. I was thinking of Australia as an all or nothing thing. I put the cart before the horses.
Relationships are not a solution for problems; they are not a solution for anything.

Today, I can also see the stupidity in our e-mail arguments.
Written words can be misinterpreted so easily. The real thoughts behind the words are often not written and what's written doesn't necessarily express what's thought. It's so unfair to make

an interpretation of what someone has written without too much thought, without giving the person the chance to explain and clarify. When I didn't like something he said, I always came to the conclusion afterwards, that I didn't really understand what he meant or hadn't read him right. Cultural and linguistic differences were playing a role as well and I wasn't really aware of it. I think people in the tropics and especially Latin people are much more exuberant in the expression of their feelings, be they good or bad. Australia is a country with a strong British influence, people are generally more reserved, more careful about what they say and emotions are more controlled. It's a challenge that intercultural relationships will always have to face. It's actually a miracle that we did manage to communicate to the extent we did.

If I could do things over, during our cyberdating months, I would worry a lot less about what he might think of me. I would be more honest about my confusion. I tried too hard to appear reasonable, someone who had things clear in her mind when that was not really the case.

If we are confused about our needs and expectations or we can't express them clearly, it sure pays off to delay decisions and take some time to make things clearer to ourselves: "What is it that I really, really want?"

To engage with people who are not interested or cannot understand our needs and expectations, is a waste of time and the only way we can find out if a relationship is going to be worth our effort is to be completely honest.

We should also have looked a lot more seriously into the areas where things could possibly go wrong: education (for the boys), work, immigration issues, transportation, housing, etc...

I would also look much more seriously at my life at that point in time, to identify the things that were working.

I have this tendency to see the entire world as useless when there are just a few things that aren't working as they should and I often realize the good things I had, only after I lose them. So, it's good to be aware of what it is that we think we will find and what it is that we are willing to sacrifice to get it.

In regards to the immigration process, I think we should have applied for residency as soon as I got here or when we first faced the prospect of marriage. My feelings for Greg the day we

married were not much different from the ones I had when my visa first expired, when we could have asked for a different visa.
I shouldn't have waited so long to see what would eventuate or to start living my life. I still think we could have gone through the whole process a lot quicker. We should have asked for an interim visa, while I sorted out my divorce. We could have saved the money of the last two trips to Vanuatu for the boys' tickets, settling into a house, our future or whatever.

As to the boys, I think I would have left Tayna in Brazil to finish Uni. He never wanted to come. I should have encouraged him to finish his study in 2001. He would have stayed with the oldies. They would have found a way. They would probably not have sold the house to the wrong people. They wouldn't be in a legal action that has been dragging for years now, trying to have the rest of the money from the sale of the house paid to them. Tayna would probably have had his Uni degree.
Would I have managed to get the boys' visas through Chile? Probably, and by the time I had all the divorce issue sorted out, the boys might have got their temporary visas too.
They could have had more time to think about everything and come in their own time. It would have been so much easier for us here to have only one at a time, instead of both together. Everything could have gone much smoother.
The boys would have had so many more good moments and happy days with their friends in Paraty.
Greg says that having the boys here has prepared them much better for life; that they have matured and become more responsible, but I still think that a lot of the loneliness and sadness they went through wasn't really necessary.

I also have to admit that many of the reasons for my coming here were not the right ones, as it has been with all my previous relationships. The main reason was that I believed that I would finally have a functional family. Greg would assume a father role and we would help the boys through their transition into adulthood. That never happened. Greg never became the father to the boys I dreamt he would be. That cozy happy family I thought we would become never really materialized. Greg and the boys go along very well, there's mutual respect and affection, but he would never become a real father and there's a very simple reason for that, the boys have got a father already.
It took me quite a while to understand that no matter how good

my intentions were, how much money and effort I put into it, without their father's support, I would only be swimming against the flow and that's how it felt like all those years.

I was always telling them one thing and their father another. There would never be a winner. You can get rid of an ex, but you can never get rid of the father of your children. I think I was trying to exclude him.

I am still not sure if from the start, his intention had always been just to undermine me, but I'll give him the benefit of the doubt. I'll blame it on my damned inability to explain to people what I really need and want. I'll blame it on my temper, on my rage that didn't let me see or think clearly.

It was hard to accept that I had fought a terrible battle for years and that it had been lost well before it started. So many tears and all I did was beat on a dead horse.

Come to think about it, I also didn't do a great job when it came to getting the boys involved. I thought I had talked enough with them about my plans of going first to Europe and then Australia, but I obviously didn't. It's pretty clear to me now, that I should have gone a lot deeper in trying to put them at ease, when I first noticed their reluctance to come.

I also haven't been able to re-connect with my sons in the way I hoped. It's only today, after so many years, after all the turmoil of the early days here in Australia seem so far away, that I realize that what I was trying to do by bringing the boys here, was to win back the time I lost while I was away from them. I wanted to do for them what I didn't do when I was supposed to, but we can't rewind life. There is a right time for everything and time doesn't last forever, it slips away like fine sand through open fingers.

So much of my motivation to come to this country was based on vague ideas of what this country had to offer and what I would achieve here. Australia eventually lost its special place in my dreams. It has become reality and reality doesn't look simple or easy or rosy.

I look back at all the suffering we went through: the years of struggle, the financial difficulties, the loneliness, the frustration, the boys' constant difficulty adapting to the new culture, constantly wanting to go back and the will to go on in spite of it all. I remember the many peaceful and lonely days when I looked at the sky so blue and it made my heart ache with the thoughts of the country and the people I had left behind and missed so much.

By coming here, none of us was really ready or aware of what and how much we would have to give up.

To be honest, Australia still doesn't feel like home to me, even though today I am an Australian citizen. I don't think any place in the world can replace the country in which we grow up. Nothing will ever taste nicer or sound more familiar than the foods and sounds that fill the sweet memories of our childhood.

I am convinced that no one needs to go somewhere else to find happiness. We don't need to cross oceans and borders, fight so hard for a place under the sun, go through all the anxieties, troubles and the bureaucratic torture to settle in a foreign country. We don't need to uproot ourselves and suffer so many cold years, feeling estranged and lonely before new roots grow, so far away from everything that's known and dear to us.

We don't need to look for happiness anywhere else, because, if we let it, happiness will come to us wherever we are.

We can travel the seven seas, leave our families and husbands behind, look for other ones, make plans and change them again. Uproot ourselves over and over... But answers will only come to us when we finally accept our life for what it is and discover beauty in what we've got.

When I look back at this crazy life of mine, all the suffering I caused to those around me and myself, I think, "If I have any wisdom in me today, it didn't come from any of the many crazy things I've done, or from all the places I've been, not even from this transcontinental cyberdating adventure. It has come from standing still."

It took me so long to finally settle down into Greg.

How many times during all these years haven't I doubted my feelings? How many times haven't I plagued and pestered myself with so many questions. Do I really love him? Am I with him because it's convenient? Am I being dependent? Is this just another messed up relationship? Another mess I've got myself into? How do I know for sure if I love him, if he loves me?

Things only started to happen for us when I finally found peace within myself and accepted myself for what I am.

One could say that my whole cyberdating adventure has backfired, somehow, if one looks at what I expected to find, but I won't. Things didn't happen the way I wanted them to happen, things turned out the way they were supposed to.

We've made it. We are still together, our love for each other, still growing...

The boys have matured so much; they aren't boys anymore. They have become real friends, real brothers. Raoni's happy in the career path he chose. We have all grown closer together, even though we are living far apart. Greg's happy in his job and I keep myself busy doing the things I always wanted.

In one of the very first e-mails, I sent to Greg I said:

"I really wish I could work only half days and spend the other half reading books, going to libraries, thinking... Try to make sense of all the things I see and don't understand..."

That's exactly what I do now. I'm actually spending a lot more time doing what I want than what I don't. Life is not a struggle anymore.

It worked for Greg and I, because we were both willing to make sacrifices to make it work.

I had made a commitment to myself when I came to Australia: I wouldn't give up at the first obstacles. One of the things that gave me strength to go on was the awareness that I needed to change.

I would try to get along peacefully with everyone. I had come here to get somewhere, to achieve something. My big mouth, my impatience, my cynicism, my anger, my sarcasm had never helped me get anywhere. I have lost count of the many times I had to fight with myself not to do or say things that would come so naturally to me. There were days I felt sorry for myself, hidden in my room for days, but deep inside I knew something had to go. I needed to find a new balance. My way of doing that was to uproot myself and lose my old me in a strange new world, trying hard to understand and assimilate new words, sounds, smells, tastes and habits. Like in Kasey Chambers' song,

I handed all my efforts in,
slammed the doors they slammed at me.
I'll just move over to your town and hide
Figure out my destiny, at last
You'll be the captain; I'll be no one (The Captain, 2000)

It has not been easy. From those first days, to where we are now has been a long and winding road.

The endless waiting for things to get sorted out, all the many little annoying problems that showed up.

I haven't told about half of them.

Every single one of my unfinished businesses from the past showed up: things I left unfinished in Holland and in Brazil, the shortcomings in the boys upbringing, my struggles with work, bad habits and health, all the skeletons needed to be removed from the closet and buried and as we survived the many anxious and painful moments, we grew closer bit by bit.

I have never been madly in love with Greg or him with me.
It never felt like a hurricane or the eruption of a volcano, it has been more like a slow dive into a calm and deep ocean, when the winds are still and the surface undisturbed, like a mirror. Today I feel thoroughly embraced by the thick warm water. Like a stormy ocean, there was something very powerful about that stillness. Think what you want. I call it love.
I realized how much I needed and appreciated the feeling of safety Greg gave me and the peace that comes with it. We laugh so much together and that's very good too.

My adventure is not about Australia or the boys anymore.
It's about Greg and me. It's about my journey of self-discovery and my commitment to the understanding of what Love is.
We both know that there will be days to lose and days to win, days to cry and days to laugh. Today I realize that my coming here has never been about Australia. I thought I had come looking for a new life, but deep inside I came here to look for myself.

Many times during all these years I imagined what my life would have been if I had stayed in Brazil or if I had gone to Holland, but it really doesn't make any difference where we are, because ultimately wherever we go, we take ourselves with us and it's what's within us that determines our lives.
I don't believe that had I stayed in Brazil, I would have regained the control over my life that I have today. I have no doubt I am better off now. Coming to Australia gave me the rest I had been looking for, for so long. The rest I needed to see things clearly, to find answers and new directions, to reconnect with myself. I truly believe I would not have found peace inside myself without this man who never charged me, who gave me space, gave me time; he listened to me and he held my hand when I needed it. He was always there when I looked for him and I know he always will be.
Would I have found a guy like this in Brazil or Holland, in

another context, outside cyberspace? Who knows? Who really cares? Does it matter?

I have no doubts any more. I'm not with Greg just because it's convenient. I'm with him because I want to be. I've never been more peaceful. I feel deeply loved and I can't think of anything better to do then to make love to him.

I have no doubt that I am where I am supposed to be.

When I think of Greg, I think of an Alanis Morrisette song,

I had no choice but to hear you,
You treat me like I'm a princess,
Your love is thick and swallowed me whole,
You're so much braver than I gave you credit for.
Thanks for your patience...
You're the best listener that I've ever met,
My best friend.
Don't be surprised if I fall head over feet...
(Head over heels, Jagged little pill, 1995).

By getting into this cyberdating adventure, I haven't found a pot full of gold at the end of the rainbow, I didn't solve all my problems overnight and I haven't found Paradise on earth, but I have found a strong sense of direction, acceptance, reconciliation with my past, peace in my heart. I've found the most important, I found myself. My search is over.

Will I ever have doubts again?

Probably, but if I do, I know that all I have to do is to get back into my heart and remember that Love is there waiting for me, remember my commitment to be who I truly am and have always meant to be.

I still have so many plans. I hope this book will lead to many other things. I want to get more serious with nutrition issues and exercise. I want to get more serious in tackling the social issues I think need to be addressed in Australia, Brazil and the world.

Much needs to be done to put better supportive networks in place, because I am convinced that, no matter how much we are aware of what we need to do and how much we want to change, no one goes forward without a little help and support.

Finally, I want to live my religious convictions more fully and more completely.

But, I have learned that life's not about making plans and

running around trying to accomplish them. Life's not about the things we want. Life's about understanding what we really need and about accepting what comes our way, small and big.

Life's about learning to love, it doesn't matter what and it doesn't matter who.

About me

I was born in Brazil, the second daughter of a Dutch mother and an Indonesian father.
I am a Brazilian, Dutch and Australian citizen and got degrees in Veterinary and Biology with a major in Nature conservation.
I speak Portuguese, Dutch, English and I understand Spanish.

In my life, I have been a singer in a rock band, a dancer, an acrobat in the circus. I worked with street children in Brazil; I took care of guinea pigs in a cancer research hospital and baked space cakes for a coffee shop in Amsterdam. I have been the owner of a natural products shop, an English teacher, a translator of Dutch and Portuguese, a counselor for Lifeline, I did research in mangroves in Brazil and national parks in Indonesia and I have worked in a remote Aboriginal Community in Cape York, Queensland.

In Brazil, I have lived in the capitals and countryside of São Paulo, Rio de Janeiro, Maranhão in the northeast and Pará in the Amazon, where my sons were born.
In Holland, I lived in Amsterdam and Wageningen and in Australia, in country Queensland, Northern New South Wales, Melbourne and finally Cairns in Tropical Queensland, where I currently live with my husband Greg, my dog Friday and my cat Kaya.

I believe all environmental and social problems in the world can be solved through the teachings of Jesus Christ.
My main interest these days is natural living.

For those living in Australia and around, you can order print copies or a free chapter here:
cr.cp.love@gmail.com